To Kim -
   All good wishes to
you always. You have
been a great help to
me throughout the years
and I wish you good
health, much happiness & love.
            Ilse / Eci

Anatomy of a Divorce
Dying is not an Option, nor is Insanity

Cover design by Joel Carver
joel@jcarvergraphics.com

ISBN-13:
978-1503278424

ISBN-10:
1503278425

"A wholesome boy married the girl next door. A successful career followed but nothing was amiss until he and his ambitious young coworker were unable to resist each other. When the desire to gain power and commit adultery overpowered him his life started to unravel. Divorce and violence do not look good on a resume, so he planned to get rid of his wife by convincing others she was crazy. With a psychiatrist's disturbing premeditated cooperation, his wife was institutionalized literally within hours without consultation or family escort. It is painful but reassuring to read how shrewdly she adapted. Surviving the mental hospital she also managed a bit of ironic in-house therapy for other patients. In unlikely surroundings she demonstrated sanity and courage. This recovery, not from mental illness but mental abuse is a triumph. Today she is a fulfilled healthy woman wishing only to help others with her story."

~Sondra Carver, Editor

"You often hear about people that come into your life and make a profound impact; however, not everyone is blessed to meet such a person. I was. She is the author of this book. Ilse Kelley has been a friend of mine since 1986. Ilse continues to be a strong woman filled with an indestructible spirit and determination driven by loyalty, love, principles, and honesty. She has overcome undeserved & despicable heartaches in her life—only to unknowingly become an even more powerful inspiration and role model to many. I am truly humbled and honored to have this noble woman in my life and to call her a true friend."

~Gina Jones

Acknowledgements

Thank you to the many people who so kindly helped me through the process of successfully writing this book. Their indulgence and patience has been neverending. Without Sondra Carver's encouragement, I never would have attempted to write the book. Sondra's endless hours of editing is most appreciated, but most of all her treasured friendship. Jim Davis was "on call" for one year generously helping me with computer issues—again this never would have moved forward without his patient assistance and the patience of his wife, Pat. There are numerous readers; each one gave suggestions and clarity to what I was trying to portray—Carol Mosser, Charleine St. Clair, Peter Court Leeds, Mary Price, Lynn Hammond, Martha Ritter, Terri White, Jeannine Zwoboda, Beau Marie St. Clair and Peggy Hoover. Gina Jones' help was invaluable with computer and publishing challenges. A sincere thank you to Karen and Karla Bausman for helping me over the final hurdles. I would like to especially recognize Dick Fleming who spent endless hours giving support, proofreading, and editing.

Thank you Joel Carver for a cover that says it all!

To others who encouraged me, who are not named, including my family, thank you!

I love you all.

Prologue

I want to tell you my story. It is a true story and I am writing it from what I vividly remember. I did not keep a journal and my calendars are vague when related to the nightmare I lived for four years. However, I made rough drafts of the letters I wrote so I wouldn't make mistakes and appear 'stupid.' The drafts I wrote were filed away with my divorce papers. I'm not sure why I saved them, perhaps to help write this story now. My time-line isn't always precise but everything I've written about happened. People's names and locations have been changed.

This is a story I finally want to tell so that people know the truth about what happened to a marriage that seemed perfect. The breakdown of the marriage happened almost twenty years ago. Ten years ago, I could not have written this but now it's time to purge myself, set the record straight that I am (and was) totally sane, and most important, help other women (or men) recognize when they are being controlled and emotionally abused. Emotional abuse can be just as damaging as physical abuse, maybe more so. I didn't realize I was being controlled and emotionally abused for years, until it was too late.

Why did I marry Robert? How could I let this happen? Let me explain how natural and 'right' it seemed.

It was the summer between our sophomore and junior college years when Robert stopped his car in front of my house. We had been close friends and neighbors since eighth grade. In the past, neither of us had considered a dating relationship. Now, when Robert stopped to talk with me, he told me that some of our high school friends were going to get together at Ray's barn, on the farm south of town. Knowing that I hadn't gone with my high school sweetheart for two years since graduation, Robert suddenly said, as though the thought had occurred to him at that moment, "You don't have anyone to go with and I don't have anyone to go with. Why don't we go together? I'll pick you up."

Hmm, I thought. As I went into my house, I told my mother, "You never will guess who asked me out tonight! Robert Kelly. YES, Robert Kelly, our neighbor."

I could see the interest that piqued in my mother's eyes. *I thought to myself, I never thought about Robert as a possible boyfriend before! Why didn't I ever think about him in this way? I think my life is about to change.*

It could be perfect. In high school, we were both popular. Robert was a natural leader. He was class president, president of the student body and on the all-state championship football team, while I was a cheerleader and Homecoming Queen. Robert was tall, handsome, nice, smart and popular...what more could anyone want? We would make a perfect couple! A dream! Soon to come true!

That was the beginning of a whirlwind romance. Robert picked me up that night and we went to Ray's. I remember every detail from that evening. The barn was well lit on the hot summer night. We settled on the floor with our backs against a bale of hay. Before long, I was sitting in front of Robert with his arms around me as we laughed and listened to stories, reminiscent of things we had all done in high school. I felt comfortable when Robert put his arms around me. It felt right. He took me home very late, so late that I felt I had to sneak in so my mother wouldn't pose questions although I no longer had a curfew now that I was in college.

It was love at first sight that night after knowing each other seven years. It was a heady young love. We realized we didn't need time to get acquainted. We already knew everything we needed to know to decide that we were perfect together.

"I want to take you to a special dance. The Stan Kenton band is playing in the neighboring town," Robert said.

I had enough time to make a pretty summer sundress with a very full skirt and spaghetti straps. When Robert came to pick me up in his parents' Oldsmobile, he came to the door with a perfect coral rose that he just picked from his mother's rose garden. I carried it with me to the dance and home again. *What a special romantic thing for him to do I thought. I also thought that Robert's mother was probably saving the rose for one of her award winning floral arrangements.*

The entire evening was romantic, dancing to the Stan Kenton band in Robert's strong

3

arms! I began to dream of what life could be like with Robert and I was in love with this wonderful young man my same age.

"When I am married I'm going to go dancing every week," Robert whispered in my ear as we danced to Stan Kenton.

Both of us loved jitterbugging to "Pennsylvania 6-5000." In spite of his 6'2" frame and size 13 shoes, Robert was graceful and comfortable on the dance floor. All smiles and full of energy, I loved every minute in Robert's arms.

"I'm going to work hard so I can afford to go dancing. I love the music. My parents never go dancing. All they do for fun is go to the movies," Robert said.

Love. It had to be love. There was no other way to explain the feelings we had for each other. We wanted to be together every free moment. We talked endlessly about our hopes and dreams. I knew that my dreams for a future were about to come true. I knew I could spend the rest of my life with this alluring young man with ambitious plans for a future that included me. It was heaven for both of us. A perfect match! I was ecstatic, ready to share a lifetime with Robert, whatever it entailed, good or bad. The possibility of anything negative didn't enter my mind.

In my dreamlike state, I didn't consider how people can change. I was not prepared for what happened thirty years later. I began to recognize gradual changes. I tolerated inconsistencies in Robert's behavior. There were subtle, selfish, personality quirks that became more noticeable as the years went by. These things troubled me, but I didn't voice my concerns to others and I learned not to question Robert for fear a confrontation would cause an argument. The abuse, which took place gradually over the years, was insidious and demoralizing.

Too late to change the failing marriage I realized I have a personality flaw of my own...a huge flaw that initially doesn't appear to be a flaw at all. *Can someone be too nice, always too accepting and too tolerant because of their love, commitment, and marriage vows? Can someone become totally blind to their husband's shortcomings?* For me it was 'blind love' not 'tough love.' I was strong emotionally, but barely strong enough to contend with what life with Robert meant. I was not prepared for the direction the marriage would go.

Robert knew I would do anything for him. Almost!

Ilse

Part I: 1992

1
"You're Crazy"

"I'm not going to talk to you, you're crazy."

"You're crazy," Robert would always say in a nasty tone filled with criticism, "I'm not going to talk to you." Then he'd hang up leaving Ilse crying on the other end of a dead phone. She didn't call a friend to talk with when this happened, but the family pet, Sasha, an Old English Sheep Dog, knew when to put her big head on Ilse's lap.

This day had begun in a normal way walking with friends. Jackie and Joyce had become Ilse's good friends and confidants over a period of years. They weren't the wives of doctors and hospital associates who had become friends after moving to Summit. They were neighbors and walking buddies as they all tried to keep in shape, stay healthy and enjoy the good life. Ilse was fifty, with brown hair, tinged with gray. She was healthy and energetic, a talented executive wife with the skills that made entertaining for her husband easy. She was also a 'people person'…always ready to listen and get to know people.

The three women lived in the same neighborhood and had similar life styles. They were also linked together with successful executive husbands. Lunch or tea in the middle of the day included long discussions focusing on their children, their backgrounds, decorating ideas for their beautiful homes, their life experiences and their dreams…rarely gossip.

Invariably their long talks would focus on their husbands. They laughed a lot, not acting like stuffy, executive, high maintenance wives. Ilse still did her own housework as she always had, even when she was in charge of special parties for her husband. Being generally the same age, these friends were not unlike the dear friends Ilse was close to before moving to Summit from Clarkston, Michigan a few years earlier.

One morning several months before this beautiful day, Ilse had walked quietly but quickly beside her friends moving as if possessed by a demon. She had been walking faster and faster the last several weeks making it hard for her friends to keep the pace.

A change in her revealed a quiet sadness. She was running away from something and although her friends had sensed the change, they had not commented. In their private discussions, they talked about why she wasn't her usual happy self. She had lost weight, which she didn't need to do, having maintained the same size 8 she had been for years. She didn't talk much about her husband although his name was frequently in the paper in connection with the hospital where he was the CEO. Her friends would comment about news articles they had seen, but Ilse didn't prompt further discussion about her husband.

This particular morning Ilse could not contain her secret. It was hard to hide because of the sadness in her hazel eyes and the tears that wouldn't go away. Her friends couldn't avoid her tear-stained cheeks and her eyes sunken from lack of sleep. These friends didn't ask questions, but waited until Ilse spilled the truth in a flood of words and tears that would not stop. Once exposed, she could not contain herself and she opened her heart. As they walked in the beautiful park, she failed to see beauty in this bright, sunny day.

Ilse told her friends that she knew Robert was having an affair, *so utterly unlike him she thought.* Throughout the marriage, he had seldom paid attention to other women. She told her friends she had confronted him about it, but he had adamantly denied it. There was disbelief amongst the friends and Ilse herself couldn't believe Robert would do this.

She had grown up with him. They had gone to high school together and were back yard neighbors. Living in a small college town in Nebraska, when it was time to go to college, they both simply walked up the street to the campus. They didn't date until the summer between their sophomore and junior year of college, but they had always been close friends.

He wouldn't, couldn't do this to her! He couldn't have turned into such a cruel person who would deny her the happiness of the good life they had built together. Logic told Ilse that Robert was

11

on overload. Maybe she was wrong about the affair. Logic also told her that there were too many signs that she was right. Caught between the clashes of these conflicting thoughts, there was a painful inner turmoil festering every waking moment.

Ilse knew the sad truth. *He no longer loved her. Unbelievable but true.* To share the insults and stories about what had been happening was difficult, but Ilse felt better knowing that she no longer had to hide her secret from these two friends. They were sympathetic, but said, knowing Robert, "he isn't the type." Why would he have an affair when he had Ilse for a wife? There must be another problem, not another woman.

For several months, Jackie and Joyce had been patiently listening on the morning walks as Ilse continued to tell them details of her life. Some days there would be laughter and a glimmer of hope that the problems would disappear and life would again be on track for a happy marriage. More often now the conversation would involve updates on efforts to come to grips with the bad situation. The friends talked about possible solutions, what could eventually happen, what Ilse wanted, counseling sessions for herself and the joint counseling she had insisted on with Robert.

Today was no different from the last two years, until a huge change surfaced in both Ilse and Robert. For Ilse, the shock and heartache of a marriage in trouble was almost more than she could bear. She couldn't conceal her feeling of emptiness, as the world she had enjoyed came tumbling down exposing her to uncertainty and a hurt impossible to disguise. Robert had been changing in his own way by forming a tougher shell around himself. He wasn't talking with Ilse except to be critical of her. His focus seemed to be on his prestigious job as the CEO of the local hospital. He vehemently denied being involved with another woman.

In spite of the beautiful sunny day, Ilse was suddenly afraid...very afraid. Robert had called, which was unusual. He hadn't talked with her in days. Now he rarely called even though they had been married for twenty-eight years. When Robert moved out of the house six months earlier, he wouldn't tell her where he was moving. He did not leave a way for her to contact him other than to call him at work, and he was adamant that he didn't want to be interrupted there. With a daughter married and living away and a son at medical school, she needed some way to keep in touch; however, this Wednesday Robert chose to call. In past months, the counselors had suggested more communication. Promises were made on both sides to talk and listen to each other. Usually when Ilse called Robert with questions or concerns, he would tell her he wouldn't talk with her.

Now, six months later when Ilse was feeling that she was getting a handle on the situation, THE phone call came. The conversation was brief. He would pick her up that afternoon to take her to see the chairman of the Department of Psychiatry. His name was Evan Frank, a medical doctor, a kind man whom Ilse and Robert had entertained in their home many times.

13

Ilse liked Dr. Frank. She did not find him intimidating and looked at him as a compassionate man. He was easy to talk with although Ilse had never seen him for psychiatric help. She had called him months earlier to ask if he could recommend a marriage counselor since he would know best who would be most helpful. Robert was furious about the phone call, although he had agreed to see a counselor if Ilse would set it up. He didn't want anyone to know that he had any kind of problem, let alone a personal issue. For Robert, it was necessary for everyone to see him in the most positive light. After all, he was a leader in the community, admired and respected. Certainly, HE wasn't flawed. To him, everything involving him should be viewed as perfect whether it was in public or private life. Heaven forbid that anyone would view him as somewhat lacking in any way. He was certain HE didn't have a problem. It was Ilse's. Everything pointed to HER with the way she was responding to Robert's rejection.

Right on schedule, 3:45 pm, Robert arrived at the house he hadn't lived in for several months. Using the garage door opener to get in, he came through the back gate, through the iron-trellised walkway and into the large remodeled kitchen. On the kitchen wall were newspaper articles, "Man of the Year" and "The Man to Watch," which portrayed some of his successes. Ilse had them matted and framed for his birthday, which pleased Robert. Ilse had been so proud of him!

Upon arriving this day, Robert went to the pantry cupboard after a curt, "Are you ready?" greeting. No food suited him except

14

some crackers, which he criticized. Ilse sat on a bar stool at the huge butcher-block counter. When re-doing the kitchen, Ilse wanted it to be the heart of the home. It became just that...warm, inviting, filled with wonderful times and friends. This day however, as soon as Robert stepped into the pleasant room, it lost its glow.

With a cold look in Robert's eyes, he didn't look directly at Ilse. He had not looked directly at Ilse for months. He barked, "Get into the car!" Shaken and confused, as she always was with his harsh manner, Ilse walked slowly out the door. A welcome school bell stood just outside the gate, placed there by friends when Ilse and Robert bought the home. Everything was in conflict: the kitchen, the home, the bell, all seemed welcoming, but today Robert seemed cold and cruel.

Ilse thought that perhaps a talk with Dr. Frank would be a start in resolving their problems and once in the car she began to relax. Although it was hard to sleep at night, she could sometimes nap during the day. Sleep was always a welcome relief, but too often sleep was haunted by ghosts, problems and the reality of what life had become. *Yes, maybe talking to Dr. Frank would get Ilse on the right track and the fact that they were going to see him probably meant that Robert had reconsidered the counseling for both of them.* Ilse had been anxious from the onset of the marriage problems to get help, which until now had seemed futile.

2
Dr. Frank

Dr. Frank's waiting room was decorated in soft, soothing colors, with comfortable traditional furniture and plenty of magazines. Actually, his office was close to Ilse and Robert's home, so the drive there had only taken about five minutes. When they arrived, Ilse was relieved to see that only a few people were in the office, and she did not know any of them. Robert of course knew the receptionist, but approached her in a brisk, business-like manner. He told her Dr. Frank was expecting his wife.

"The appointment is for Ilse," he emphasized.

In just moments, Dr. Frank came out and ushered Ilse and Robert into his large study. The couch Ilse thought he'd have for psychiatric sessions was missing, but there were relaxing chairs and light filtered through a window.

"It is nice to see you again," he began. He looked at Robert and said he'd like to talk with Ilse alone first, then Robert alone, and then the two of them together. This didn't seem unusual, as there had been a similar pattern with the counseling sessions they had attended earlier. Dr. Frank had recommended a doctor in Princeton, which was a long drive for counseling, but it was private and no one knew them there, so Robert had agreed to go. After several sessions with the psychologist in Princeton, Robert said it wasn't helping, he couldn't afford the time away from work, and he wouldn't go any more. He also told Ilse that Dr. Rule, the Princeton psychologist, suggested to him that she probably would need to be hospitalized in a state institution. There was a mental health unit at the Summit hospital, but Robert said that he couldn't have Ilse there because of his reputation. Robert reminded her of the high school field trip in Nebraska to visit the State Mental Hospital when they were high school seniors. He laughed and *Ilse thought he was just making one of his sick jokes. Was he setting her up? Was it a part of Robert's plan?*

There hadn't been any more sessions for any type of joint counseling until now with Dr. Frank. Ilse was encouraged as she thought this doctor was the best of the best, so when Robert was shown to another office, Ilse was relieved to be able to talk freely with Dr. Frank.

Ilse immediately began quietly crying. She also began to quiver, then shake. This involuntary shaking that had begun to plague her earlier now started again in Dr. Frank's office. It was uncontrollable. She tried to will herself to stop the shaking, but it got worse. There was a pain in her chest and she felt sick to her stomach. Her head felt like it was splitting. *This was a fight. Someone had to believe her, to*

18

understand her, and help her. Dr. Frank could do that if only he would listen to her.

Then the questions began. "What is upsetting you? Can you stop shaking? Do you know what makes you shake?"

Ilse felt comfortable with Dr. Frank. He had always been easy to talk with at social functions, but it was obvious that this day his interest was purely medical. Dr. Frank could usually draw Ilse out with just a few comments, although trying to control her emotions today wasn't working. He said he was concerned about the things Robert had told him. Wondering what story Robert had already told him, Ilse began to panic when she told Dr. Frank about her troubled marriage as she saw it. Whimpering, she sank down as far as possible in the large leather chair seeking comfort. She told him that Robert had left and he simply didn't want to be around her anymore. It confused her because he said he didn't want a divorce. He told her he couldn't live with her because she was crazy.

She knew exactly what Robert was doing. *He was living a lie. He was telling associates and the other doctors, especially Dr. Frank, that he couldn't deal with her accusations of an affair that he insisted didn't exist.* He said she was making it increasingly difficult to focus on his work, and she was an embarrassment to him. None-the-less, on occasion he still took her to social functions and acted as if nothing were wrong. Robert kept telling her she was crazy, so Ilse tried frantically to convince Dr. Frank that she wasn't. *If only I could keep from crying, she thought. She had to convince this doctor that she wasn't crazy.* She had heard that word repeatedly from Robert and hated all that it implied. *Couldn't he use another word to describe her?* She knew she wasn't crazy and she tried frantically to be convincing.

Dr. Frank looked at her with compassion and concern, but Ilse could tell he had already drawn conclusions based on whatever Robert had told him when he made the appointment. Ilse knew Dr. Frank would believe Robert without question because Robert was an executive with power over employees and even the physicians who were affiliated with the hospital. Ilse had no trump card. She was afraid her pathetic pleading for the psychiatrist to believe her wasn't going to work.

Ilse was thinking, please, please, please give me a chance. Believe me. I'm not crazy. I've been trying to piece together what has happened. What I know has made me sad, depressed and emotionally upset, but not crazy.

Daringly, she decided to reveal her suspicions about the other woman and her identity. She knew that Dr. Frank would know this woman since she worked at the hospital in an administrative capacity. When Ilse told him it was Carrie, Dr. Frank didn't say anything. He just looked at her. Aside from his knowing Carrie, she wondered if he was surprised and shocked, or just the opposite, that he had suspected the same as she. Could it have been too early for a stray rumor or two? She knew Carrie was well thought of throughout the hospital and Robert had told Ilse she was brilliant. He had promoted her in a very short time from an administrative resident to a vice president. Robert, Dr. Frank and Carrie were all hospital connected, and Ilse had no influence over any of them.

Looking back on this critical session with Dr. Frank, Ilse had lingering questions. As part of a professional diagnosis, Ilse was never administered even a simple questionnaire to assess her emotional state. Why did he not examine her before drawing conclusions? Wouldn't some medical tests have been helpful? What if she had been diabetic, had a heart condition, or was anemic? Her shaking alone needed to be evaluated, to say nothing of the crying, headache, and pain in her stomach. It seemed to her that professionalism had been trumped by expediency.

Dr. Frank kindly told her he was leaving her alone for a few minutes. Neither his facial expression nor voice gave any indication of how he interpreted Ilse and what she said. Left alone, she looked out the window and began to calm. The sun was still shining, and she could see the leaves were gone.

There would be a few moments of peace before having to face Robert for the joint counseling session. The tears didn't stop, nor the quivering, but the situation seemed like a bad dream. Perhaps it was.

Robert met with Dr. Frank next. It was brief. Dr. Frank told him of Ilse's accusation about another woman which appeared to be the cause of her depression. Robert said it was wrong, unfounded, absurd, and that his wife was mentally ill. Working with the medical community all those years, he told Dr. Frank, he knew the signs of an emotionally wrought woman. His rejection of her, he said, had put her over the edge. He couldn't deal with it anymore. He couldn't and wouldn't.

Ilse assumed this was the essence of their session, but she realized more might have been said. *She wondered how Dr. Frank could simply believe Robert but not her. What would be a more 'sane' reaction to Robert's rejection?*

With all three back together, the two men looked right over the top of Ilse's head discussing her and what was to be done, as though she weren't there. Serious and intense, they ignored her crying, shaking and attempts to interrupt. It was as if she was stupid and didn't know what was going on. Ilse tried to reach over from her chair to Robert, just to touch him, to get some strength. He pulled away. The one person that used to love and protect her had now turned, withdrawing from her touch. She knew that instead of helping her he was trying to destroy her. *Why? Why? Why? Dr. Frank was supposed to see these things, to understand.* But instead, it was as if she weren't there. She couldn't believe what was being said.

Looking at Robert, Dr. Frank said, "There is a place about an hour from here. It's nice. The staff is good; in fact, some of our doctors are on staff there part-time. I can make a call since we affiliate with them, and see if they can admit her today."

Dr. Frank looked at Robert, not at Ilse. Her look of disbelief might have persuaded Robert to reconsider, but he didn't look at her. As cold as ice he replied to Dr. Frank, "Do it!"

Was she hearing correctly? It couldn't be. She knew she was right; *they were wrong,* but she was going to be put in a hospital, not the

22

beautiful local hospital of which Robert was the CEO, but in an unknown mental hospital an hour away.

"Oh no! Oh please, no!" *"Admit her" to the hospital or "commit her" to the hospital. Was there a difference?*

Dr. Frank left the room to make the necessary call. Robert didn't say a word while Ilse's body was racked with sobs. Moments later the doctor was back.

"It's all set," he told Robert who shook his hand. Then Dr. Frank gave him directions, telling him the hospital would expect them in about two hours. Robert turned to Ilse with obvious relief. It was settled. *It seemed her hospitalization was prearranged, although Dr. Frank and Robert talked as though it was a new idea. Was it really Robert's idea that she should be hospitalized and he had previously suggested that to Dr. Frank?*

"Get up. Quit crying. Someone will see you, but above all, quit shaking!"

Didn't he know she couldn't make the shaking and crying "come and go" whenever she wanted? It wasn't an act. It made him uncomfortable and now it would not bother him, for a while anyway. He could work long hours and continue his affair with Carrie with his problem wife gone. She followed him out of the office, head down, crying, trying to take his hand, still hoping for a bit of comfort. As they left, Dr. Frank wished her well with a sad, solemn look on his face. He told Robert that he could call on him for any questions, concerns, or support and Robert should keep him informed about Ilse's progress.

23

Back home Ilse lay on the bed in what had been their master bedroom, which now felt foreign to her. She lay down on the bed in a state of disbelief. Soon Robert came into the room to say he had to take care of some things at the hospital, and she should be ready to leave in an hour.

As soon as Robert left, *Ilse thought briefly of getting in the car and driving away, anywhere, to disappear. However, she knew he would find a way to come after her. She couldn't get away. Ilse thought, I'll refuse to go because I know he manipulated the situation without me realizing what was happening. I'll simply refuse to leave. I'll stay here.* Then she slept. It was a fitful short nap and she woke suddenly with the horror of what was happening. Cold...she covered with the afghan her dear Mother had made for her.

What would her mother say to her? What should she do? Be strong and THINK of a solution to this nightmare. She was not able to comprehend what had just happened in such a short time. She was a fool to have gone so agreeably to see Dr. Frank, thinking Robert was looking for help for both of them.

Any fool who knew how Robert's mind worked would know what he was up to. Maybe she could call someone who wouldn't be affected by Robert's wrath. Who wouldn't be intimidated by him? Maybe she should call one of her friends from the town she had moved from, Clarkston. She knew they would help her, but they were too far away and she needed help NOW. There wasn't time. She didn't have any warning. She was trapped.

Shortly, Robert came home and snapped, "You're not packed!"

Would I pack myself to go to a mental hospital, she thought. He was angry but it didn't matter anymore. Ilse usually did whatever it took to keep him from being upset, but not now.

He took a suitcase out...the biggest one they had. Ilse moved to a chair they had bought when they finally could begin purchasing permanent things. It was a safe place from which to watch Robert as he methodically emptied lingerie from the chest by removing the drawers, dumping them into the suitcase.

He went to the built-in closet shelves and took out neat stacks of sweaters throwing them in with a few pair of hanging pants, all a jumbled mess. He brought Ilse her tennis shoes and told her to put them on. She moved like a robot, but then thought to grab a bag of toiletries, hairbrush...and a purse. She had to have a purse. At the last minute she grabbed the small white afghan her Mother had made for her years ago, the one she had wrapped up in moments ago on the bed. There was a teddy bear their son had given her for Christmas to add to her collection.

Her son was in medical school and the bear wore a doctor's white lab coat. She tucked it into her purse as a child would who needed a security blanket.

"You need a coat and other shoes. You'll be there awhile, maybe the rest of your life. We've got to go," Robert snapped as he picked up the big suitcase and carried it downstairs.

When Ilse didn't follow, he hurried back upstairs, took her by the arm, and pushed her ahead of him. By now, listless, Ilse stumbled in front of him.

"Wait! Wait!" Ilse said. "I have company coming next week. I can't leave. They planned this trip months ago." Robert made a phone call saying that because Ilse was sick, she had to go to the hospital. It set off questions, but he said he was brief because he was in a hurry. Ilse was crying too hard to talk on the phone.

As they left the house, they walked through the back-gated breezeway looking out to the large trees and snow. If it were spring, she would look out on pink impatiens. *Ilse wondered when she would see her home again, or if she ever would.* Now it was winter. There were no pretty flowers. In a few months, it would be time to plant flowers that would look pretty against the stone with the blue shutters and doors.

When she was planting the impatiens last spring, kneeling and loosening the rich black soil, the neighbor from across the street came over. He said he hadn't seen Robert around much; why was she doing all the work herself? He was on the hospital board, a nice man, with a lovely, kind wife. Tears began to come as she put her head down, continuing her planting job to cover her emotions. She simply said,
"He's left me."

With no questions, he replied, "I'm sorry. I've seen you coming and going in the Lexus and wondered why Robert was never with you."

A short time later his wife came over, sympathetic but looking for answers in a kind, caring way. She had been a good neighbor and friend. Having two grand pianos, they had

26

asked Ilse and Robert if they could store a Steinway piano in their large living room. It looked beautiful and fit right in. Everyone enjoyed it at parties. Ilse appreciated the neighbor's concern then and later.

More than a year before, Robert had wanted to look at a new luxury car. It was a Lexus and together after looking at it, Robert bought it on the spot. It was only a few years earlier that Molly, their daughter, totaled her car on the way to Michigan. Robert decided to give her Ilse's car and said he'd buy Ilse another, a Toyota Camry. For the first time he agreed to automatic windows and then said, "This is probably the last car you'll ever get." At the time, Ilse just laughed as *she thought, what a strange thing for Robert to say. I wonder what he means by that.*

Then he bought the Lexus on a whim but it became Ilse's car because Robert had a hospital car, which he said had to be American. Still he couldn't resist driving the Lexus. People would stop and ask him about the car since there weren't many in the area. The car made him proud. It helped to show he was successful.

Now, as he shoved Ilse into the Lexus, there was no satisfaction for her in its luxury. To her a car didn't equate with humility, and there was no need to flaunt one's prosperity. This day her gray mood matched the gray leather upholstery. Robert was in a rush and they were bound to get caught in traffic with people now going home from work. Ilse had stopped crying. She was just tired. After about ten minutes and no conversation, she put her head down on the armrest next to Robert. He didn't push her away. He even put his hand on her shoulder, which was momentarily comforting. It was starting to get darker, but Ilse didn't notice with her eyes shut. Everything was already dark to her. Once during the trip Robert stopped the car to check the directions Dr. Frank had given him for the hospital.

3
The Mental Hospital

The hour passed and the car stopped. Ilse would not lift her head. Robert became almost gentle as he prodded his wife to get up and come with him.

"This looks like a nice place," he said, "sort of like a bed and breakfast." There was a porch on the front of a white clapboard building with carriage lights by the front door. Helping her up the steps, Robert opened the door and pushed her inside. Ilse sat down on a sofa, confused and afraid. She knew what was happening, but realized she no longer had a voice or any control. Always interested in history and museums, Robert's attention turned to the memorabilia on the walls. He tried to draw Ilse in a little by telling her that one of the doctors they knew from Summit had grown up in the house and his father had been the administrator of the mental clinic.

"Come and look at these pictures to see how it used to look," he said, but Ilse didn't care. She was not interested in the pictures but did notice the overstuffed furniture was what she thought of as "old rich."

A kind, middle-aged lady approached and asked both of them to come into her office for paper work and Ilse realized she was expecting them. Again, she began to cry and quiver. *Was this really happening? No. It couldn't be!* It was as if it was happening to someone else, but why then did she have a sick feeling?

After they began the paperwork, Ilse didn't say anything until suddenly she blurted out, "No! This is a mistake. This is WRONG!" *She couldn't stay here.* Everyone ignored her as Robert signed the paper, then lifted Ilse's hand and told her she had to sign. She knew she had no choice as he held his hand over hers while she wrote her name.

Today was Wednesday and Robert said he would come and see her on the weekend. He said she'd be okay, and he would call her. He told her she had to be there. He was being nicer than he had been in months. With a quick hug, Robert was gone, and Ilse felt empty, totally alone, and deserted.

A large, slovenly young man came into the room and said, "Follow me." He said his name was Frank and that he was an attendant. He wasn't dressed like an attendant. He had on jeans and a wrinkled long-sleeved white shirt. His hair was black, unkempt, and he needed a shave. Frank's demeanor rubbed Ilse the wrong way even in her state of shock and confusion. By this time it was dark, but Ilse was to be taken to another building where her room was to be. Her head was down as she followed him, and she couldn't help noticing his big, dirty white tennis shoes with bright, chartreuse green shoelaces. She guessed he was nineteen or twenty.

Everything was bewildering and overwhelming but Ilse's tears had temporarily dried and she was observing what was happening. They followed a well-lit path past several low white buildings. Lights were shining from the windows. At one of the buildings, Frank stopped and said in a low gravelly voice, "we're here." They walked into an entryway with imitation leather chairs and wooden arms. Off the small entry area were closed doors, maybe offices Ilse thought. Before a double door, there was a window with a buzzer to the left. To the right was a bathroom, which Ilse said she needed to use.

"No, No," Frank said, "you have to wait until we take you to your room." Frank pressed the buzzer and a serious looking young woman came out, took the paperwork and opened the locked doors. Frank and Ilse followed her. She locked the doors after them. *Ilse wondered how she was supposed to get out if there was a fire (or if she wanted to leave).*

Patients were standing around with their eyes focused on the newcomer, checking her out. Some were talking, some laughing, all curious about the new patient. *She felt like a spectacle.* Ilse began crying again, but softly now as she followed Frank and the other staff member.

Rooms lined the hallway. All the walls were an off-white color without a single picture on the walls. As they walked down the tiled hallway, Ilse saw two or three beds in each room. Four doors down to the right, Frank announced, "You're home." The light in the room was dim,

but Ilse saw three beds. She was told the one by
the window was hers. Beside each twin bed
stood a nightstand with a lamp. Ilse was
assigned one section of the closet. Without
saying anything, Ilse began to go into the
bathroom and shut the door. The woman asked
Frank to step out, but she insisted on standing by
the open door while Ilse used the toilet. *This
humiliation was dreadful, worse than she
imagined. She couldn't believe that this was
actually happening.*

After Frank came back in, Ilse started to
open the suitcase on her bed.

Again, Frank said "No! No!" He opened
the suitcase while Ilse sat on another bed, tears
now streaming down her face. He began to take
out her lingerie, examining each piece by piece.

"Nice things" he said, "nice things."

*Sick, Ilse thought, this guy is the one who
is crazy!* He went through everything removing
a belt from Ilse's bathrobe. Then he had her
take off her shoes and he took her shoelaces and
the strap off her purse.

*Ilse thought, they must think I'm going to
kill myself…first the bathroom door has to be
open, then they take my things, and now my
cosmetic bag. He's actually taking the tiny mirror
from a lipstick case and the razor for shaving my
legs. Unbelievable. If I wasn't disturbed before, I
will be now, she thought.*

A staff member named Pat came in and
told Ilse she could put her clothes away. She was
anxious to lie on the bed because she was
exhausted and wanted to sleep, but Pat said she
couldn't sleep. Not yet. She was going to show
Ilse around. Hanging in the main hall for

everyone to see was a big green chalkboard marked with names and schedules. Already Ilse's name was on it. She recognized a doctor's name that she knew from Summit. She decided she didn't want him to know she was there, so she erased her name when Pat turned to continue the tour.

Pat took Ilse to a lounge, more like a library with books and games on the shelves, comfortable chairs, and a sofa next to a wall of windows. There were two game tables and only two people there, both young women. Next, Pat showed the new patient where she would go to get her medications morning and night.

As Pat led Ilse down the hallway, they passed a long line of patients waiting to use the common phone. An unkempt girl with tight jeans and a tighter sweater was being harassed by another patient for talking too long. Others were arguing about whose turn it was to use the phone next. Past the phone line, Pat led Ilse to the main lounge where there was a TV and plain metal chairs lined up in front. This room didn't look comfortable, but most of the patients congregated here. Three men in the front row were watching TV and arguing about which channel to watch. One guy was fat and his pants crept down showing his "crack" from the back of the metal chair. *Gross and revolting, Ilse thought.*

Part of this room was a kitchen with a refrigerator and sink. One lady had purposely poured out a pitcher of iced tea and another was yelling at her to clean up her mess. Ilse smelled popcorn and Pat said that they put only a certain number of microwave packets in the cupboard every day, but cautioned not to hoard it. She said if you were lucky enough to find some in the cupboard, you could pop some. Associated with that room and the people there, Ilse didn't think she'd ever want any, so it didn't matter. The room was noisy and about half the people were smoking. It was the only room in which you could smoke, but being a non-smoker, Ilse didn't intend ever to go in that lounge. She found out later that she should go in there because records were kept of how patients spent any unregimented time and socializing was considered important.

Pat said that Ilse needed to have something to eat. Ilse had not been aware that she hadn't eaten all day. She wasn't hungry, but a food tray was brought to the smoke-filled room. Pat sat with Ilse at a table as she picked at the food and then pushed the tray away.

All through the tour, Pat tried to make Ilse feel comfortable, but Ilse shook and cried the whole time. One of the patients came up, laughed and said, "You're scared!" Yes, she was, so Pat took her hand and asked her questions, trying to calm her. She had been assigned to familiarize Ilse to the clinic routine and make her feel "comfortable."

Ilse knew that when the door closed behind her, it had been locked. Meals and activities were to be in other buildings. For a while, she was told, someone would go with her to the dining room, or any activities away from this building.

"Walk, I want to walk in the morning," Ilse said. It was part of her routine. Pat told her someone would be with her at all times until she was released from "watch." She was told she would get used to it and it would be okay.

I wonder how quickly I can be released from "watch," Ilse thought. She knew she had to find a way of getting out of the clinic as soon as possible. Getting out would be her goal, but first she would do what she had to do to get the privilege of being trusted to come and go without a watchdog at her side.

It had been a long, long, horrible day...the worst imaginable. Ilse begged to be left alone to go to bed. Finally, she was taken back to the room. They weren't letting her out of their sight.

Now a roommate was in the room, sitting at a desk, writing in her journal. Her name was Nanci. She seemed "okay" but young, only twenty-two. The new roommate said "hi" but didn't talk much. She told them she was a nurse. Normally interested in other people, Ilse wasn't even curious why she was there. Nanci was about 5'8" with dark curly hair, cut short. Her complexion was ruddy and she seemed nervous, but *Ilse thought, who wouldn't be?*

Ilse got out her nightgown and headed to the bathroom to change, but there was to be no privacy this first night, not even to change her clothes.

I'll go without a shower until I get out of here, she thought. She wanted to be left alone. Modest by nature, it was just another infringement. *Were they going to take what little dignity she had left?* She wanted to sleep and find some peace. The night nurse gave her two white pills that would help her sleep. Ilse told her she didn't need anything to sleep, but she took the medication since the nurse wouldn't go away until she saw the pills go down. The roommate left with an aide to go to the lounge to smoke as soon as Ilse climbed into bed. Immediately she fell into a fitful sleep.

Just moments after Ilse went to sleep, a team of two came through the already open door and said "room check." They looked at Ilse, wrote something down and left. Ilse went back to sleep immediately but was awakened again, this time with a flashlight shining directly in her face for "room check." *Now Ilse knew they thought she was suicidal.* It didn't occur to her then that they were also checking Nanci's bed and every room down the hall. Furthermore, it didn't occur to Ilse at this time that there was a reason an aide went with Nanci to the smoking lounge.

4
Orientation

Awakened with bright sun coming through the window the next morning, Ilse was groggy as she examined the room in the daylight. It looked different but still intimidating. The walls were bare except where Nanci had made some weird drawings. Nanci, the roommate, was already gone. Ilse considered staying in bed, maybe forever. She had no idea what the day would bring until a cheery lady named Marie breezed in to tell her to "rise and shine" and to follow her to get her meds. Ilse had been on Prozac for several months to ease the depression so she knew that would be what they would give her. In her long pink robe, minus the belt which Frank had taken, Ilse followed Marie down the hall to a little gated cove they called the nurses' station. They gave her a little cup of water and watched as she took the pill. Then Marie said that after Ilse got dressed, she would go with her to have breakfast in another building.

Always in the habit of making the bed and keeping everything organized, Ilse slowly made the bed, trying to think of the easiest way to have a little privacy to get bathed and dressed. She put her bear on the pillow, folded the afghan she had brought along, then went to the closet to get something to wear. Marie sat on the bed while Ilse chose a pair of beige slacks and a colorful sweater. Since her tennis shoes no longer had laces, she decided to wear the loafers she'd brought along and wear pantyhose under the slacks since her socks wouldn't fit into the loafers.

Going into the bathroom, Ilse decided to forego a shower and quickly dress, brush her teeth, wash her face, and put on a little pink lipstick.

Funny, she thought, as she put on the pantyhose, that they let me keep pantyhose. Couldn't she hang herself with them if she wanted to? They're quite strong. She thought that crazy Frank was careless when he was so busy enjoying her lingerie. Frank probably made a lot of blunders and she decided not to mention the reckless pantyhose oversight. At least she could wear pantyhose because he was so stupid. Besides, she didn't like him and those psychedelic green shoelaces kept flashing through her mind.

Marie led the way; there was no crying and shaking this morning, but a sense of listlessness as Ilse followed her. After Marie unlocked the door, she stopped at the window and signed Ilse out, explaining that when she came and went she would always have to sign in and out with the time even when she was no longer guarded.

A short walk brought them to an attractive building housing the dining room with a buffet line and only a few people. It seemed that Ilse was getting a late start the first day. There were fruits, breads, cereal, eggs, bacon, etc. Nothing appealed to Ilse although the food was nicely displayed and the people serving were pleasant as Marie introduced her to everyone. She was told that they were part of her "family" and she would soon get to know them all. There were tables throughout the large dining area; some smaller ones had groups of four, five or six eating breakfast or having coffee. They were obviously doctors or other staff informally discussing their patients and work. They glanced up when Ilse came in, but didn't let their gazes linger. Just the same, Ilse knew that her presence was noted which made her uncomfortable. After eating as little as possible, Marie gave up on her and together they headed back to the dorm.

Ilse headed right for her room after getting through the security gate. The bed looked like a haven, and she flopped on it going right to sleep again. Moments later Marie was telling her she had to have blood drawn and visit the on-site internist. Back down the hall, past the empty lounge to another office, a nurse drew blood. She wasn't very adept, having to stick her many times to get the needle in her vein. *What a bunch of misfits, Ilse thought.*

Next was the doctor's office. It seemed darker than it should be but the darkness fit with Ilse's state of mind. In fact, she was more docile now...not crying or shaking or even talking unless asked a question. A nurse told her she didn't have to undress but to lie down on the examining table and take off her shoes. When the doctor came in, he didn't introduce himself. He didn't really talk with her, and only made comments to the nurse who was charting his words. He acted as if Ilse didn't know what was happening. He took the waistband of Ilse's pants and lifted it. Ilse knew her pants were now too big since she had lost so much weight in recent months. Now she spoke up.

"There is nothing wrong with me," she said, "not physically, just my messed up head." He laughed but didn't have a reply. Finally, she was back to the room and the bed she didn't like, but it was to become her haven. It wasn't a haven for long. Marie was back, this time to take her to her assigned doctor...her "shrink."

5
Dr. Joan Morrison

Dr. Joan Morrison was a tiny lady dressed in a fabulous outfit, a brown suit with a peach silk blouse and high, fashionable shoes. Her jewelry was simple and she wore glasses that framed kind, compassionate eyes. Ilse was aware of how people presented themselves. This was no exception. There was a business-like quality that could not be overlooked as she asked Ilse to sit in the soft wing-backed chair by the window. All the counselors seemed to have high wing-backed chairs in their offices, Ilse noted. The floor-to-ceiling bookshelf was laden with medical textbooks and a coffee table held magazines and tissues. Instead of the wing-backed chair, Ilse chose a leather swivel chair opposite Dr. Morrison's desk.

Soon in tears, Ilse began talking about her situation. Dr. Morrison didn't take any notes and didn't comment on what she was telling her. Ilse decided not to hold back since she was already in a mental institution. She blamed Robert for putting her there and began to tell the doctor a little of what brought her to this point. Thank goodness, she wouldn't have to be in Dr. Morrison's office longer than an

hour, not the first day anyway. The doctor
would need to allow time for other patients, plus
she was the physician in charge of the entire
clinic. It seemed that Ilse had been assigned to
the best psychiatrist they had; whether it meant
she was more disturbed than the other patients
remained to be seen. *Maybe Dr. Frank had
requested Dr. Morrison for her.* Whatever the
reason, Ilse instinctively liked her and thought
she could learn to trust her.

Walking back to her room Ilse noted
someone had put her name back on the large
green chart and now the hours were all filled in
with a schedule Ilse was to follow. Every hour
there was something she was supposed to do:
exercise, crafts, group therapy, group therapy,
group therapy, group therapy...and visits with
Dr. Morrison. Free time was allotted during
evening hours or one could choose an evening
activity. It was exhausting to even think about
it.

Ilse knew her way back to her assigned
room and decided to go there to sleep it all off. It
seemed like a good idea. There weren't any
patients around and it was nice not to have
anyone trying to talk with her. She wanted to be
alone to analyze what was happening in this
place.

Almost immediately, Marie was there
again, this time to take her to lunch, through the
locked door, along the walkway to the cafeteria.
This time the dining room was loud, packed with
patients. Some teen-agers from another building
didn't seem disturbed in any way.

"Why are they here?" Ilse asked. Many
had drug addictions and some had family

problems. *Thinking about her own children, Ilse was glad her daughter and son had never had to be hospitalized in a place like this.* They had never been addicted to drugs or had unusual emotional problems.

The lunch, served cafeteria style, was presented nicely but the smell made Ilse nauseous. She couldn't eat much, but took a little salad and a Diet Coke. The chocolate cake looked good. It was an effort to eat, but Marie told Ilse that they consider what you eat as a measure of improvement. Ilse became an expert in taking food, cutting it up, eating a little, and throwing the rest in the trash can. She was not anorexic and she knew that. She simply wasn't hungry.

She had taught her students about anorexic behavior and the consequences when she taught high school in Michigan, before moving to New Jersey. Personal relationships, marriage and family, health and nutrition, childcare and development were among the units she included in the home economics curriculum she taught. She was strong in all those areas, confident, and a good example to students. Ilse's students, both boys and girls, called her Mom or Mrs. "K." She related to her students feeling she had been a better than average teacher. That was another world from the one she was a part of now.

Her students would never believe where she was, or the predicament in which she now found herself. She knew she was emotionally troubled but it was related to the rejection by the husband whom she had adored all those years...not just the rejection, but also the denial on his part that there was another woman. Why couldn't he be upfront, rather than assert that Ilse was crazy and needed hospitalization?

6
Making a Plan

True to her nature, Ilse quickly decided to make the best of the situation and begin to figure out what she would need to do to be released from this "cracker factory" as soon as possible. In fact, it was at lunch with her counterparts, when Ilse decided she would do whatever she was supposed to do to get out. She would cooperate, get involved and use it to her advantage. This wouldn't happen without some trust that the system was going to work for her. *All she could do was be herself, be honest and be willing to take any help she could find to get OUT of this place. Whatever it took!*

Part of the process would have to involve thinking about Robert, their life together, and maybe her life before Robert. She would have to look at her past, meld it with more recent years as a wife and mother, then focus on what had happened in the last two years, and finally what was the future to be. Choices. Whatever it took is what she would do, but first she just needed to rest. Without any physical exercise, she felt exhausted.

7
Help!

Help! After lunch, Marie left her for a while to rest since Ilse begged to have some time alone. After Marie left the room, Ilse ran to the phone. She remembered the number of her good friend, Rene, in Clarkston.

They had taught school together, along with two other women, and had bonded as "sisters." Over the years, they had done many things as couples, including a cruise, visiting a resort in Mexico, and more recently a trip to England and Scotland. The four couples traveled well together, but once in awhile there was a glitch...usually related to Robert's unrealistic, selfish expectations. If Robert didn't feel like eating, he didn't think anyone else should want to.

When Ilse told their friends, Rene and Josh, that she thought Robert was having an affair, it was hard for them to believe that Robert was unfaithful. Nearly a year earlier, before Robert had moved out, Ilse had forewarned them that there were problems. Since then, Ilse had talked with Rene, along with other mutual friends from Summit. None of the group could quite understand what was happening with Robert or why he had left their home since he was so unyielding in his insistence that he just wanted to be alone to work and pursue his career and there definitely was not another woman. They had thought that Ilse's fears of his infidelity were probably not true because he never seemed to pay attention to other women; however, doubt crept in since there was nothing else that would cause their friend such anguish. Robert refused to talk with any of these close friends when they tried to call him.

Now, at the phone with no one guarding her, she dialed and thankfully, Rene answered. Happy, cheery, always upbeat Rene soon was frantic calling for Josh to come to the phone. They heard Ilse pleading.

"Come and get me out of here. Please, please, you have to help me. They took my shoelaces. Robert put me in a mental institution. You know I'm depressed, but I shouldn't be here. He gave me no choice. He framed me and I have to get out of here. I don't know who else to call." Crying hysterically so Rene could barely understand her, Ilse begged for help. She gave Rene the number on the phone, but hung up when Marie hurried back, telling her that she wasn't allowed to use the phone yet. She had trusted her to stay in her room to rest, but she wasn't sure if Ilse had made a call or not. She saw, however, that Ilse was visibly upset again and out of control. Now Marie sat in the room while Ilse was given a moment to rest.

8
Group III and the Routine

Marie said that there was a group session that Ilse needed to attend; she would take her there. The others in the group would already be there. She showed Ilse on the green chalkboard that she was in Group III with five other people. Going into the group was like going to kindergarten the first day, not knowing anyone, the teacher or the school. It scared Ilse to walk into the little room, but by now she was becoming calmer, although there were still tears in her eyes.

The group leader was a young lady, a psychologist. The group had four women and one man in it. All at ease, they had no problem talking about themselves. The leader, Ms. Loren, asked Ilse to introduce herself. Ilse was nervous. After muttering her name and where she lived, she said she didn't feel like talking about herself. The psychologist told her it was important that she "share." She got "off the hook" that day but it wouldn't be like that for long. *Ilse was beginning to realize that being cooperative would be a key element in showing she was well enough to be released.* At following sessions, Ilse opened up a little about herself, but she was more interested in the other members of her group and why they were there. She was quite adept at turning the group focus on the others. *If she got the others to talk, she wouldn't have to "share" except a bit here and there. She had already told her walking buddies at home, her Michigan friends and others what was on her mind. She didn't feel the need to keep talking with people who couldn't help her.*

In her group was a police officer named Peter, a tall well-built man about Ilse's age. He had gray hair, deep blue eyes and a nice smile. He said he had left his wife who was fine with it, but he had terrible guilt feelings about leaving her after a long marriage and three children. The guilt made him sick. There was a parallel in their lives, but Ilse was the one who felt guilty because she could no longer make the marriage work. She was now putting blame on herself.

What had she done or not done to make Robert look to another woman for what he needed? It was something to think about. Robert didn't think he was the one that needed to be put in a hospital. He had no guilt about leaving his wife while this man, Peter, did. Ilse and Peter ended up talking some after most sessions; she could understand how he felt and in turn, he was sympathetic to her.

A thirty-some year old beautiful black woman was also in the group. She had a successful career as an administrative assistant somewhere in Philadelphia. She was married, she said, to a wonderful man. She talked about her addiction, a sex addiction. Ilse didn't know that there was such a problem. It embarrassed her to hear details of the woman's sexual encounters. At one point, Ilse asked her if she wasn't afraid of not only losing her husband but of getting AIDS or some other venereal disease? Ilse told her that thinking of the probable consequences might deter her.

After being at the clinic for a week, Ilse began to interject ideas and solutions for everyone else. *Distanced from other patients' problems, she thought she could put herself in their situation.* She had empathy for her group mates. Sometimes she thought she should be the one leading the group instead of the young psychologist. She wasn't afraid to ask the other patients questions about their problems, which prompted discussion and ideas.

The adults who were addicted to drugs or alcohol were in another unit nearby. The only interaction with these people was at mealtime with one exception, Julie who was also in Group III. Young and attractive, she had been through detoxification for drugs in another unit. Now she was regrouping to go out into the world away from a restricted environment. Ilse thought she was very together. In one session, Julie told about how difficult it had been to go through detox and how much she looked forward to staying straight. She said she had promised never to go back to the drug scene.

Ilse had been taking a silver jewelry class for several years in Summit and was wearing silver bangles she had made. She really liked Julie. She could have been her daughter, so she gave her two of the silver bracelets. Julie hugged her and told her she would make her proud. She'd stay straight.

A few days later, loud music was blaring from one of the cars in the parking lot. Julie was in her bikini underwear dancing on top of a car. It didn't matter that it was cold. The doctors determined that her boyfriend had brought in drugs for her and she couldn't resist, even after all the therapy and promises. Ilse cried for her and began to fight for her to have just one more chance. She even went to Dr. Morrison who had made the decision to send Julie home this time. It didn't help. Julie would have to wait until a later date to try to detox again. There were now only four others in the group besides Ilse.

The other two women in the group had been around awhile. They seemed to enjoy being in the hospital. Ilse never did figure out what their problems were, if any. Maybe they liked having no responsibilities other than to show up for the numerous sessions.

Ilse thought the two women looked at the hospital as a nice reprieve from their difficult home lives. She did note that if you weren't troubled, the entire clinic would make a nice spa, complete with good food, clean linens, an exercise room and beautiful grounds with shrubs and trees. It could be turned into a luxurious retreat by redecorating the bedrooms and improving the lounges...soft chairs, a little paint, pictures on the walls, fluffy pillows on the beds, etc. Robert wasn't one to encourage unnecessary pampering and Ilse never expected it, having come from a working class, no-frills background. She did appreciate the setting, however, as it reminded her of the ranches and farms of her California childhood.

Ilse went to the lounge to read and try to think things through. An aide entered and wrote something on a pad in her folder. Twenty minutes later, she was back again making another notation. Curious after the third visit, Ilse followed her to the smoking lounge where most everyone seemed to be gathered. The aide was making checks on paper to note where everyone was. It caused Ilse to stay in the smoking room for the next notation even though Frank was hanging around with the patients in the smoking lounge. It seemed that it was important for the patients to not be alone in the other lounge. Frank said "Hi" to Ilse with a leering smile. Being polite, she replied and went back to her observations that night. It was interesting to see how everyone was acting...a lot of loud voices, bragging, smoking, fighting, cursing, some singing, angry faces, sad faces and many faces devoid of emotion. Ilse's face was one of the sad, confused ones but she was not crying this second night there. She was simply studying the situation and making a quiet plan. She went back to her plan: *to cooperate, interact with the other patients and staff, be pleasant, show up for sessions, participate as openly and honestly as she could, and GET OUT!*

The plan took shape and Ilse quietly executed it. It was only a few days before Ilse began to earn some freedom. She was trusted enough to go with others to the dining room and even allowed to go for a walk without a private escort. But she still couldn't have her shoelaces or bathrobe tie. Dr. Morrison had added possible activities to her chart: crafts, gardening, exercising.

Frank was assigned to accompany groups to various activities. His favorite was to go to the exercise room. This was Ilse's first adventure out, about the third night of her hospital stay. Frank arrived as sloppy as ever, with his dirty shoes and bright shoelaces. *Ilse was embarrassed, still thinking about how he had gone through her personal things.* When they got to the gym, she was happy to see they had a Nordic Track. In addition to walking in Island Park near their home, Ilse had used a similar machine forty to sixty minutes a day at home. This seemed a long way from the familiar room at home but ignoring the other machines, Ilse went right to the Nordic Track and began.

Frank watched, amazed that Ilse even knew how to work it, let alone keep her balance, telling her he wanted his turn. She said, "The exercise times are for the patients, not you... maybe you could use a machine that no one else is using." Not a fighter by nature, but mad at Frank for his intrusion, Ilse decided not to give in to him. Frank still insisted that he should have a turn. *Why should Frank get a turn? He's an employee.* A verbal fight ensued. Ilse stayed on the machine and Frank pouted. It was the beginning of a war between the two. Ilse stayed on the machine for the whole session because she felt empowered. As stupid as he was, Frank got the point.

I'm not through with him yet, Ilse thought. And she wasn't. *She knew that Frank could not influence the staff or deter her plan to work her way back home.*

Every evening, the single telephone in the wide hallway was busy with the usual line-up of people arguing to make a call. People could call in if they could get through. Right after dinner the phone wasn't as busy. Rene had tried to call Ilse with the number she had given when she sent her S.O.S. She never got through, but Rene told Ilse later that Josh called Robert at work to ask him what was going on. Robert convinced him that it was necessary to commit Ilse, that she was suicidal. He told Josh that he had to remove the guns from the house because Ilse was crazy and one never knew what she might do.

9
What is Robert Thinking?

Before Robert had moved out of the house, he made a fuss of removing all the guns, not saying why but *Ilse knew why. He could tell friends that he had prevented her from doing something stupid.* Living in Michigan years before, when Robert was at the Henry Ford Hospital, an associate's wife had used a gun to commit suicide. She had postpartum depression after the birth of the second child. Ilse had been good friends with her, bringing over meals, encouraging her, taking care of her children and befriending her. It was a heartbreaking experience, which left a scar. It had affected Ilse in many ways but in particular, how she felt about guns. She hated them and would never use one to hurt anyone, let alone herself.

Robert collected guns and pistols. Ilse had given him some for birthdays or Christmas after he showed an interest in a particular make or model. Some of his hunting buddies helped her find just the right gun for hunting pheasant, quail and deer. She didn't know or appreciate much about the guns, but could admire a beautiful stock or barrel.

The favorite gun in his collection was a Civil War gun with a bayonet that Robert had bought from an elderly lady in his hometown. He would often tell the story of purchasing the gun as a teenager with his father for twenty-five dollars. It truly was a treasure and Robert liked all history of the Civil War, as did his father. On the evening he took all the guns so she wouldn't hurt herself, he removed that gun too, but it is doubtful that it would even work. The antique gun had been displayed on the mantle over the fireplace in every home Robert and Ilse owned.

Skeet and trap shooting was a hobby for Robert. In fact, one year he was club champion for skeet shooting when the couple belonged to the Country Club in the Detroit area, the only club with a shooting range. He would go there and shoot with one of his favorite doctors, the chairman of the Department of Radiology, his very good friend. At that time, Robert began to load his own shells. Ilse had bought him the machine, and after the move to Summit, he often spent time in his basement workshop loading shells.

Yes, he had a thing about guns but Ilse would not handle them. He kept them under the bed. *He knew very well that Ilse would never use one and wouldn't know how to shoot one if she wanted.* In spite of knowing that, he made a show of removing the guns. It was incongruent with his other behavior, even early in the marriage breakup. *It occurred to Ilse that he was making a backhanded suggestion that there were other ways to end one's life.* Ironically, he even said that shooting oneself would be too messy.

"Remember Elaine?" he remarked in an offhand manner about their friend's wife who took her own life with a gun. Ilse had helped take care of her two little boys left screaming alone in their house.

How selfish it was to do this, she thought, but was this what he was hinting she should do?

What else was he thinking? Wouldn't it be easy if Ilse were out of the picture? Robert could openly grieve that Ilse took her own life. Then Carrie could arrive on the scene, support him, help him to again find happiness... they would live happily ever after... a thought that kept creeping into Ilse's mind as he continually told Ilse how crazy she was.

While Ilse was in the hospital getting therapy, she tried to look into Robert's mind. *She decided that Robert had been planning to leave her before he even realized it himself. She had an inkling that he felt if he played his cards right, if things didn't work out with Carrie, Ilse would always take him back.* For a long time, in spite of the verbal and emotional abuse he had inflicted on her, she would have. The love she felt for him could not be denied, regardless of how he felt about her, or how he treated her. *Yes, she realized that she had blindly let him have a powerful influence over her.*

Over the years, there had been a gradual change in their relationship. The changes were so miniscule, spread over such a long period of time that they had gone almost unnoticed. She was aware that as he became more important and powerful he was never satisfied. There was

59

always another goal that could only be realized through his continual climb up the ladder of success.

Ilse was also aware of her important role in helping him climb that ladder to the very top. They began as a team, and until now, the career advancement had been a team effort. Her methods were kind and gentle support. His methods were often ruthless and aggressive. Their approaches to getting ahead were different. Maybe this was because they came from very different family environments.

Part II: 1940-1990

10
Families

Ilse spent many hours talking to Dr. Morrison, her psychiatrist, about her heritage.

Ilse had been born in Nebraska to hardworking German immigrants. She never knew her paternal grandparents but her mother's parents lived in Janesville, a neighboring town. Her grandparents had moved off the farm to retire in town, but the farm was still theirs. Ilse's mother, Ella, was an only child.

As a young couple, Ilse's parents followed their dream to California where they worked hard to develop the highest yielding vineyard in the San Joaquin Valley. While there, twins were born to them. Sadly, Donna and Donald lived only a few hours and were buried in Reedley. These first twins were rarely mentioned. The couple went on to have two more boys, a redhead named Walter and a blond named Steve. This move to California provided a wonderful life except for the loss of their twins. After five years, the family moved back to Nebraska to be close to Ilse's maternal grandparents. It was in

Nebraska that Ilse was born and another set of twins, James and Jacob arrived.

When Ilse was five, her parents were tired of the cold Nebraska winters and decided to return to their beloved California. The couple sold their Nebraska acreage on which they had developed modest homes. They gave away all their frivolous possessions like dolls, toys and unnecessary items. They literally packed one trailer with all the belongings for their family of seven. The old car pulled the overloaded trailer for the trip west. Four little people were piled in the back seat with big brother and parents in front.

Ilse remembered many experiences growing up in California. First, they worked in the orchards, cutting apricots for the drying trays while their father sought property to develop with his brother who would be moving from Denver. Ilse was five, but she cut apricots along with the adult women.

When Daddy (as the children all fondly called him until the day he died) found suitable land for development in Los Gatos, the family lived in a small trailer house with no bathroom facility. There was an outhouse they had to use for several months until they moved into the "big" house. On the property was a nice ranch home into which the family moved when the former owners left. Having been confined to the trailer, everyone appreciated the space and especially the bathroom. Then, as part of the development, Daddy and his brother built lovely homes next to each other with four bedrooms each. Since Ilse was the only girl, she always was given her own room. The boys had bunk beds, one set in each room.

For Ilse's mother, the Los Gatos home was her favorite place. She could look out at the beautiful Santa Cruz Mountains from her kitchen window. She had pretty flowers and the garden was full of artichokes and other California specialties. Looking out of the dining room window that framed the entire room, she could see a bank of crimson ice plants, which flowed down the backyard terraces.

For the children, it was wonderful too. They took the bus to school and had nice teachers. They walked to town on Saturday mornings for folk dance classes. Every Saturday their mother baked bread, enough loaves and rolls to last their family of seven for the entire week. The most delicious smell permeated their house and the children were never denied a hot roll with butter, fresh from the oven.

Saturday was the time to shine shoes and the kids all took turns. Each family member owned a pair of good shoes. But finally, Daddy bought Ilse a special pair of patent leather "Mary Janes" which didn't have to be shined, but she still was expected to take her turn rubbing the brown paste on everyone else's shoes.

On Sundays, the family attended the Presbyterian Church. Sunday night they enjoyed huge bowls of popcorn with milk...a treat and a family tradition. On rainy Sunday afternoons, they all helped pull homemade taffy or made popcorn balls. Goodies were not usually in the house, but there was always sugar or syrup for candy making. They played Monopoly by the hour inside or 'Hide and Seek' and 'Kick the Can' outside. There were balls and bats, trees to climb and two bikes to be shared.

The oldest brother and his friend taught Ilse how to ride a bike by sending her down one of the steep dead-end streets in the development. It was one of Walter's meaner tricks followed by many others. In this same house, he tied her to a fence by the street. Cars drove by and people waved until several hours later, when Steve rescued her. With so many children, one didn't always show up missing until a chore was to be done. No one had missed Ilse at all. With the freedom to run and play when there were no chores, Mother didn't find anything amiss. If Ilse complained about the things Walter was doing to her, her mother said that was his way of showing love.

All five children took piano lessons and had definite practice times. Ilse didn't like the lessons or the practicing. She would rather be climbing trees or organizing her room. She had a sense of rhythm and loved to sing, but a visiting lady had laughed at her when she sang. Embarrassed even at that age, she was hesitant to sing out. Dancing was more fun and Ilse begged for dance lessons like her neighbor, but her parents said she couldn't take lessons. She thought it was because they didn't have enough money for such extras.

When they lived in Los Gatos, Ilse became ill one night. Her father had traveled to Florida with Uncle Matt. Ilse found her mother in the laundry room with an endless stack of ironing. As Ilse fell to the floor, her mother knew she was sick, very sick and directly called the family doctor who was at their house in twenty minutes. He said Ilse had to be taken to the hospital. On the way out of the house, Walter was laughing from his bedroom nearest the door.

"Is she going to die?' he yelled.

Her mother replied, "I don't know." She had a ruptured appendix and almost did die.

After the surgery, Ilse again asked her mother if she was going to die. Always honest, her mother replied, "I hope not, but I don't know. Only God knows." Other than to give birth to her children, Ilse was never sick enough to be admitted to a hospital again...until now.

Her parents ran a "tight ship" but they were steering the family on a clear course of hard work with rewards that would last a lifetime.

Their father often said, "All work and no play makes Jack a dull boy." He made sure the children had plenty of both work and play. They had platitudes for everything it seemed. Respect for their parents and elders was demanded. Every child in the family was treated the same. If the twins got a nickel, the other three would get one too. If there was one chocolate bar, it was divided five ways (with some argument that one piece was bigger than another).

Sometimes, when needed, strong discipline was used. After church one Sunday, Ilse received a good spanking she never forgot for talking during the service to her twin brothers. Her mother was usually the disciplinarian, but she got a firm spanking after breaking a piece of wooden molding her father had been soaking to bend and fit in a corner.

When it broke, Ilse tried to run, but her father spanked her hard...to this day it still hurts. This was the only time her father raised a hand to her.

Earlier, while working on a farm cutting apricots and living in a motel, Ilse saw three dimes on the table. She took the dimes one night and spent them on candy on her walk to school the next day. Every dime in the room was to be accounted for, so they knew one of the children had taken the money. They figured out that Ilse was not only taking the coins at home but also stealing candy from the neighborhood store. Both parents took Ilse, kicking and screaming, to the store where she apologized and told the clerks she would never come in again. It was horrible for her but she never stole another thing. "Live and learn" was another of their platitudes. She learned!

After building homes on the two streets in Los Gatos, the family moved to the San Joaquin Valley where farmland was rich. Daddy loved the white ash soil for the crops. First, they purchased a chicken ranch. Yuk! Carrying a chicken in each hand by its feet to be vaccinated while it pecked at your legs was not pleasant. Cleaning the eggs by sanding them was not as bad because the youngest four children talked and laughed while they worked sitting on low stools around the basket of eggs Walter and Steve had collected. That ranch was sold as soon as it was improved.

They moved to another run-down ranch with an orchard of grapefruit and orange trees, run-over with grape vines. The vineyard was taken out, the land cleared and cotton planted.

Daddy bought a cotton picker, shared it with neighboring farms and all the children worked, hoeing weeds and picking cotton in the fall. Their mother made large bags with straps, appropriate to their sizes, so they could work in the field alongside the hired field hands. Weighing their bags when they were full, the foreman kept a record so they could collect their pay. At the end of the day, they would be able to jump onto the cotton trailer before going home for supper. The two older boys had to work the hardest by running the tractor and milking, but everyone helped, bringing in shingles for re-roofing the house or straightening nails to reuse in the new machine shop.

Ilse's mother made most of her clothes and usually the shirts for her brothers, many times out of matching feed sacks. She didn't mind if Ilse used her machine and fabric scraps to sew something. Ilse started making little things such as doll clothes. She was attached to the sewing machine with a determination to create.

Her long straight hair was put into braids every morning by her mother for as long as she could remember. Her mother carefully parted her hair down the middle, and brushed and brushed and then began to braid, tying the ends with a rubber band. For special times or church, she fashioned French braids and sometimes ribbons. With her long braids, she looked like a little old-fashioned girl.

One summer Ilse begged to have her hair cut and her mother finally relented IF she could take care of her hair herself. It was so straight, her mother ended up giving her a permanent.

Ilse struggled until she could fix it herself. Even as a young girl, she was concerned about the way she looked. From being out in the sun every day, Ilse had freckles. And then there was that nose inherited from both her mother and father. They tried to tell her that it looked aristocratic, but Ilse knew it was just plain big.

During the hot summers, all five kids were hired out to pick grapes. Sometimes they were put into a box and sometimes directly on trays for drying in the vineyards. It was hard work, but they were paid, and the best part was riding their bikes to the swimming pool after work. They didn't realize that their mother liked that too because they came home squeaky clean after the dirty grape-picking job.

Any money earned was given back to Father. It wasn't to be used for frivolous things, but was kept in each child's account....their college fund. It was accumulating bit by bit and each child had his or her own savings account book so that he or she could watch their money grow.

On the last ranch in California, Daddy helped Steve install a regulation size basketball hoop at the correct height on the barn. They used the dirt barnyard for a gym floor. Everyone played basketball, but Steve practiced every free moment into the evening hours. It was a wonderful, innocent time.

You would think that with four brothers Ilse would be spoiled, but that was not the case. There was plenty of work for everyone, whether on the ranches in California or in the garden or house after the move to Sidney.

The family moved back to Sidney to be close to their aging grandparents who now had failing health. When Ilse's family moved to Sidney, her parents bought a house around the corner from Robert's home not knowing that he would be the love of Ilse's life. Soon after buying the house, the maternal grandparents moved in with them. Luckily, there was a downstairs bedroom and adjoining bath for them to use.

Now, as an eighth grader and a California girl, Ilse began school in Sidney, along with her three brothers. The oldest brother remained in California to attend the University of California at Berkeley. Steve was a sophomore. The twins were starting the sixth grade.

Ilse's parents selected a house in a limited attendance area that would feed the laboratory school associated with Nebraska's State Teacher's College, only two blocks from their home. It was important to Ilse's mother and father that their children have the best possible education, so they looked for a house in this area.

Ilse's mother had earned a two-year college degree from NSTC as a young girl and then she had gone back to school in California to get a four-year degree. She worked around the five children and the ranch work, traveling twenty miles each way, with her family scarcely aware of her absence until she completed her studies. In later years, Ilse marveled at how she managed it all. *How did she?*

Her father had never been to college because he never had the opportunity. As a very young man, he quit school to become head of the family and take care of the farm when his father died. He had later gone for his high school diploma and taken numerous adult education classes. With a quiet modesty, he was one of the most intelligent men Ilse knew. He was also the hardest working man she knew. He expected no less of his five children. Because he had not had the opportunity to go to college, he expected that his children would all go to college. So, a two story older home was purchased near the college. The four children that remained at home would go to school there.

On the property, a barn complete with a haymow had been converted to a garage and tool shop. The loft became a favorite hangout for the younger brothers and their friends. A rope ladder, which they raised and lowered, provided privacy since it wasn't easy for the parents to get up to the loft.

Beyond the garage were a huge yard to be mowed, a big garden, a little gazebo and flowering shrubs bordering their neighbors, the Kellys. Neighboring on the other side of Ilse's home was a family that included Judy who would start school at TCHS (Teachers College High School) at the same time as Ilse. Judy and a girl across the street, Dorothy, had moved in from a one-room country schoolhouse. Dorothy was the prettiest, Judy the smartest and Ilse the friendliest. These country girls were pure gold and became close friends.

The Kelly home that bordered Ilse's back yard was immaculate. The grass was perfectly manicured. The flowers were beautiful and there was not a weed in sight. Mrs. Kelly was a perfectionist about her garden and house. Very sweet, she was distant, maybe shy or insecure. *Was she also abused? Ilse wondered later.* She had one very good friend living across the street with a daughter in the same school class as Ilse. Dr. and Mrs. Kelly had no social life, but Mrs. Kelly was active in her Women's Club where she excelled in creating floral arrangements for competition, representing her club at the fair. Being artistic, she usually earned several blue ribbons, which were written up in the local newspaper. It was the focus and joy of her life. When she met Dr. Kelly, she was working as a registered nurse and for a while, the Kellys worked together in his private practice. In later years, she helped with the books.

Dr. Kelly, Robert's father, was an important otolaryngologist in town. In addition to his ear, nose and throat practice, he specialized in eye surgery. Even though a serious, rather odd man, he was well thought of as a physician. Yet, he was unapproachable. Aloof. Those who visited his office as patients said he rarely spoke, but took the time to meet their medical needs. He was brilliant, having graduated from medical school second in his class at the University of Nebraska. Performing surgery as it related to his specialty in the local hospital, he spent endless hours at home studying medical journals and often dissecting pig's eyes to maintain his skills. The Wall Street Journal and the Kiplinger Report were read religiously. With more money to invest than most people in town, every year he worried about his federal income tax report. It made him nervous, but not enough for him to hire an accountant he could trust. In Sidney, the Kelly family was considered wealthy, the result of hard work and frugality combined with a successful career choice.

Robert's house had every modern convenience that money could buy at the time. Their family had the first TV and an antenna tower was placed on their roof for everyone to admire. *It seemed the Kellys wanted to impress others.*

Robert Kelly had gone to the lab school since he was in kindergarten. He was bigger than a lot of the kids. He had brown curly hair and in eighth grade was already tall and lanky. When he walked, he ambled. Brown eyes and perfectly white teeth made him a very 'cute' neighbor. When he showed up for school that first day, he sported a black eye and broken nose, which he had received after "mouthing off" to a passing college student. It made him look tough.

In contrast to Robert's family, Ilse's family didn't have a TV, but they were invited next door to the Netherland's on Friday nights to watch "Amos and Andy." They didn't have a dishwasher or fancy furniture, but the house was clean and well maintained. Ilse's home, although modest, was a meeting place for friends and relatives. The large living room was friendly and welcoming but it was usually cluttered with the weekly accumulation of newspapers and notebooks. The over-sized dining room table was where the kids spread out their homework, which their mother monitored. She was a taskmaster keeping track of assignments, proofreading, and demanding the best from each child. *How did she have the time?*

Sandwiched between those plain walls was a fierce family cohesiveness and loyalty, established over the years. They learned to share one bathroom on the second floor, banging on the door occasionally to hurry someone along. Robert had his own bathroom next to his own bedroom; he didn't have to plan his time around his lone sister or parents. In reality, Robert and Ilse were living next door, but their family life was worlds apart.

Over the years, with intelligence and strength, Ilse's father built a sizeable nest egg. Because of their modesty and frugal nature, people did not realize that they had a growing bank account. When the children asked what they should write down for his occupation, their father said, "self employed." He was semi-retired, managing the grandparents' farm and going to the stock market every workday. With his excellent mind and cunning, he had invested successfully in the stock market with profits from the sale of each ranch. He also subscribed to The Wall Street Journal. Without the children knowing, he was putting stock in their names.

The family could have lived differently, but they had been used to living frugally and Ilse's parents would do so the rest of their lives. It was a trait that they passed down to all of their children. A college education for all five children was at the top of their priority list...that and instilling good morals and high family values ...hard work, respect, honesty, integrity, trust, love of God and each other. That is what Ilse and Robert, years later, had tried to give their children. It seemed that they had been successful

until the marriage began to collapse. *They were no longer a good example Ilse thought.*

11
Reflections with Dr. Morrison

Meeting again with Dr. Morrison, Ilse found herself thinking about how her predicament now fit into the scheme of things. Dr. Morrison would probe, and it seemed that when Ilse talked about her family, their hard work, their camping trips and all the fun they had together, she was happy. Ilse liked remembering how things had been as she grew up. These memories weren't part of her depression; instead, they were comforting.

Whenever she had to talk about the last few years with Robert, her mood changed. Confusion caused her to shake and cry. She told the doctor about meeting Robert. She talked about mutual acquaintances from their years in high school and college together and about their subsequent courtship and marriage. She told her stories about friends...what they meant to her as she reminisced. It was pleasant talking to Dr. Morrison every day until she was reminded of where she was and what was happening. The memories were comforting.

After the move to Nebraska, a favorite memory was when school began that fall. A neighbor, Ilse's age, stopped by Ilse's house when she was pushing her little brother in his stroller. Lucy talked about classmates who lived in the neighborhood, as well as others who lived on farms. She said she would stop by and walk with Ilse to school the next morning. The next day they walked up the street to an old building on the college campus, which housed the junior and senior high students.

Although it was difficult being a new student, Ilse was anxious to meet her new classmates. It would be the first day for Dorothy and Judy too, but the way had been paved for Dorothy since everyone thought she was the prettiest girl ever to be in the class. Everyone was looking for her, not for Ilse or Judy. For a few days, the new friends were few but everyone was friendly.

Meg Olson was also to become Ilse's close friend...a life-long friend. Meg lived in one of the nicer homes, a modern ranch home her father built. Only two blocks away, the two friends could run back and forth to each other's homes. They left messages in a bridge railing, slept over at one another's houses, walked up the hill to school, and got into mischief together.

Meg's young mother wore nice dresses and was pretty with a slight figure, short brown hair and expressive brown eyes. Meg looked just like her. In contrast, Ilse saw her own mother as much older with her braids wrapped around her head. She was plain, somewhat stout, and used lipstick only when going to church or the PTA. She was usually in a housedress even if she was working in the garden. Her mother had only one pair of nice shoes and they were old fashioned;

brown with a tie and a short thick heel. She had worn the same pair for years with any dress to church or 'dress up' affairs. Her mother's dowdy dress was somewhat of an embarrassment to Ilse but she never criticized her.

Although their families were different, the two girls became the best of friends. Spending time at each other's homes, often hidden away in their bedrooms, the two could share confidences knowing those secrets would go no further. Meg had another close friend she had known for years. Ilse often found herself jealous of Gloria when the other two spent time together. Three friends together didn't always work. One-on-one seemed better from Ilse's standpoint.

A new laboratory school was being built when Ilse entered the eighth grade. The students left the college campus and moved into their own new building for high school. It had been fun to "hang around" the college, playing "chalk the arrow," (a game which required snatching chalk from the college classrooms and leaving directions to be followed by the opposing team), or going underground through the pipe system. Ilse and Meg got involved with "chalk the arrow" but never got caught. They were "too chicken" to go underground which was more for guys like Robert. Hours could be wasted with these so-called games. Fortunately for Ilse, her parents never knew about them, but she found other ways to get into trouble...non-serious pranks like laughing in class or tricks on the teachers.

Robert, on the other hand, got into big trouble for hurling chunks of plaster of Paris onto the drama department stage. He was even taken into police custody for one of his misdeeds. His father had to get him out, but interestingly found it amusing. Ilse's parents would have let her sit in jail.

The new school had a huge indoor swimming pool so everyone had to learn to swim. Boys and girls took physical education separately, but the girls had a male swimming instructor. It was mandatory that the girls wear old college issued swimsuits. They were wool and often had holes in them. Ilse hated those suits. They were humiliating especially if you didn't have much of a figure, which Ilse didn't. Even more humiliating was the open shower room. Miss Morton, the strict P.E. teacher stood guard making sure everyone showered. Ilse would hurry through, then wrap up in a towel to protect her modesty. If she were more developed, as most of the girls were, she thought she would have been more comfortable. Sometimes the boys and girls had a co-ed class to learn to dance, bowl or canoe on the river.

When Ilse arrived in eighth grade, she became aware of a group of girls who called themselves the "Sexy Seven," all well developed for their age and probably having early periods. They were in Ilse's class, but they had attended school together for a long time. Being almost flat-busted with a thin but firm body on a 5'2" frame, Ilse didn't mind not being a member and she didn't care that she didn't have cramps like those girls, but she wished she had breasts. That was soon to change as her figure rounded, but she remained small. That was okay with her since she was able to keep up with her brothers and she was competent in sports.

In high school, Ilse teamed up with Robert and others to run around the campus and escape campus security. After almost getting caught, Ilse gave it up. Other times, when her mother discovered her being with boys instead of sleeping over with a friend, she confronted her. It was embarrassing to have her mother scold her in front of her friends. Ilse's mother could be quite intimidating because she expected excellent behavior from her children. It was fortunate she never knew what trespasses Ilse's younger brothers committed using the barn loft for headquarters.

Ilse's favorite subject was an elective, home economics. She was adept in the sewing classes since she had been making her own clothes for years. Her mother had told her she would not be able to buy her many new clothes, but she would always buy her fabric to create her own. She showed her modern sewing machines in the store windows, and said when Ilse made all her own clothes, she would buy her a new 'Singer' sewing machine. When the class didn't have a clothing or food lab, the teacher, Miss Judd, lectured, and that was when Ilse got into trouble for laughing, snickering, and whispering. Ilse was just acting like a normal teenager.

Robert was on the football team along with his best buddies from childhood. Their coach motivated them beyond belief by yelling and screaming. Pete was small but dynamite. As the team quarterback, he could dodge in and out and run like the wind. Robert was a lineman. Coach Bill led the team to become all-state champions. After this, some of the guys got "cocky" leaving the school whenever they wanted for a coke or a haircut. The principal insisted they meet with the school psychologist to reduce their arrogance, but it was a waste of the administrator's time. The team buddies decided to stick together. They'd get out of school to go to the session but agreed they wouldn't say a word.

When the family first moved to Nebraska, Ilse's brother Steve went out for the basketball team. With all the practicing in the barnyard, he had become a tremendous shot. He never missed a jump shot. Immediately he was put on the varsity team to become the star of the team. By the time he was a senior, he was averaging twenty-three points a game. It was fun to have a brother in the limelight.

The gym teachers held a clinic to teach cheerleading, so any girl who wanted to try being a cheerleader could practice. Ilse had been watching the junior cheerleaders her first year at the school. The most popular girls were cheerleaders. The three from Ilse's class were all members of the 'Sexy Seven.' College professors' daughters, they had gone to school together since kindergarten. Ilse practiced for hours in her back yard, especially the jump, which was the most difficult part of the cheer. She used a stump in the back yard to support her hands, allowing her to practice getting high in the air. A loud voice and enthusiasm were her added ingredients…and her smile.

Tryouts for cheerleading meant being on the stage in front of the student body, first with a group and then alone. The jump turned out well and she felt she had done her best. Ilse was voted in as a junior varsity cheerleader as a freshman, not necessarily because she deserved it, but because of Steve's friends. All the basketball and football games were attended with considerable interest and excitement. Her parents were at the games to support her cheerleading efforts, but also for their son, Steve, the star basketball player. Vital and enthusiastic, Ilse remained a varsity cheerleader her sophomore, junior and senior years, one year as head cheerleader.

James and Jacob, the twins, didn't play basketball but chose wrestling for their sport. Ilse was able to cheer for them too her senior year, when they were on the varsity wrestling team.

These memories seemed like yesterday. As she thought of where she was now, it felt like she fell from heaven into a deep pit.

12
Robert Visits and Ilse Remembers...1991

When Robert finally came to visit on the first Sunday Ilse was in the hospital, she was pleasantly surprised by how nicely he treated her. He hadn't called since he left her that horrible night she was admitted. She wasn't sure he'd come for the promised visit but he arrived, gave her a big hug, which everyone observed.

"He must care for her," they all thought and even said how fortunate she was to have such a loving husband. Those remarks came from people who weren't in Group III with her.

First Ilse took her husband to the lounge, not the smoking lounge. Soft, easy listening music was playing and Robert commented on how nice the place looked. Then they went to her room and Robert lay down on the bed. He said he was exhausted from working so hard, and the trip cut into his day.

Disappointed, Ilse realized *nothing had changed. She was just a nuisance to him.* But, always trying to make amends and wanting to make him feel better, she began to rub his back. When they were together, she used to rub his back about twenty minutes every night before he went to sleep. He always liked that and it was a time to talk with one another. It had been months since she had given him a back rub. He made a comment while she was rubbing his back that maybe he was the one that should be there. *Ilse thought that he could use some counseling, but did not reply. This was just another contradiction. Maybe he really couldn't decide if she was the crazy one or perhaps he was.*

Before leaving after the first brief visit, he told her that he couldn't hide the truth from people. He was telling them she had checked herself into the hospital. He thought it would be a good idea to call her parents in California since it was routine to call them every Sunday, but he said not to tell them where she was. She agreed it would only worry them. Robert dialed the number, then stood there while they talked. All the crying and sniffling made Ilse sound as if she had a cold and that is what Ilse told her mother when she asked if something was wrong. When they asked about Robert, Ilse told them that he was working as hard as ever. This would be a pattern every Sunday whether Robert was there or not. Her mother and father were now old and rather fragile. Ilse didn't want them to worry about her. In fact, she decided not to tell her brothers either. *If she could get out of there, none of the family would be the wiser.*

Before he left, Robert said it wasn't a good idea to have any jewelry there because the people didn't seem too trustworthy. He took her money, the gold bracelet she was wearing, the diamond earrings he had given her and her diamond engagement and wedding rings. She had kept her rings and earrings on at night and didn't want to give them up, but he insisted, putting them in his pocket. *Ilse again felt stripped. Why was he taking her jewelry? Especially her rings? Did he want her to feel she no longer had a husband? She already felt alone with him gone.* He let her keep some silver pieces she had made in jewelry class.

Ilse didn't want him to go but was somewhat relieved when he did. *He wasn't going to help her.* She couldn't hold back the tears when he was around. *The things he said did not encourage her. The things he said scared her.* Before he left, he said he thought they would have to give her shock treatments. Ilse hadn't heard of shock treatments being used these days. She had only been there five days and no one had mentioned it.

Ilse had thought she was already doing better. She wasn't on "watch" anymore.

Robert left before dark. Ilse didn't feel like sleeping yet. She felt like talking if she could find Pat, the lady who was so nice to her that first night. *She could ask her about the shock treatments. She didn't want to give Dr. Morrison any ideas by asking her.* Pat wasn't in sight so Ilse began to worry. *She thought they'd have a special room for such a procedure, with straps on the table to hold a patient down.* She knew there was a strange room down the hall. With no furniture, pads covered the entire floor and walls. They had dragged one of the big guys there and locked him in. It took three attendants to drag him to the room. You could see him through a thick glass window, like looking at a caged tiger. It was frightening. *So was the idea of needing shock treatments.*

I think he is just trying to scare me, she thought. Why? Why did he want to be so mean? The sad part was that he managed to upset her by what he said and his refusal to talk with her. Either way she was devastated. *He could shatter her under the best of circumstances. This was going to be difficult.*

After Robert's visit, Ilse was upset about several things. First and scariest was the threat of shock treatments. Second, he was telling people SHE had checked herself in to the hospital. That wasn't fair. Third, what was he saying about stealing jewelry? No one could take the jewelry that she was wearing, she thought....unless they took it off of her to give her shock treatments. Ilse thought back on the gifts Robert had given her over the years. He had been generous buying jewelry, even when they didn't have much money.

Her first engagement diamond was one/half carat but of good quality, purchased at Zales on a whim. They were looking in the jewelry store window and Ilse liked a simple white gold ring with a star-like setting. Robert went in the store, bought it and took it home to give to her at a later date. That was between their junior and senior years in Nebraska, after spending the summer in California with Ilse's parents. In the kitchen with his mom, Mrs. Kelly, the next day, he talked about the ring he had bought, and asked his mother if she wanted to see it. She did, and rather offhandedly, he asked Ilse if she wanted to keep it. It wasn't the romantic proposal she had dreamed of, but she said "yes." They called Ilse's parents right away to tell them of the engagement.

"How soon?" her mother asked. She must have thought Ilse was pregnant. You could hear the relief in her voice when they said they would get married the next summer right after college graduation.

They had been 'pinned' right after they began dating between their sophomore and junior years. Unlike the engagement proposal, when Robert gave Ilse his fraternity pin it was very romantic. It was a clear summer night with a sky full of bright stars. Robert took Ilse to the base of the college campanile while it was chiming, declaring his love for her as he pinned his fraternity pin on her blouse. It was the first promise of a lifetime that they would share. They went back to classes surprising their friends since they hadn't dated before that summer.

Ilse had moved into the dorm and had watched many pinning ceremonies from her dorm window. Robert was a TKE and Ilse heard them singing "Sweetheart, sweetheart, sweetheart, sweetheart of TKE." Robert participated in the ceremony for other girls but never had a ceremony for Ilse. She always wondered why, but never questioned Robert even though she was hurt. He had been very active in the fraternity. *Maybe it was because she wasn't in a sorority.* She had gone through rush for his sister sorority and a few others, but decided sorority life was not for her. Her roommate and now dear friend was in the sister sorority, but never said anything about it.

Nevertheless, Ilse proudly wore the fraternity pin until she was engaged that next summer.

For Ilse's birthday, the first summer after they were married Robert gave her a watch. There was no traditional wedding gift such as pearls, but Ilse knew he didn't have a lot of money and would be saving for graduate school. For a wedding gift, he gave her a large painting by a sorority sister of a dark raven, which she thought was ugly. Robert openly bragged that the oil painting only cost $25. *Was there early on a hidden meaning with such an unromantic wedding gift? A huge raven filled the dark canvas with a moon behind it. It was strange and made Ilse uncomfortable when she graciously accepted the gift. Ilse felt like a phony acting as if she liked the gift.* She got rid of it after one of the moves. A far cry from pearls!

Tom, one of Robert's best childhood friends, helped Ilse order a watch that Robert had coveted. Ilse thought her wedding gift was appropriate and Robert seemed pleased.

When they moved to New Hampshire the third year of their marriage, he began to buy nice gold jewelry for her...a beautiful gold rose for Mothers' Day after Molly was born, an enameled turtle broach, and earrings after she had her ears pierced which he didn't want her to do. She surprised him by doing it anyway. An administrator's wife who was a nurse pierced her ears with a needle one day in the kitchen. Robert accepted it right away and then bought her some good earrings, handmade by a local artist, which was approval enough.

There were Mikimoto pearls given for Christmas one year, and a long strand to match

90

another year. On beach vacations, Ilse bartered her watercolor paintings for gold charms or chains. Robert would suggest they go to a favorite jewelry store there, and sometimes he would buy her something. The most recent was a gold chain and matching bracelet. It was one of Ilse's favorite gifts. With Robert's interest in jewelry, she began to appreciate it as much as he did.

While living in Michigan, as he became more and more successful, he said he wanted her to have diamond stud earrings and he wanted her to have a bigger diamond ring. She liked it all, but was embarrassed when he would proudly make a point of telling friends to look at the new piece of jewelry he had given her.

Ilse had also given jewelry to Robert. Together they found an amazing new wedding band for him of fourteen-carat gold, rimmed with twenty-two karat nuggets. Before that, she had surprised him with a large nugget ring she had custom-made for him by a jeweler. She had hoarded away money to be able to make the purchase as a surprise. He also liked watches and would covet the Rolex that his friend Joe had. On a business trip to Chicago, he bought a stainless steel Rolex, then Ilse bought him a gold and stainless one. The most recent watch gift was a Patek Philippe which he had Ilse order. It was more expensive than both Rolex watches combined, but he loved it.

In Summit, with an even more prestigious job, Robert wanted Ilse again to have bigger diamond studs to show off, and he replaced her engagement ring again. This time it was a radiant cut, set again in gold. Gold was always her choice and his. Spoiled now by the jewels, she was no longer embarrassed by wearing them. After all, most of the doctors and board members' wives all had more jewelry than she did, more unusual, more expensive, and more impressive.

A lot of good all those jewelry gifts did her now in the mental hospital, she thought. He had taken away her engagement and wedding rings. She wanted to wear her wedding bands. After all, even though he wasn't living at home, they were still married. She had been stripped naked of hers, but he was still wearing his wedding ring. Odd that he would keep wearing it, she thought. He could continue his ruse of a good husband (even though he had a crazy wife) when he was at work but he probably wore it when he was away from Summit with Carrie. People would just assume that he was married to Carrie. Ilse wondered if Carrie wore her old wedding band too even though she was now divorced. The thought left Ilse silently fuming, especially when he took her rings away.

Ilse was also thinking about a jewelry gift that she knew Robert had given to Carrie. When they were still living together, he had come home from work early one day. In the kitchen, before they had a chance to have dinner, he said he wanted to go to a good jewelry store to get a 'little gift' for Carrie. He wanted her to go along to help him choose something.

"She has been so supportive over the past months, with all the extra stress of my promotion." The past months he had often talked about Carrie saying he was her mentor...she was brilliant...she was following in his footsteps...he had already promoted her...and on and on and on. *Ilse thought it unreasonable to buy her something since he never did anything for the many others who had helped him*, but Ilse didn't question him. *She also thought a personal gift was inappropriate for Carrie.* She always went along with whatever he wanted. *She was thinking back to other "coincidences" that involved Carrie but as usual said nothing. Since he was involving her, she thought he planned to buy a small item.*

When they got to the jewelry store, he began looking at gold chains and then bracelets to match the set he had given Ilse at the beach. He wanted Ilse's opinion and she asked him, "Don't you have a hospital policy about giving gifts to employees over a limited amount?"

"This is different," he said. *As soon as he started looking at the chains, she KNEW this wasn't right; it was more than an appreciation memento.* When he assured her that it was okay, she went along with him, again feeling brainwashed. She suggested he buy the one she liked LEAST, one not as pretty as her rope chain. The price was almost $400.

Some memento, she thought, but at his suggestion, she wrote the check, *knowing full well what he was doing.* She even wrapped the box beautifully and made pink satin ribbon roses for the top as she had made for Molly's wedding.

When she came home from volunteering the next evening, there was a car in the drive and Robert was already home. Ilse was still wearing her pink volunteer smock and as she walked through the house, she realized the car parked outside was Carrie's. A beautiful evening, she found the two seated side by side on the porch love seat. Carrie had just opened her gift and she thanked Ilse for wrapping it so beautifully. She was wearing her new necklace and bracelet.

Soon Robert excitedly said, "Come and see Carrie's new car." He bragged that she had bought the car without consulting her husband. This happened before she was divorced.

Sure, Ilse thought. What would Robert say if she bought a car without consulting him, or even a piece of furniture? She thought of one of the doctor's wives who went out and bought a new Jaguar. Everyone thought that was funny and it served him right for all his infidelity. Carrie was married to a teacher and it seemed that she had the higher paying job. A few months later, Robert, who had said he had to drive an American-made car, bought an Acura, which matched Carrie's. It was suddenly acceptable to drive a foreign car provided by the hospital.

The concern about jewelry and the scare of shock treatment, made it difficult to sleep after the first visit from Robert. Before going to bed, Ilse went to the smoking lounge because they would be checking who was socializing. She asked a few of the patients if anyone had to have shock treatments but they didn't know.

That night Ilse found out that one of the young women, Betty, was going to cut another patient's hair, so she asked her why she was able to keep the scissors. Betty bragged that they didn't know she had them and they also didn't know that sometimes she slept in another person's room. *These people were weird, Ilse thought. They had problems. Ilse thought she would never do anything to deter her release* and she asked Betty if she wasn't afraid of getting caught.

"What are they going to do? Keep me here another month? How bad is that?" she said. *With the nighttime bed checks, Ilse wondered why they didn't realize Betty was sometimes in a room other than her own. And what about the scissors?* Ilse wasn't going to tell. Betty seemed nice enough. Betty told her she'd give her a manicure if she'd come to her room.

"Thanks but no thanks." *Maybe she was lying, Ilse thought. It didn't make sense. She had no reason to trust her.*

She could no longer trust Robert. Trust was a cornerstone of their marriage but there was too much pointing to infidelity. She thought she knew immediately when he had become involved with Carrie. If he no longer loved her and wanted out of the marriage, why not be honest about it? Why try to convince her that she was imagining it? Was she? She had been thinking back, over and over, when did this begin? It was before he would not sleep with her.

Ilse had trouble going to sleep that night even with medication. She tried, unsuccessfully, to convince herself that Robert was just trying to scare her with his subtle suggestion she might need shock treatments. *He knew it would haunt her, maybe put her over the edge.* She remembered that he had similarly frightened her when he told her the Princeton psychologist said she might have to be hospitalized. That had happened. Here she was. *Would his shock treatment threat materialize too? She was second-guessing herself. She couldn't let them strap her to some table, put electrical wires to her brain, then*

send charges to her brain and body. She didn't
have a mental disorder that required this horrific
procedure. She felt utterly helpless and scared.
Now she decided that maybe it was another part of
Robert's plan. So cruel! **She finally went to sleep**
thinking *she had to get out of here before they*
gave her unnecessary shock treatments. **She had**
to!

13

Climbing the Ladder

The previous winter Robert began to complain that he was almost fifty and "feeling old." He had always complained that he hated working so hard, but both of them knew he was driven to keep climbing to the top of his corporate ladder, stepping on anyone in his way and doing whatever it took to reach the pinnacle. He had come to Summit to be the CEO of the Valley Hospital. Another smaller and older hospital, Summit General, was in town, as well. They were both under a parent company, Health I. The CEO of Health I was Robert's boss and the CEO of Summit Hospital was his counterpart rival.

Upon their arrival in Summit, Ilse and Robert were wined and dined by influential people in the community. Robert immediately made changes and improvements at his hospital. He got along well with the board members, department heads, doctors and administrative people. In return, they entertained and Ilse began, at Robert's suggestion, to volunteer at the hospital, both on the cancer floor, and in the gift shop.

After being in Summit a short time, Health I decided to merge the two hospitals. The Summit General CEO was about the same age as Robert, but had been there longer. One of them had to leave, and there was concern but not the same concern as when Robert was passed over for the top job in Detroit. Ilse felt that was the most difficult time of his career. It prompted him to seek another job, which had led to the position in Summit.

They selected Robert to fill both spots as the CEO of the merged hospitals. There was political, behind the scene maneuvering, but he was up to the challenge of running both hospitals as one.

After being CEO of the merged hospitals for only a few years, rumors began that they were going to drop the parent company. One of the two remaining CEOs would have to go. At a social gala, Robert sat next to the Health I CEO's wife, his boss's wife. She was outspoken and asked him point blank if he was after her husband's job. He assured her that the idea was absurd, but told Ilse about her comment, and then went aggressively after the top position. He had already been planning his move. He did whatever he needed to do to make it work. He was not going to be left behind, as he had been in Detroit. He was going to be on the top. He became more focused than ever, working longer and longer hours. He won the race and became the top man for the hospital and a respected leader in his field. With his expertise and ability, he had proven his worth from the day he set foot in Summit, getting the hospital out of the red in just months and then running both hospitals and the parent company as one. What an accomplishment! He had worked so hard to attain his goal. Ilse was thrilled for him and ever so proud in spite of what she knew about him.

14
More Reflections: 1950's

As a young girl with a ponytail years ago in Nebraska, Ilse saw Robert as a leader. He was class president and a popular football player. He was friendly, but never interested in Ilse as a girlfriend. Ilse had a boyfriend in high school, a lovable farm boy and football player. It wasn't serious enough to continue, but she always cared about him.

Robert had a girl friend from another school. She was well developed which was always important to the boys. He quit dating her when he went to college and then dated a few sorority sisters for fraternity activities. Socially he was shy, like his mother and father. By college, he was 6'2", thin, handsome...and smart. There was no doubt that he would be successful, although he went to college on probation because he had not applied himself. He often frustrated the teachers and his parents, particularly his mother. She didn't seem to have much control over his wild behavior.

During high school, Meg and Ilse worked summers at a drive-in as "car- hops." They walked to work together but could sometimes "bum" a ride home at night. Now and then, Meg drove her dad's red pick-up truck to work. When the drive-in wasn't busy, they sat on the tailgate and talked endlessly about anything and everything. They also loved to talk to the owner's handsome son who managed the small enterprise. Both had a crush on him, but he was engaged to a girl as pretty as he was handsome.

Their senior year the two good friends both detasseled corn for the few days the corn was ripe. It was the hardest physical work they had ever done. Ilse's brothers and other kids from school, including Robert, worked in the cornfields because the pay was good for those few days. Robert worked for a Dairy Queen during high school and before that, he had two paper routes. Although his parents seemed to have more than others did, he always had a job and worked hard. When he wasn't working, he was with his girlfriend except at detasseling time. Everyone was too tired to go out after working in the fields.

Starting early in the morning when it was a little cooler, the teenagers went to the assigned farm to detassel the corn. Sometimes they walked, pulling out or stomping out suckers. The suckers were extra shoots from the roots of the corn stalk. That was the hardest because the leaves cut your legs and arms and often the foreman had to yell to hurry everyone up. The job meant riding on a platform above the tractor in the hot sun with a bar across the front to keep you from falling. As the tractor went down the rows, the workers reached over and pulled the tassels out. By the end of a few hours, and certainly by the end of the day, everyone was hot, sunburned, exhausted, hungry and thirsty. They would dream about pulling tassels all night. Hard work but good money. Yes, but car hopping was much more fun!

For Robert graduating from high school was important, but not as important as the football games. Robert's father attended only one, but his mother never went to any. When he graduated from high school his mother attended the ceremony, but his father was "too busy."

By the time they were graduated from college, Ilse's parents had moved back to California. They proudly returned for the graduation ceremony and were staying for the wedding. Robert's mother went to the graduation with Ilse's parents, but his father "was too busy" again.

"Besides," he said, "you haven't done anything yet. Don't get a big head."

During her senior college year, along with living in the Home Management House and student teaching, Ilse planned their wedding. Mrs. Kelly, Robert's mother, wanted to know everything that was going on. First she didn't like the color for the bridesmaid's dresses, so Ilse changed to pink, then she said 'Robbie' couldn't have Ilse's brother, Steve, for his best man although Robert had already asked him. She thought he should have his sister's new husband. He ended up asking a good school friend named Ray to be best man. Ilse felt bad about the best man conflict, but went along with what Mrs. Kelly wanted without a word. After all, Ilse thought, Mrs. Kelly hadn't had a chance to plan a big wedding for her daughter since she had avoided the entire dilemma and eloped. Besides, it wasn't to be a fancy wedding, but a nice wedding by small town Nebraska standards. Ilse's mother sent yards and yards of satin and lace so Ilse could create her own wedding dress.

Ilse asked her best friend, Meg, to be her matron of honor. Now married, Meg had remained a best friend, even though their lives had gone in different directions.

Throughout college, Ilse worked in a drugstore stocking shelves and waiting on customers. The pharmacists let her work a few hours every evening and on Saturdays. With the savings from her work, along with her father's college fund, Ilse was able to pay for college. She worked at the drugstore until the summer after her wedding.

While living in the home management house and doing her student teaching, Ilse began work on her wedding dress. She looked through the bridal magazines endlessly, planning to make her dress prettier than those in the glossy photos. With a design in mind, she fashioned a pattern and then cut it out of old white sheets. Sewing it together, to get the proper fit and the opinion of her friends, she happily modeled her mock dress. It was going to turn out as she planned, so she spent hours sewing perfect seams. The bodice was lace over satin cascading down the center of the dress to the hem. The rest of the long dress and train was made from a heavy ivory satin. She planned to wear the pearls Meg had given her. Tiny satin covered buttons were lovingly sewn down the back and on each pointed lace sleeve. The tulle her mother had sent would make a fingertip veil attached to fresh flowers. It would be perfect.

The two bridesmaids, along with Meg, the matron of honor, looked like southern belles. The men in black tuxedos were handsome, especially the groom.

With all the work and fuss, it was a proper Nebraska wedding for the time. To make it perfect, Ilse consulted 'Emily Post' over and over. The invitations were correctly addressed and sent out at the appropriate time. As the centerpiece, the cake was beautiful with tall candles and floral arrangements on either side. Mrs. Kelly's neighbor and close friend prepared the table with the pink net over-cloth Ilse had made. Cake, nuts, punch, tea and coffee were served in the church basement after the service. It was all Ilse had wanted. Most of Ilse and Robert's friends had similar weddings and Robert seemed pleased.

Ilse's big disappointment was not the wedding but the rehearsal dinner, which was Robert's family's responsibility. She expected Mrs. Kelly would go all out creating beautiful arrangements for the table similar to her blue ribbon award winning arrangements. There wasn't a flower in sight.

Another glitch was the reaction Ilse had to the high dosage birth control pills her new father-in-law Dr. Kelly had prescribed for her. She was nauseous during the college graduation ceremony and the hectic following week before the wedding. Dr. Kelly was making sure Ilse wouldn't get pregnant before she worked two years to get Robert through graduate school.

Everyone was happy about the actual wedding and they were a happy couple. Robert was twenty-two and Ilse would be the same in August. The young couple left for Niagara Falls the night of the wedding in the little red VW bug that Robert purchased before he student taught, as an undergraduate student. He had sold stock inherited from his grandmother to pay for it, which annoyed his father. Feeling independent, they thought they had the world ahead of them as they left for their honeymoon and their life's adventure.

Dr. Kelly had not attended high school or college graduations, so one night when Ilse was having supper at their house, he casually mentioned that he wasn't going to go to their wedding. For once, Ilse asserted herself.

"If you aren't there when the wedding is ready to begin, the people will wait while I personally come to get you and drag you there!" He couldn't believe she would talk to him in such a disrespectful manner and she couldn't quite believe she spoke up to him either. He did go to the wedding and he acquired a new respect for Ilse. It seemed he approved of what she had said.

Off to a happy start with cans hanging from the car and 'just married' all over the windows, Ilse and Robert stopped at a diner for a wedding dinner of hamburgers and fries, all dressed up. Ilse wore a beige raw silk suit she had made, with a little bow-hat and veil. Matching shoes, gloves and a corsage completed her outfit. Robert had changed from his black tuxedo to a beige suit, white shirt and tie. There they were all dressed for their wedding supper.

The other diner patrons tried not to stare, but shot amused glances at the couple. Out of place but undaunted, they went to find the motel their best man had reserved for them. It was what both would later call a dump, but they could afford it and Ray, who could arrange for anything, had selected it.

As bad as the room was, it wasn't as bad as their disastrous wedding night. Robert turned on the TV and lay down on the old brown iron bed. The black and white TV, the smallest one possible on a tiny dresser across from the bed, did work. Ilse was trying to size up the situation and decide what she should do. Although he had always seemed to be in pursuit of her the entire time they dated, he suddenly wasn't paying any attention to her. She was confused. There was rice everywhere, falling out of their hair and clothes, a nice reminder that they had just been married a few hours before. She decided to take a shower and put on the pretty blue nightgown from Meg and college friends. Robert just wanted to watch the western on TV so Ilse snuggled up to him and waited patiently for some response. What a disappointment! He finally decided that quick sex would be fine. No romance, no endearments, leaving Ilse more confused. *Why all the pursuit before and now this? She thought that Robert would be a good lover but that didn't seem to be the case.*

The rest of the honeymoon wasn't any better. When they got to Niagara Falls, Robert spent hours and hours taking pictures of the falls day and night from every angle. He bought her a little statue of a nude that ended up on the mantle or a tabletop for many years. They found a cheap hotel room not far from the falls on the American side, browsed the shops and had picnic lunches after stopping at a grocery store to get bread and lunch meat. Every night was disappointing. Robert was not very interested and after Ilse asked him why, there would be quick sex, which seemed to satisfy him but left Ilse frustrated. She had feelings she wanted to explore and express. He was anxious to get out and take more nighttime photos of the falls.

After a few days, Robert said he wanted to head home. He had a summer job waiting for him working on a road construction crew. It was excellent pay and he could start as soon as they got back. Ilse could go back to work at the drugstore whenever she wanted. So, they turned around and headed back to Nebraska singing most of the way, harmony when possible, as they laughed. She knew, without him telling her, that she couldn't stay on key. Later, in church, he would lean over and say 'mouth it.' So she did.

15
Married Life: 1962

Back in Nebraska, they arrived in the late evening at the studio apartment, which was a half block from Robert's parents' home. They couldn't get in it before their honeymoon, but they thought Mrs. Kelly would clean it up a bit after the last renters. They arrived to find all the unopened wedding gifts in the middle of the floor and the mess the last renters had left. They opened a studio couch on which to sleep. It was a typical hot summer Nebraska evening and the window air conditioner wouldn't work. To get through the night would be the goal and then Ilse would clean and begin to make a home.

Robert was up at five and after a breakfast of eggs and toast, he took his lunchbox and headed to work. They had stopped to get some of the basic staples to get through the first day, but Ilse could walk the short way and get more groceries. So, their first summer as husband and wife began. Ilse cleaned and made the little furnished place look good. She prepared dinner for the Kelly parents on Sundays, usually a pot roast she put in the oven before going to church. She was doing what her own mother had done for years. The Kelly's seemed happy to come to the younger Kelly's for meals. She could take the laundry to the Kellys' and in return for using their machine, she helped Mrs. Kelly weed her flowerbeds. It was strange to call her Mrs. Kelly since Ilse was now Mrs. Kelly too. Neither parent ever told her to call them anything else. After children were born she decided to just begin calling them grandma and granddad. That would seem more comfortable.

During the last year of college, Robert received a letter from the government. He had already planned to avoid the draft by going on to graduate school. Ilse interviewed for teaching jobs near Lincoln where Robert would begin to work on his master's degree in hospital administration. It had just been made into a two-year program, so Ilse could commit to two years of teaching. She got a job thirty miles away from the University of Nebraska. The school was a large consolidated school with many farm students. The boys were bigger than Ilse, towering over the petite new teacher. She fit into a special vocational agriculture and home economics program. It would be a ten-month contract, so Ilse began two weeks before the other teachers and worked two weeks after the others in the spring. She was very excited and made plans all summer long.

Mid summer, Ilse and Robert took a day to go to the little town to look for a small, furnished apartment. They found a place with old furniture and dark aqua walls. It had a bedroom, bathroom, small living room and kitchen on the main floor of a cement block building. The owner of an old hardware store had converted the back of the building into two apartments. Underneath the apartments was a dirt-floored basement with a washer and dryer. It was only a short walk to school, so it seemed ideal. They didn't have money to buy furniture so this was perfect. The owner told them that if Ilse wanted to paint the walls, he would provide the paint. The place was a mess but for only $60 a month including utilities, they grabbed it.

When it was time for Ilse to begin school, they moved all their belongings. They took almost all of their wedding gifts, clothes, and Robert's desk. Dr. Kelly let them use his big car to move and they were able to borrow a trailer from a farm friend. Robert hauled in all the boxes and put them into the living room. Ilse began to clean the filthy kitchen, starting with the cupboards and oven. It was a Sunday and Robert was anxious to get back to Sidney so he could be up by 5 a.m. to continue his road construction job, not wanting to miss any much-needed income. He moved back into his old room at the Kellys' and would be eating every night with his parents. Before he left, he wanted to "try out the bed" but as usual, he was in a hurry.

Working late in the evening to help shed the uneasy feeling she had, Ilse pondered her loneliness. Keeping busy seemed to be a good way to take away any misgivings. She made good progress on cleaning the kitchen cupboards and the few kitchen utensils, pots, pans and staples fit easily in the limited space. Next Ilse tackled the oven and refrigerator. It's amazing, she thought, how anyone could leave it so dirty. The next day she spotted two cockroaches. Even living on farms, she had never become used to spiders or other creatures that didn't belong inside the house.

School was going to be good she thought. She reported early the next day after the short walk. All dressed up in a summer suit and high heeled shoes, she was given a tour of the school and shown the offices and her classroom. The stock room had everything you would want for the bulletin boards or your desk. Other teachers were not around yet, but the principal and even the superintendent came by to check several times during the day. The classroom was big with six kitchen labs fully equipped, tables for cutting fabric and twelve sewing machines, many of them new. It was so neat. There was a washer and dryer so the towels and aprons from foods labs could be laundered. Ilse also liked the idea of having a huge chalkboard and two large bulletin boards.

Her students were high schoolers except for an 'exploratory' class, which included seventh grade boys and girls. Already a committee of women was going to meet with Ilse about what she would teach for an adult education class, one in the fall and another in the spring. She was told she would be the advisor for the FHA club (Future Homemakers of America) and she would be working with the vocational agriculture teacher who would advise the FFA (Future Farmers of America). With that teacher, she would have co-responsibility for the concession stand for all the ball games. Getting refreshments and coffee ready for community events and PTA would also be part of her job. It promised to be a challenge but Ilse was anxious and ready to begin.

Robert drove down the following Sunday, staying for a few hours, taking enough time to try the bed again. "It was amazing," he said, how good Ilse had made the place look. Already she had cleaned from top to bottom. She had the kitchen and bathroom shining and had painted the living room. Robert said he'd help paint the bedroom and bathroom, but never had the time before going for graduate school orientation.

As soon as graduate school began for Robert, Ilse's students arrived for classes and life was busy for both of them. Robert left early everyday, dressed in a suit, white shirt and wing-tipped shoes. The hospital administration program strictly observed a dress code. It had been a strain on their finances, but sport coats were not acceptable. Part of Ilse's responsibility was to starch and iron five white shirts every week and shine the size thirteen shoes. It irritated her to have Robert put on a shirt in the morning, find he didn't want to wear it, then throw it on the floor. She complained about that and even mentioned it to his mother who laughed and said, "Oh, does Robbie still do that?" She soon hated ironing white shirts, but she did it to save money for twenty-three years. Finally she talked him into letting her take them to the laundry when she had a large house to maintain, was teaching full-time and taking care of two teen-agers.

Another job Ilse hated almost as much as ironing white shirts was cutting Robert's hair every few weeks. It started the first summer, again to save money. He bought electric clippers and she gave him as good a haircut at home as did a barber. He loved the convenience of being able to have his hair cut whenever he felt like it. Often it was late at night. He even came for haircuts after he had moved out of the house. The last time was very late on a Sunday night. He was harassing Ilse while she was cutting. It was all she could do not to run the clippers right down the middle of his head. When she told her friends about it, they laughed and said it was good she held her temper or she'd probably be dead. They may have been right. Anyway, he never asked after that.

Big Eight football games were the highlight of the fall during the two years of graduate school. Going in to Lincoln, the couple would have a wonderful day sitting with other graduate students and their wives for the ballgames. After parking the car, they walked a long way with other spectators, absorbing the excitement that radiated from the crowd. The favorite event was the Homecoming game with a pre-game party. Ilse was happy for this social interaction and for the numerous other get-togethers with the married graduate students.

Often Robert went back to the university library on the weekends and Ilse worked on preparations for her adult education classes. All her classes were going nicely. She enjoyed the students and she had great support from the parents and faculty. They made her feel like she was doing a good job. Once in awhile Robert would go to the high school football games, reliving his time on his high school championship team, and having a hot dog from the concession stand assigned to Ilse.

It wasn't long before both Robert and Ilse decided they didn't want to stay in 'cockroach heaven' as they called their apartment. They hung their slippers on dresser knobs so they wouldn't step barefoot on a roach if they got up in the middle of the night. In the kitchen, they found empty beer bottles left under the sink half-full of roaches in the morning. The mice were coming in from the nearby corn field as it started to get colder, so they set several mouse traps and heard "snap, snap, snap" minutes after setting the traps. Ilse hated mice traps, so at school she organized the junior high boys to take turns on "mouse patrol." The boys loved checking and setting the traps every day and Ilse didn't have to admit she was a coward.

The roaches and mice were bad enough in their apartment but worse yet were the rats in the laundry room under their bedroom. When they moved the bed, they discovered a hole leading to the basement, which they boarded up, but that wasn't enough to calm Ilse, and Robert agreed to look for a new apartment.

It wasn't easy to find another apartment in the little town, but they did. Unfurnished, $85 a month, it meant a two-mile walk for Ilse to school everyday. Already there were bitterly cold days, but sometimes Robert could drop her off at school, and she arranged to have another teacher drive her to and from school in exchange for babysitting his five children.

The new apartment was a nice change. With two bedrooms, Robert now had an office with room for his desk and bookshelves. There was one major problem however; they had NO furniture other than the desk and very little extra money with which to buy any. They bought a mattress and springs from the furniture store, which was owned by the local funeral director. They placed their suitcases side by side on the floor using them and a linen closet for extra folded clothes. Someone told them there was an old used refrigerator at the hardware store. They bought it and tried to paint it, which didn't work out well, but when they were buying the refrigerator, they spotted two chairs hanging from the ceiling rafters. The owner almost gave the metal chairs to them so now they were all set. They would use Ilse's sewing machine table for their kitchen table. It would be fine with a card table sized cloth, and it was great to be away from the roaches and rats! Besides, in the spring they could plant a huge garden in the back yard. Ilse was in paradise.

During class one day the principal called Ilse to his office by intercom.

Oh no! What have I done? Ilse wondered. Nervous, she made a quick trip to the office to find the principal laughing. It seemed that the teachers thought it was funny that they were sleeping on a mattress on the floor. He said he had a bed frame, which he was leaving on their apartment doorstep to use as long as they needed it.

What a relief and how very nice, she thought.

During the summer between the two years of graduate school, they decided to drive the little red bug to California to visit Ilse's parents. They took the Kelly's tent and two sleeping bags and were off. In California, they lived off Ilse's parents for a few weeks, enjoyed her brothers, and took a trip up to Washington, Oregon, and Vancouver with her parents. Her mother bought her beautiful wool fabric to take home to make some new clothes. She also bought enough green Harris Tweed wool for Ilse to tailor a sport coat for Robert.

Teaching and all the activities became easier the second year. She had good rapport with the students and other faculty. But Robert was angry about one student's disrespect for Ilse. She monitored a study hall in the cafeteria at the end of a long hallway. For a few days when the board president's son walked down the hall behind her on the way to the restroom, the senior boys in the back of the room would snicker. Ilse thought she knew what he was doing, so she chose to ignore him. One day, she accidentally turned to see him giving her the finger. She had to react. She didn't say a word to him but walked directly to the principal's office. Since he wasn't there, she went next door and told the superintendent that Bob Morgan gave her the finger and someone needed to deal with it.

Later she found out the old, kind superintendent went into the teachers' lounge and asked what "giving the finger" meant. The faculty was amused that he needed to ask. Bob Morgan was suspended from school for a week and had to apologize in front of the school board and Ilse before he could get back into school. Even though the student was adequately humiliated and disciplined, it seemed this was not enough for Robert, who still wanted to "beat him up."

117

Typing became a challenge for Ilse since Robert was writing many papers besides working on his thesis. They rented an electric typewriter, and most evenings and weekends were spent getting papers letter perfect. The thesis was the biggest challenge because of spacing and footnotes, so Ilse was relieved when they hired a professional typist. Robert was becoming more and more intense as he felt the pressure mounting. One day he came home to report that the head of the program had met with him to tell him his work was good, but he had a nervous habit, which concerned him. He told Robert that he needed to stop shaking his foot. Robert did, in fact, shake his foot enough so the floor would shake. He wondered if Robert would be able to take the stress of hospital administration. Robert realized he would have to work on hiding his nervousness.

Robert passed his orals and the thesis was accepted. The couple was relieved and thrilled anticipating a new adventure. The program chairman had connections with hospitals throughout the country and he arranged for the students' internships following graduation. Robert said he would be willing to go anywhere and there was an opportunity to go to New Hampshire. The couple had to get a map to see exactly where New Hampshire was since neither had traveled East.

Graduation was a special time. The graduate school classmates had some end of school picnics. Ilse convinced Robert that they should splurge and have the group for steaks on the grill. She made her special potato salad and brownies and everyone brought something to share. By now, they had a $25 sofa in their apartment and the Kelly's had given them a chair and a window air conditioner. It was a Godsend. They purchased a new console TV and life was good.

The graduation ceremony was the final crowning glory of the two previous years. Ilse sat with some of the other wives and their families who came for the occasion. It was bittersweet without Robert's parents there. He had worked so hard and they would only have had to drive eighty miles to be there, but Robert "hadn't done anything yet." To add insult to injury, Dr. Kelly had encouraged Robert's friend Ray, who was best man in their wedding, to go to medical school while he discouraged his own son from that choice. Robert said his father didn't think he was smart enough for medical school, but thought Ray was.

Ilse was concerned that Robert's parents were never supportive of him. *She thought they didn't deserve to have a son that was so motivated when he had had no show of admiration or affection from them.* Robert didn't complain about them but Ilse knew he felt bad that he could never do enough to please them. Ilse tried to make up for their attitude by doubling her efforts to give him strokes. She had no trouble recognizing his many good qualities and enjoyed building his ego. Because of his family background and their expectations without positive reinforcement, Ilse began to smooth over or overlook Robert's rough edges letting unacceptable behavior slide. She knew you couldn't expect to change someone after you married him.

There were tears and questions after the graduation ceremony. Ilse had heard stories about how sometimes wives were abandoned after putting their husbands through school. Robert said the idea was crazy. Pushing these thoughts aside and undaunted by the elder Kellys' attitude, the young Kellys headed for New Hampshire to meet the friendly New Englanders. They had been told they weren't friendly, but that wasn't true. Upon their arrival they were treated royally, taken to a special meeting for introductions and told they could stay in the intern residence until they found a place to live.

It had taken most of Ilse's teaching salary to pay for their living expenses and put Robert through graduate school. They had no help during that time except the few pieces of furniture Robert's parents had given them. They were resolved to be financially independent, but when they got to New Hampshire they knew Robert's $4,000 a year salary wouldn't be enough. The administrator of the hospital used his influence to get Ilse an interview at the junior high school. She walked down the hill from the hospital for the interview in her suit and three inch heels and was hired. She would earn $4,500. Wow! It was 1964 and the $8,500 combined income sounded wonderful after feeling so poor when Robert was in graduate school. They thought they were going to be rich. At least now, they would have enough to rent a nice place to live. They found an unfurnished apartment within walking distance from school. Robert could take Ilse to school on his way to work and she could walk home.

The apartment on a hill with windows looking out toward the mountains was spacious compared with what they had in Nebraska. They even had a garage now. With about ten apartments in the building, they became friendly with their young neighbors. They also became very good friends with the administrators and their wives, some their age and some ready to retire. It was wonderful to be a part of the hospital community.

Soon after arriving in New Hampshire, the Director of Nursing hosted a Halloween party. Nebraska didn't have liquor by the drink and the couple wasn't prepared for this kind of party. After many martinis, the group told Ilse she should take Robert home. The men helped Robert to the car and Ilse took the driver's seat, as he got sick all over the side of the car. He had long ago told Ilse about getting sick on beer at home. His buddies had hauled him home then and his father had been furious with him, shoving and hitting him.

The weather was already getting cold in the Northeast, and Ilse felt cold as she drove home to the parking garage. She tried to convince her drunk husband that he had to get out of the car and she would help him to the apartment. Robert wouldn't move. Ilse was afraid to leave him because it was so cold. Frustrated she tried to threaten him. Another apartment owner drove into the garage space next to their red VW, and Ilse tearfully asked if he would help her with her drunk husband. He convinced Robert to get out of the car, but was not prepared to handle someone so big. Robert went with him, falling down several times. It was humiliating to Ilse. She didn't know how to handle a situation like this. Robert slept it off. The next day Ilse told him what happened. Robert didn't think he was that bad until he went to the car and saw the mess. He'd clean up the mess, but he wanted HER to bake cookies and thank the neighbor. He didn't want to face him. Ilse did.

As time went on, there were numerous incidents of behavior that embarrassed Ilse. She always had to make the excuses and do the apologizing. For example, she would call and give regrets at the last minute if Robert suddenly didn't want to go to a dinner party for an invitation he had previously approved. Rude! In later years, she told him to call himself when he wanted to back out at the last minute. Then he'd relent and go rather than make the uncomfortable call.

Living in New Hampshire turned out to be a wonderful experience, giving Robert and Ilse memories that would last a lifetime. Robert had an excellent secretary whose assistance, along with the help from other administrators, provided Robert great on-the-job training. He was willing to work hard and tackle any assignments given to him. He had the energy to apply the principles of hospital administration he had learned in graduate school and the spirit to be creative and offer new ideas. He had the time to connect socially with the people he worked with and he enjoyed being with them. As a couple, they fit right in, loving their opportunity to unburden themselves after the difficult years of graduate school.

Without the responsibility of typing papers for Robert and less preparation for Ilse's classes, the couple embarked on a new lifestyle. They began to ski in the winter, to play bridge, go to the lake for bonfires and songfests, and tour the beautiful countryside. They decided they could purchase a home, spending many weekend afternoons looking at houses. They especially bonded with Robert's secretary, her husband and six children, witnessing a love that had lasted with vitality through many years. These friends became life long friends and confidants. Losing Milly in later years was like losing a mother.

The couple had arrived in New Hampshire with their meager belongings still using boxes for chairs, their mattress and box springs without a frame and side-by-side suitcases for their clothes. With both of them working, they decided to buy a sofa and matching chair, a Lane coffee table and end tables...all Danish modern. What fun to be able to buy some furniture after the spartan two years in Nebraska!

Everything wasn't perfect, but rarely would they argue. In fact, throughout their marriage, they seemed to have fewer disagreements than other couples did. Ilse willingly deferred to Robert and if she had an opinion when others were present she usually wouldn't voice it, especially if the discussions were work related or political. On religious matters, she was more confident that she could offer her ideas.

Ilse had the responsibilities of managing household expenses and she handled most of the choices related to their budget. She paid the bills and kept good records. Growing up, her father taught her to keep a balanced account book. In later years when it didn't seem to matter so much, Robert would still insist that the checkbook be reconciled to the penny. There was NO room for error.

Any major expenditure would be discussed or in some cases quickly decided by Robert. After all, he had been a business major in college and had the expertise. Ilse, on the other hand, received on the job training growing up, allowing her to stretch the dollars. She could almost 'make a silk purse out of a sow's ear.' There were occasions when Robert went out to 'look,' but came home proudly announcing he had bought an appliance, a large woodworking tool, or once, a car for which he had to have Ilse put up stock certificates as collateral for the loan he wanted. In the future, he wouldn't buy a car unless he could pay cash.

Ilse had come to the marriage with stock that her father had purchased for her over the years. Robert insisted that they live on whatever they earned themselves and Ilse thought that was a good idea. Dividend checks were put aside, not to be used for living expenses. They agreed that selling stocks or using dividend checks would encourage living beyond their means which neither wanted to do. The dividend checks became a source of dissension however. Ilse, although she managed the household account, wanted some money of her own to buy gifts for Robert or personal items for herself. It didn't set well with her that she had been working for three years but had no discretionary fund of her own.

Quarterly Ilse received a $100 check from the hundred shares of General Motors stock, which her parents purchased for her. Her mother told her she should sometimes indulge and use the dividend money. The first Christmas in New Hampshire, Ilse took the $100 and bought Robert a watch he had admired at the local jewelry store. He was pleased and began to relax on some of the extra expenditures.

He drew the line when she wanted to open her own checking account. It was an ongoing argument throughout their marriage. He would say, "It's all yours. You don't need your own account. End of discussion." His check always went into their joint account. They had early on established the habit of paying themselves first, putting away money in a savings account they could draw on if necessary. They were always in agreement on that, but having her own checking account continued to be the biggest point of dissention between the two. They had the same argument over and over throughout their marriage. In the end it came back to haunt her. She should have defied her husband, opened an account and fed it with part of the money she earned. Like getting pierced ears against his wishes, he would have had to learn to accept and live with it.

Dr. Kelly gave the couple $2000 for a down payment on a house and the couple found one under construction. It was in a nice neighborhood, not too far from the hospital. What a dream to be able to purchase a home of their own! They would be able to choose the wall colors, finish the entire downstairs and half bath and do all the landscaping. It was a small three bedroom, one bath home, with a living room and small dinette and kitchen area opening onto a back deck which looked out on a rock ledge with birch trees...a raised ranch. It was the only money the elder Kellys ever gave the couple, but it was a huge boost. Oh yes...there was a brick fireplace in the living room. When they finished the big downstairs area, they used bricks from the old hospital and a huge barn beam to create a fireplace mantle. The mantle was soon adorned with Robert's Civil War gun. Complete with a large bar, barn board walls, and burnt orange carpeting, it was a great party room and future playroom.

16
Starting a Family: 1966-1970

Before they moved into the house, Ilse knew she was pregnant. The pregnancy was planned to correspond with the Vietnam War draft. The first draft was avoided with college deferment when Robert was headed for graduate school and now, with a baby coming, he would get off the hook again. Robert was adept at organizing his life and actually, Ilse found it reassuring to be able to plan ahead for what could be controlled in her life.

Ilse and Robert were both thrilled about the pregnancy. After visiting the doctor, Robert immediately announced to everyone that he was going to be a dad. Ilse had dreadful morning sickness for several months. Dr. Duffee told her that he had never seen anyone who vomited so hard that the blood vessels broke on her eyelids. She managed to continue teaching until the end of the school year. She was truly enjoying teaching the junior high classes, an adult education tailoring class, and supervising a student teacher. Her curriculum included clothing construction, home decorating, grooming, and personal relationships, her favorites. It was also a good time to take some college courses at the University of New Hampshire, just blocks away.

As Ilse watched her body grow, she began to make some maternity dresses. Sally, one of the administrator's wives, loaned her a few outfits, which she would wear over and over until she was quite sick of them.

When Ilse was four and a half months pregnant, Pam and Tom Curry came to visit. Robert had been Tom's best man at Tom and Pam's wedding. Robert and Tom had gone from kindergarten all the way through college together. Pam and Ilse had become close friends too, so as couples they would continue their relationship for years to come. They had planned their first trip together, heading off to Cape Cod. They found a hotel room with two beds that they could share. With an electric frying pan, they managed many meals in their shared motel room. Laughing into the night, they heard each other moan and groan about their sunburns.

What always came to mind when Ilse later remembered the Cape Cod trip, was the new shift type maternity dress she made. It was thin red and white stripes, shirred at the top of the bodice to fall comfortably over her newly bulging stomach. She thought it was pretty and couldn't understand what upset Robert about her wearing her first maternity dress. He said it looked awful. He said she looked fatter than ever and she should take off the new dress. He had never before criticized the way she looked. In contrast, he had always seemed proud of her. Embarrassed and tearful, with Pam and Tom hearing Robert's criticism, she changed her clothes to suit him.

At school, as she got bigger and bigger, the students began to giggle when her stomach rolled around with the active baby. At home in bed, Ilse would excitedly ask Robert to feel her stomach, but he would turn away. It made her sad that he didn't share her wonder and excitement about this miracle growing inside her, their precious baby. He said it "spooked" him. Ilse remained happy and excited, anticipating motherhood even though Robert didn't share her enthusiasm about the changes in her body except her larger breasts which he liked. She was thrilled with the whole pregnancy process, a true gift from God she thought. She was healthy and after the first several months, she felt wonderful.

Ilse's hairdresser said he could tell she was going to have twins because she was so huge and carried the baby out in front like a bowling ball. He said he knew because he had seven kids of his own. Ilse thought she would love to have twins, after all her mother had given birth to two sets of twins. Dr. Duffee said he only heard one heartbeat. She just looked big even though she had only gained the twenty pounds he allowed. On her last exam, she told the doctor that she was slowly leaking fluid. Because of that, he said he thought she would have her baby the next day.

Another week came and went. The water never broke because of the slow leak. When she began to cramp and pains came closer together, Robert helped her to the car and drove through a snowstorm to get her to the hospital. On the way, Ilse and Robert were still talking about what they would name the baby. It would be Will after her father if it was a boy, but they weren't sure about a girl's name. After Ilse was checked in Robert went back home. Although it wasn't common at the time to have fathers present for the delivery, Dr. Duffee told him, because of his position at the hospital, he could gown up and stay for the delivery, but he didn't want to.

At the hospital, Ilse was taken to a room, prepped, and began the wait between contractions. Ilse was concerned for a girl screaming next door for her mother. She asked the nurse about her. The nurse said it was a young girl from the home for unwed mothers, located in town. Ilse was so grateful that her baby was going to have a good father and a loving mother. It eased any pain she felt as her heart poured out to the young girl in the adjoining room. Their baby girl was born at 6:30 in the morning. Dr. Duffee watched as an intern who was brand new on the obstetrics rotation delivered their baby. The intern's wonder of it all added to the excitement Ilse felt. As soon as the baby began to cry, the intern danced around the room smiling with new life in his arms. That incredible miracle had touched him too. Robert missed both of his children's births by choice. He could have been there, but chose not to be there for the amazing events.

Robert came to see Ilse and the baby on his way into work, all dressed up in suit and tie, ready for the work day. His office was in the same hospital, so he ran up to check on Ilse and the baby several times a day. He was very excited and told Ilse she had done a good job. She was overwhelmed by the generosity of the beautiful roses he brought her. They would be the only ones he ever gave her until many years later for their twenty-fifth wedding anniversary. It was a waste of money, he said, but Ilse thought the flowers were a beautiful gift expressing a love that was shared.

When darling little Molly was born, Ilse was an ecstatic mom. Robert was pleased to be a father and he was proud, offering to hang the diapers since the doctors said she shouldn't go up and down stairs. The pregnancy and delivery were normal, but the doctor had strict rules. Without a dryer and not able to afford a diaper service, Robert was willing to help. He hung diapers once and then bought a new dryer from Sears. Ilse got a dishwasher, a portable one, the same way.

Molly was a good baby, healthy and happy. She had thick, soft, light hair, very straight with wisps of curl at the nape of her neck. She grew fast in spite of projectile vomiting whenever she ate. Ilse loved staying home to take care of her, walking her in the stroller, even in the snow. Robert was there in the evening for her fussiest time. Ilse soon found it was best to have the little one bathed and ready to put to bed when he got home. He enjoyed holding her, and immediately thought she was very smart. Since he was insistent that Molly shouldn't be spoiled, he said the best thing was to let her cry. To a point, Ilse agreed, but she was more inclined to hold and soothe her. Robert left most of Molly's care to Ilse. Still, she was careful that he got plenty of attention, making his favorite meals and catering to him whenever she could.

When Ray, who had been Robert's best man, came with his wife from Boston to ski, the guys said they would take care of Molly so Ilse could ski. Together they changed one messy diaper and that was the end of that. He never changed another diaper.

"It isn't part of my job description," he said. It was also the end of Ilse's skiing days. On weekends Robert would go with hospital friends to ski and Ilse enjoyed being home with little Molly.

The next winter she was pregnant again. Staying home with the children was never burdensome for her. Before the second child was born, Robert was tired of his place in the pecking order at the hospital. He decided to leave the hospital and work for the Regional Medical Center, which involved traveling around the New England states, promoting the hospital and good health care. He would fly out on a small plane and be gone only a day or two at a time. They still had only one car so Ilse would take Molly in the middle of the night to meet him at the airport. She worried about the danger of his flying on small aircrafts, especially in the unpredictable winter weather.

A wonderful couple who lived only two houses away became friends with Robert and Ilse. Of all the people she had met, Ilse was particularly fond of Melanie. She was smart, practical and fun! Before the children were born, they had tea almost daily and worked on every imaginable craft, making wreaths from pinecones and other things they collected.

Pregnant at the same time, once the children were born they traded babysitting or got together for playtime. They also got together as couples to play cards or Password. Ilse refused to try bridge again after Robert told her in front of everyone how stupid she was. With tears of embarrassment, she decided she'd stick with easier card games of chance.

Before the children were born, there were a couple of outbursts that Ilse had never forgotten. She couldn't remember what brought on the first one, but she remembers vividly what happened. Sitting on boxes in their apartment, beginning to eat dinner, there was some complaint about the food. Ilse picked up her glass of water and tossed it in Robert's face. He raised his fist, got red in the face and screamed at her, but surprisingly only walked away, staying mad for several days. Ilse sat back down and ate her dinner, proud of herself for standing up to him. The second time was in the new house. A handy neighbor often came to help Robert with the project of finishing off the downstairs. Robert was extremely handy and could handle almost any home building project himself, but was glad to get help with the carpentry work. The biggest problem was finding the time. Ilse usually worked right along with him and became pretty handy herself. This particular Sunday Mike was there, working with him all morning and into the afternoon. Ilse had made spaghetti and meatballs from scratch. It was ready, and ready, and still ready. She kept calling Robert to come up to eat. When he finally got there, hungry, and looking for the spaghetti that smelled so good simmering all those hours, there wasn't anything left. Ilse had eaten what she wanted and put the rest down the disposal. Robert was livid and his anger was evident with his beet red face and clenched fists. His friend, Mike, thought it was funny. It was a good buffer for Ilse to have Mike there, but she never attempted anything like that again because it was sure to endanger her.

Carefully planning their life, as he had planned graduate school and then the baby to avoid the draft, Robert wanted a second child. Ilse wanted the second child too and Will was born twenty-five months after Molly. He had colic and both parents couldn't wait for the worry and screaming to abate. Robert held him on his stomach as he stretched out on the sofa to try to calm his crying. Little Molly teetered out in the middle of the night to sit by her mother and little brother while he was fed. She was the sweetest big sister, always.

Years later, after the divorce, Ilse's sister-in-law and brother tried to remind Ilse of an incident when their family visited New Hampshire at Easter time. For some reason, Ilse had no recollection of it at all and the story they told her frightened her. *How many things had she put entirely out of her mind so that she could live in harmony with Robert all those years? Why wouldn't she stand up to him if the children were endangered?* The story they reminded her of was when they all went out for a drive to enjoy the spring day and Molly began to fuss and cry. Ilse had little Will in her arms. Robert stopped the car, took Molly out, put her in the middle of the road, got back in the car and drove away leaving the crying two year old alone.

After Steve and Liz told about that heartbreaking incident, Ilse recalled that on every trip he invariably stopped the car, pulled both children out and spanked them for fighting. As hard as she tried, she could not recall his leaving Molly on the road. She knew that he would drive faster and faster if she said anything when he'd had too much to drink and he wouldn't let her drive. There were other incidents, but Ilse held her tongue unless it seemed he was being too severe; then she would pay a price for several days for intruding on the discipline he doled out. He would lash out at her with nasty comments. Ilse would respond by being silent. *She knew in her heart that sometimes his behavior was irrational.*

Ilse no longer taught school after Molly was born, except for substituting, but she began to take in sewing. She didn't enjoy alterations, but had a wonderful time making wedding dresses, special dresses for the brides' mothers, bridesmaids' dresses and beautiful, unusual ball gowns for her favorite customers. It was such fun and nice to bring in some extra money. The neighbors asked her to teach sewing to their teenage daughters who didn't have home economics in the parochial school they attended. Next, the adults wanted their own class. Ilse scheduled sewing or classes around the children, continuing to feed her artistic passion. Part of the passion was making clothes for little Molly...coats and hats with fur trim and dresses that matched the lining. Another passion was decorating her home and helping friends with theirs.

When she was still teaching, she made a complete maternity wardrobe for the art teacher. They bartered a watercolor painting for the clothes. Robert enjoyed the extra income, encouraging Ilse to pursue her career in this way. He told people how talented she was which fed her ego. It was nice to be appreciated and admired.

Ilse made a promise to herself that she would compliment Robert in some way every day, whether it was about how he looked or something he did. She thought, in spite of his successes and good looks that he was insecure. He could never do enough to please himself and she couldn't do enough to please him either.

Whenever they were out, Robert would put an arm around Ilse, or hold her hand. He showed a lot of affection in this way even though he wasn't inclined to be romantic at home. Yet, they were a loving couple. Ilse never moved over in the car until they had a baby car seat between them. There was closeness, always a goodbye kiss in the morning, a hello kiss, and the daily "I love you." There was never the romance that Ilse had dreamed of, but Robert showed his love for her by his attention and affection.

Robert seemed proud of her endeavors as a mother, homemaker, and her friendliness and interest in others. Both of them were well groomed and attractive. He used her for a buffer when they were in social situations. She was more comfortable in social situations than he was, whereas Robert's strength was related to work. Because of this difference, they worked well as a team, understanding the strength of each and how to use that strength in their respective roles.

Both of the children were baptized at the Congregational church they had been attending since they came to New Hampshire. Other hospital people that Robert admired were also members so Robert and Ilse joined and became involved. They taught a Sunday school class of teenagers together with Robert keeping order, not too successfully. In undergraduate school, he had student taught; after many conflicts, he decided he never wanted to teach again, but he never forgot one student, Stephen Phillip, who drove him "up the wall."

After being in New Hampshire almost five years, Robert became restless with his job. He began to look for other opportunities, becoming interested in a position in Detroit as an administrator. He traveled by himself for the interview, calling Ilse to tell her he was taking the position as an Assistant Administrator at the Henry Ford Hospital. It meant living in a big city and it intimidated Ilse. He quickly found a two-bedroom apartment on the second floor. Reluctant to leave New Hampshire, but anxious to further his career, their house was sold to the first people who looked at it and they were on their way. This time a moving van was necessary, as there was now an accumulation of furniture. Leaving the friends and good neighbors behind was the hardest part.

Living in the small apartment proved difficult. With only one car and no place for the children to play, Ilse took them on long walks, struggling to get the carriage down the steps from the second floor. Robert bought oil paints for Ilse to give her something to do in the small quarters. Some of the hospital wives befriended her, many having children the same age as Ilse's. Apartment living didn't last long. Ilse was unhappy and Robert hated the weekends since he didn't have a workshop for building projects. Also, the skiing wasn't very good compared to New Hampshire...besides, none of the other hospital people skied.

Ilse and Robert found a four bedroom, two story, older home closer to the hospital. It needed a lot of work, and that made it a perfect choice. The house was a decorator's delight. Robert would go with Ilse to approve wall paper choices, then Ilse papered every room. They bought used furniture at house sales. Together they fixed the house up, always working side by side unless Robert was at work. He liked the people at the hospital and became friends with many. Both of them sharpened their social skills and they began to entertain more than they had in New Hampshire, often having guests for meals. They started going downtown to see the Detroit Lions play, getting caught up in the excitement of the pro ball games.

It was during this time that their friend Elaine committed suicide, using a gun to shoot herself. She began saying strange things that concerned Ilse. Not wanting to intrude on the relationship Elaine had with her husband, but knowing she needed to speak up Ilse decided to call him at work, first calling Robert for approval and a 'go ahead.' Ilse called to tell him the things that Elaine was saying. They were already getting help but it wasn't enough, soon enough.

Elaine's horrible death and the devastation to the lives of her husband and two boys was always a reminder of how cruel it was for the ones left, to selfishly take your own life. After his mother shot herself, the little boy Molly's age was found at the bathroom door crying "Mommy! Mommy!" The younger little boy was found screaming in the playpen. Robert had taken Elaine's husband home from work that evening and ended up going back to clean up the blood while Ilse tried hopelessly to comfort the children.

17

Living in the South: 1970-1972

Not too long after their friend's death, Robert had the opportunity to work at MUSC Hospital in Charleston, South Carolina. Ilse went along when Robert interviewed for the job. She loved the open spaces, the trees, the people and the opportunity for Robert to advance his career. The hospital paid for the move, which was a luxury in itself and they found a new home under construction in a beautiful area.

When they arrived at their new Charleston home, neighbors stopped by with food. They met a wonderful couple from across the street. Roy was a doctor at MUSC and Kim was a stay-at-home mom. This couple had a boy and girl, the exact ages of Molly and Will, and they became inseparable playmates. Kim and Ilse also bonded immediately. When a third child was born, Ilse and Robert were her Godparents. Life couldn't have been better.

Robert and Ilse knew they could finish and decorate the unfinished house they bought to suit them perfectly. Robert sanded all the hand-made kitchen cabinets and together they finished them. Ilse happily hung wall paper everywhere, making the children's rooms suitable and special. The builder kept coming by to check on the progress, not quite sure they would meet the challenge. One day he asked Ilse if she would make a list of all the colors and wallpaper she used so he could duplicate them in another house. Ilse didn't want choices duplicated, but told him that she would choose and coordinate others for him.

That was the beginning of her decorating career. After the first house she decorated for the builder, he brought her a list of all the houses he was currently working on. He fired his decorator and Ilse was in her glory, picking, choosing and coordinating while she was spending someone else's money. Kim watched the children while she spent a few hours at the paint and wallpaper store. She asked another neighbor artist to join in the venture after a short while. On the way to the stores, they planned their basic color scheme and the feeling they wanted to create for each home. A morning would include choosing carpet, paint, wallpaper, lighting fixtures, tile or linoleum, appliances, bathroom fixtures and sometimes the exterior colors for the siding, shutters and roof. It was such fun and great money for a few hours of effort.

It was in the South that Ilse began to paint in watercolors and acrylic paint on plaques. She had been working in acrylic or oil since Robert encouraged her in Detroit. There she had begun to enter art shows, selling paintings with frames Robert had made. He was always excited when her paintings sold, and Ilse was flattered that people wanted them. She was selling the plaques to a local shop, hoarding away some of the money so she could buy extra gifts.

Living in Charleston, the family found they could go to the beach for the day or long weekends. Another hospital family wanted to go to Myrtle Beach to camp over Easter weekend, so they got out their tent and headed to the campground. It turned out to be very warm for springtime and they loved it. The ocean water was warm, so different from Cape Cod and Maine on the northeast coast, or the cold water of the Pacific Ocean where Ilse's parents lived. The children loved it also. Ilse and Robert felt they were in paradise as they walked the beach hand in hand looking for sand dollars. They knew they would go back as often as possible. In the fall, they went to the Outer Banks with their long time friends Tom and Pam and their two children, after a turkey dinner in the newly decorated home. Traveling to the Carolina beach became a yearly event for the two families. Some years they went in the spring for a week and another in the summer. Those family trips left the fondest memories, with everyone relaxed, even Robert.

Life in the South was wonderful, both at work and at home. Robert thought the children should have a dog and Ilse thought that was a wonderful idea. They had a black cat named Midnight in Detroit, but it turned wild and wandered off. Now they had a mushroom colored cat named Blondie, who was an indoor cat. They had it declawed to protect the new furniture they had purchased.

The children had the exciting task of choosing a little beagle and they named him Skipper. It was agreed that the children would help take care of him, but since the weather was mild, Skipper was to be an outside dog. Robert made a big doghouse with siding and shingles with two assistants, Molly and Will at his side. He put up a long lead line into the woods so the dog would have plenty of room to run. Sometimes, however, the dog would be left in Robert's workshop, getting sick and leaving messes after getting into the children's poster paint.

The family had the dog about four months when Ilse was reading to the children in the Carolina room that overlooked the woods. All at once, Molly started to cry and pointed outside. Someone was stealing their dog. Will started to cry too. Ilse went out to confront the man as he was loading up the doghouse. He said Robert had given the dog to him. He lived in the country and the dog would have plenty of room to run. *Why would Robert do this to the children without consulting her?* When he came home to find the children upset, he brushed it off by saying the dog would be "happier in the country." *Ilse thought it was a cruel thing but she would never voice that to the children.* When she told him later how she felt about it, he just shrugged.

"Forget it!" he said. Ilse, Molly and Will never forgot it. After that, whenever there was talk about getting another dog or cat, Ilse would recall this cruel, uncaring incident, afraid there might be a repeat performance.

Several nights while living in the South, Robert came home concerned about union problems at the hospital. One night, after the children were asleep they left the house for a short walk up the dark street. A ditch covered with groundcover separated the house from the road. When they were at the top of the hill, a car approached, turned off its lights and made a U-turn following them down the street back toward their house. Ilse and Robert walked faster and faster, not knowing what to do except try to get away. Whoever was in the car recognized Robert and wanted to scare them. Ilse could only think of the children alone back in the house.

As soon as they were across from their house, Robert said, "Run for it." They stumbled in the ditch and rushed through the door. In a panic, he said, "Lock the door." Ilse said she'd call the police. He said "no" as he loaded his gun. The car disappeared but the scare remained.

When they hurried across the ditch, they tore up some of the groundcover. Only a few weeks before the little neighbor girl came to the door with her beautiful collie dog beside her. Robert answered the door and began yelling at Molly's friend.

"Keep that dog at home! It is tearing up the ivy we planted. If you bring that dog back here again, I'm going to shoot it!" Katie ran home crying to tell her mother who immediately came over to confront Robert. Robert told the mother the same thing. Ilse listened from the other room horrified. Molly or Will didn't know why the neighbors thought they had such a mean daddy and couldn't play with them anymore.

At the hospital, Robert was a popular administrator. He was invited to teach classes in hospital administration at the local university, which had an impressive graduate program. Lacking a dress code like the one in Nebraska, he thought the students were sloppy and needed more discipline if they were going to enter the field of hospital administration. Robert came home to tell Ilse about a particular student who pressed him rudely with questions after his lecture. The student who gave him a difficult time was Joe Hawk. It wasn't too long after his encounter with Joe that Robert had an exploratory call from Detroit, enticing him to go back to the Henry Ford Hospital in a higher position with more money. Joe and Robert's paths would meet again and they would become the best of friends. By questioning Robert, Joe had somehow won his respect and admiration.

Robert had aggressively looked into the hiring of outside cleaning services for the MUSC hospital deciding to bring in a new non-union company based in Chicago called Service Master. Involved with the union group, Robert was often threatened reminding them of the night on their walk. Ilse and Robert became good friends with Mario, who Service Master Company brought in to manage the cleaning service. A bachelor, he often came to the house for dinner or to help. The children loved him and the pizza or spaghetti dinners he would make for them.

"Eat! Eat! God love ya!" he would say to them as they clung to his legs waiting to be tossed in the air.

The cleaning company was so new that Robert found himself working with the president of the company. He convinced Ilse that it would be good for her to sell some of her other stocks to invest in this new company which she did, putting the stock in both of their names. The company grew and the stock split, then split again. It was a good financial decision.

One Sunday evening there was a call from Robert's mother, Grandmother Kelly, in Nebraska. It was one of those calls that one always dreads. Ilse wrote to them almost every week, but they didn't talk on the phone often. Grandmother said that Granddad had been rushed to the hospital and Robert should come. Not long before, he had caught his fingers in the snow blower; he was depressed because he could no longer do eye surgery.

When Robert asked his mother if he had tried to commit suicide, she said,

"Of course not! Why would he do that?" The next morning Robert flew to Nebraska. He was soon on the phone asking Ilse to come and bring the children. His Dad was going to be okay but he had tried to take his own life. Ilse and the children were soon on the plane joining him. It was a sobering experience. Robert needed Ilse there. He was shaken. They talked to the neighbor across the street, a good friend, who wanted to help, but had questions. The suicide attempt was hush-hush. Mrs. Kelly was adamant that no one should know what happened. By now, Robert's sister and her husband had arrived too. Granddad had been taken to the local hospital where everyone knew him. It was hard to keep it a secret, but Ilse thought that honesty was the best policy, even though it was painful. The family relented and told the truth, but only when it was necessary, ashamed that anything like this would happen in their family.

After Robert's father got well enough, he was moved to a mental health facility in the neighboring town. With the entrance examination, they found that not only was he depressed, but also that he had colon cancer, telling the family that he probably had about a year to live. He was also addicted to numerous medications, self-prescribed so that he could sleep or perk himself up in the morning. With that news, Robert went back home to work leaving Ilse and the children there to take care of his parents. Robert's sister Amy and her husband also left. Surprisingly, the colon surgery went well and Dr. Kelly was able to "get off" addictive medications.

Over the years Dr. Kelly had displayed some erratic behavior, from stealing pop and beer cans from neighbors' garages worth a nickel apiece, to side-swiping a car in the church parking lot and leaving, to taking small items from stores because he didn't want to wait in line to pay. Mrs. Kelly had been trying to hide visits from the police from her family and her few friends.

The weirdest thing that Mrs. Kelly told the family was that Dr. Kelly had used a small drill and insisted he could drill his own teeth. No one could believe that he would do that but she swore it was the truth. *Was he trying to save money or did he think he could do anything? And what about the pain? If he was a dentist, not an eye doctor, it might be a little more understandable. He was clearly disturbed.*

The family was used to having Dr. Kelly bring out the syringes for flu shots every Thanksgiving or Christmas. He did that until Robert and Amy told their parents they wouldn't come on holidays if he made that a tradition. It ruined many family get-togethers for the children *and what sort of memories would they have of their holidays with their grandparents?*

Before the family left after the suicide attempt, they went through the house to find all the hidden medications. Full bottles of pills were thrown out, many flushed down the toilet. Pills were everywhere, in pockets, in boxes hidden under the bed and when the ceiling tiles in the closet were removed, they found his biggest stash. It was a big job to rid the house of the medications.

"How could he have so much?" they thought. Being a physician, he could order medications direct which he had been doing for a long time. Robert said, "The old man is nuts," and headed back home to get on with his life.

The young family had become active in the Methodist church. Robert attended regularly, but Ilse became more involved, working with the Auxiliary ladies making things for their holiday bazaar, joining a bible study group, and finally becoming a church deacon. Robert didn't mind going because he liked the minister's thought-provoking sermons. The Methodist church had a Moravian Christmas service, which was a new experience for them,

149

and they visited the Moravian Village in North Carolina.

With Robert's encouragement, Ilse looked into buying a franchise for "stretch sewing" which was popular at the time. Not long after they began to look into the possibility of this business venture for Ilse, another phone call came from the Henry Ford Hospital in Detroit.

18
Detroit and Clarkston: 1972-1986

The phone call from Detroit changed their life again. They wanted Robert to come back to the Henry Ford Hospital with a promotion and more pay. Robert laughed and told Ilse they would never give him the money he wanted to get him to move back. They did, however, and Ilse was soon packing boxes to move back to Michigan.

The children had already started school. They rode the bus to the public school and had the opportunity to be in classes that weren't segregated as they had been just a few years before. It was wonderful for them to see a side of life their parents had never seen until they moved to the South. They were in the habit of saying "Yes Ma'am" and "No Sir" and calling their friend's mother "Miss Kim." Some of their acquired southern courtesies pleased Ilse. It seemed to add a softer, gentler demeanor, and showed respect for others.

Balking somewhat about leaving the sunny South, Robert softened the blow for Ilse by taking her to High Point to buy new furniture for the children's rooms. Going back to Detroit was going to be hard after having an almost perfect life in South Carolina. There were the beautiful trees, a nice home and neighborhood, a church family, a wonderful decorating job, great hospital friends, best buddies for Molly and Will, the South Carolina beaches nearby and it was only three hours from their favorite North Carolina beach. *What more could anyone want?* Ilse and the children had it all, but Robert was ready to continue his climb. With that adventurous spirit, and the willingness to do whatever it took to help him reach his goals, Ilse faced the new challenge happily. He didn't need to bribe her with furniture for the children, but she wasn't going to turn the offer down.

The move back to Michigan went smoothly with everyone settling into the new routine. The only problem was the day the moving van arrived. Their cat Blondie was seen outside, but later she wasn't to be found anywhere. The children asked the neighbors, but no one had seen their precious pet. The children mourned and it bothered Ilse to see them so sad, losing another pet.

Winter came not long before Christmas. Robert suggested they all go to the pet store and buy a new cat. Molly and Will agreed on a little black and white kitten. She already had her shots. They would have to have her fixed when she got a little older. She was supposed to be litter-trained, but after a few days it was obvious she had been taken from her mother too soon. They named her Noel because she was an early Christmas present. She charged all over the house, making messes on the carpet, and tipping over the Christmas tree. The children loved her, but had to leave her on Christmas day to fly to California to celebrate with Granny and Grandpa Mueller. They were excited to be with their favorite grandparents, but sad to leave Noel so soon. Robert had promised to feed her and clean the litter box while they were gone. They put her bed in the bathroom so she could stay there during the day while Robert was at work.

Every few days Robert called them in California to see how everything was going. He missed them, he said, and "Oh, by the way, tell the children I had to give Noel away."

"What do you mean you had to give Noel away? You can't do this to the children!" Getting rid of the pets in this manner was becoming a cruel pattern.

"I just did," he said. "The stupid cat isn't litter trained. I don't know why you're so upset. Anyway, I gave it to the police station. I told them it was a stray."

How selfish! Ilse thought.

Back in Detroit, Robert was again immersed in his work at the hospital. With season tickets for the Lion's games, Will was old enough to go to some games with his dad. Ilse went to others.

Robert had bought a little blue sports car just before returning to Detroit. With two cars, and a nice house, they again 'kept up with the Jones.'

Ilse made friends in the new neighborhood. She did the usual painting, wall papering and decorating. She had morning coffee with the neighborhood women, mostly stay-at-home moms. Becoming bored, she began to teach the popular 'stretch sewing' techniques with a demonstration booklet she wrote to give her students. At first she taught in a fabric shop, then adult education at the high school and then at home where it was the most lucrative. Robert bragged about how much money she made teaching sewing.

In the early spring, with snow still on the ground, the next-door neighbor-girl came over and asked about the cat they had lost when they moved in. She said there was a cat in their garage, almost dead. Ilse and Robert had long ago given up on the cat ever returning, but the cat in the garage was their old cat Blondie. Although almost dead, Robert allowed Ilse to spend the money for a vet and put Blondie in 'kitty intensive care' until she got better. *Ilse thought that maybe he was willing to spend the money on Blondie because he gave Noel away at Christmas.* It had taken all winter for Blondie to find her way back to her family, where she was petted and pampered enough to make up for lost time.

Neighbors asked Ilse to help them hang wallpaper and soon she partnered with a friend. She found time to be a Brownie leader and Girl Scout leader. Robert joined Indian Guides with Will. They were named 'Big Trouble' and 'Little Trouble.' Actually, Will was very little trouble but Robert was a lot of trouble. When they went on overnight cabin trips with their tribe, Robert showed up at home, having left Will with the other fathers because it was too uncomfortable to sleep there. He would go back in the morning. *What did those fathers think? Ilse wondered.*

Because Robert's father didn't attend any of his school functions, Robert always went to programs and school conferences for the children. He knew it was important to them. They heard all the things parents like to hear about their children...how smart they were, how nice they were to their classmates, how polite and well adjusted they were. It made Ilse and Robert feel good about trying to instill wholesome values. There was plenty of love and affection plus time to help with homework or school projects. They were a happy family. *Ilse had a satisfying feeling of contentment. Life was as it should be.*

Ilse began to commute for graduate classes. She coordinated classes with school for the children and Robert's work as best she could. She was about half way through a master's degree in clothing and textiles when Robert said he wanted to move to a nicer area. She had a strong four-point average going and had already taken the classes that were the most difficult for her like statistics and chemistry of textiles. She had worked hard to get this far and didn't want to give it up. Robert convinced her that she needed to go back to teaching, that she should substitute teach until there was a full time position available. It was about money. With all his success and saving all these years, they needed to save even more aggressively for college.

With every promotion in Robert's career, there was a corresponding move to a bigger, better, showier house. As he was promoted to Associate Director at the Henry Ford Hospital, life became more complex, social circles changed and there was more money. He had never made a gigantic salary, but life got easier financially.

When they first returned to Detroit, Robert hired Joe Hawk, the troublemaker from the MUSC class he had taught. Joe came to interview with his attractive wife Marilyn. There was something about Joe that drew Robert in. First of all, Joe didn't let Robert intimidate him or push him around. He was a Vietnam War vet who had been injured during two tours of duty. Before that, he was recruited to play football for West Point. Robert admired everything he had done. The men became best buddies, but Robert was always treated as the respected boss.

Joe gave Robert suggestions on how to dress, which Robert took, such as wearing long socks so the skin wouldn't show when he crossed his legs. Joe had a Rolex and it soon became an obsession for Robert to have one too. They bought the same kind of Scotch after Joe taught Robert the difference in taste.

Ilse didn't understand it and yet she did. Robert wanted to be like Joe. Both the men were smart. Robert had already proven himself to be a very good hospital administrator. Robert was better looking, Ilse thought, but Joe was definitely smoother. He could charm anyone, including Robert. She couldn't help but like him, and she and Marilyn became close friends.

The family had been driving to Nebraska to visit Robert's parents every summer. Robert wasn't happy there, always leaving Ilse and the children to talk with his mother while he wandered off to the college campus or another old haunt. The first time they drove from New

Hampshire when Will was a baby, Robert was anxious for his father to see his son. When his father entered the room, he started talking to Robert about the stock market economy before he said 'hello' to the rest of the family. Robert said, "Don't you want to see your grandson?"

Dr. Kelly glanced down at little Will and replied, "He looks okay." He was a disappointing granddad. Grandmother made up for his behavior somewhat, but not enough for it to go unnoticed. He was one of the coldest men Ilse had ever met but she continued to try to engage him with friendship.

When they were back in Detroit, Robert's father again tried to take his own life. Robert went to Nebraska for only a few days and Ilse was left again in Nebraska to take care of his parents. The children stayed with neighbors so they wouldn't miss school. In the end, many years later, Dr. Kelly died of old age. He had survived the colon cancer without radiation or chemo.

Their family didn't hug, not even to greet their grown children they hadn't seen for a long time. Ilse prodded Robert to give his mother a hug and then he would respond, but it wasn't natural for them. Grandmother would try to hug the children in response to their warmth, and Molly would climb up on her granddad's lap, unaware that it made him uncomfortable. Robert was good about hugging Ilse and his own children, but he hadn't learned that growing up.

Ilse's family was warmer, hugging one another in greeting and when they said goodbye. Ilse hugged most of her friends; it seemed the natural thing to do. Molly was also full of hugs and kisses, but Will was more reserved with his affection.

When Robert was with his father, talk was always serious between the grown men. There wasn't any laughter or reminiscing about good times together. *Ilse thought there hadn't been many good times.* They talked of Robert's work most of the time. He had every reason to be pleased with his son's success and contribution to the health field. There was NEVER a compliment and it seemed Robert never won his respect. Ilse knew that Robert thought his father was brilliant, but *Ilse thought he had a weird way of showing his intelligence.*

Robert wanted everyone to know he had smart children. Sometimes it was embarrassing when he bragged so much, particularly about Will. In Ilse's family they had been taught humility, and she wanted their children to be taught the same. Being intelligent was great, but how you used your gift was what was important.

19
Conflicts and Concerns

Back in Detroit, the family made the move to a new house in Clarkston, where they had a huge yard and a shared pond with other people on the street. The house was again unfinished, and again Ilse went to work. Robert had very little time to help, but he mowed the yard with his John Deere and Will was now old enough to help him. They kept the same friends from the hospital group, but made a lot of new friends too. Again, life seemed better than ever.

The family continued their trips to the beach. They met Ilse's brother Steve's family and their parents in Michigan to camp, which Ilse found to be fun but a lot of work. For the Michigan trip, Ilse's parents were going to sleep in the back of their station wagon. Robert and Ilse would use her parents' old tent.

When it started to storm in the middle of the night, the children kept right on sleeping. Rain was coming down hard, it was thundering and lighting flashed repeatedly. Water started seeping into the tent. All of a sudden, Robert said, "I'm going to sleep in the car. You're on your own. I'm out of here!" Before she had a chance to reply, he was gone. There was no way she could get the children out of the tent alone with the storm raging around them.

The next morning Robert said, "I slept great. Did you get wet?" Ilse saw the look of disapproval on her mother's face but her mother never said a word. There had been two deaths in the campground that night because of the storm. *Ilse knew she had again been treated badly, without concern or respect*, but she didn't want a scene. *It seemed easier to let it go.* There was always a good time to balance the bad, or so it seemed.

The fall after moving to Clarkston, Ilse put her name in to begin substitute teaching. Molly was starting eighth grade and Will sixth. It worked out nicely to be gone when the children were at school. On days she wasn't called to substitute teach, she would pack up her worktable and go with her friend from the old neighborhood to hang wallpaper. They couldn't keep up with the job offers. Besides making better money than substitute teaching, they were having fun, laughing their way through difficult jobs. One of their customers asked if Robert Kelly was Ilse's husband. Ilse shouldn't have mentioned it to Robert because that was the end of hiring out to hang paper. He said he "couldn't have a wife doing such menial work." Never had he complained before. *How could honest hard work make anyone look bad, she thought.*

Then fate smiled on Ilse. A substitute-teaching job turned into a full time position in a school about a thirty-minute drive from home. It was perfect! The hours coordinated with Molly and Will's. The faculty was great and she met a teacher she especially liked, Rene, who became a good friend. She could quit ironing Robert's shirts if she would take them to the laundry he said.

Ilse always kept a clean, neat house. Robert had never complained, but was becoming more and more particular. He was actually angry if he found any scratches on the furniture or dents in the walls from the children's friends. He would confront them about a spill or mark on the wall, yet surprisingly they still came every day after school to their home.

One of the more embarrassing times was when Robert invited a new employee to the house for dinner. They were having a lovely evening together when all of a sudden, Robert got up, brought out the vacuum and began sweeping the carpet. Ilse couldn't figure out what he was thinking, but *she thought he was acting like his father.*

When they finally reciprocated by inviting some teaching couples to their home, Robert got up after dinner, wound the clocks and again got out the vacuum to sweep the floors. Ilse wanted to disappear since she really enjoyed this new group of friends, unrelated to his hospital work. Yet, the couples tolerated Robert's strange and rude behavior over and over. Ilse was embarrassed. *It was infuriating, humiliating and downright outrageous!*

Ilse, years later, was told about several incidents concerning Robert's odd behavior. One was on a golf outing hosted by Robert and Ilse. Robert wanted to treat some couples to dinner at the country club and the men to golf before dinner. Before they finished golfing, it began to rain. When Robert got out his golf umbrella, it was broken. He went to another club member's golf bag, put in his broken umbrella, and took one that looked like his. There was an embarrassing verbal confrontation, which was witnessed by the rest of the foursome. He always pretended to be honest to a fault. At the hospital, he made Ilse pay for even a stamp...but here he was being dishonest. In this case, he wanted something, so he took it, even though it belonged to somebody else... like his father would have done.

Living in Clarkston was wonderful. One summer vacation was coordinated with a trip to meet Ilse's family in Utah. Robert suggested they fly to Salt Lake City and rent a car to join Ilse's family, then tour.

Robert didn't enjoy the camping without a comfortable bed or indoor plumbing, so he said he'd meet Ilse's family for a week if they could stay in a motel not too far from the campground. The motel had a swimming pool and a trampoline for the children. Ilse's parents decided to stay at the motel too. It was fun for all the cousins to come to the motel for swimming after their picnics and hikes.

The cousins had a great time. Being the same age, Will and Tony hung out together.

"Dad, may we have the keys to the trunk to get out the ball?" Will asked.

"Whoops!" they said as they accidentally locked the car keys in the trunk.

"You idiots!" Robert screamed at them. His voice got louder and louder until everyone at the motel was on their balcony watching him berate the boys. He couldn't get himself under control, continuing to holler at the stupidity and lack of responsible behavior.

Ilse and the rest of her family tried to calm him saying, "We'll take the seat out and get at the trunk that way."

"It won't work. They have ruined the trip." He went on and on while Ilse's brothers took the back seat out and retrieved the keys.

The damage was done. Everyone was embarrassed and Will and Tony had been humiliated in front of everyone. People were shaking their heads and protecting their children, not sure what this 'mad' man would do next.

The family went on to have one of their better family vacations driving to Bryce, Zion, the Grand Canyon and Yellowstone. Everyone was careful not to behave in any way that would cause another outburst.

Ilse could never figure out what made Robert sometimes go berserk and other times keep control of his emotions. It was frustrating. After his tantrums, it seemed Robert was unaware that anything unusual had happened. He'd never mention them and Ilse had long ago decided it wasn't worth the hassle.

Many years before Robert had told Ilse about a family camping trip his family attempted when he was young. They were headed to the same National Parks Ilse and Robert were going to with Molly and Will. Only a few days into the trip, Dr. Kelly turned the car around heading back to Sidney. It was because he heard on the radio that the stock market was going down.

They had fixed up a huge family room downstairs with a pool table on one side and a big sectional sofa, TV, and computer on the other side. It was the hangout for Will and his two best friends. Ilse preferred to have them at home and they loved it. The boys would come in after school, select their individual Stouffer's pizza from the freezer, put them in the oven, and head downstairs to play pool while their pizza was baking.

Molly didn't have as many friends come to the house. She was more likely to be out riding bareback on her friend's horses next door. The girls also liked to use the kitchen to bake or make supper for the family, all of which was encouraged.

Out of the blue, Robert said (again) that he wanted to get the children a dog. They hadn't forgotten what had happened to their dog when they were little, but no one mentioned it. Ilse said she voted against it thinking she would be the one to take care of it. But Molly and Will got excited and began to discuss what kind they should get, promising they would help with the care. Robert said he would walk it. Ilse knew that meant he'd walk it once or twice or when he happened to feel like it. Anyway, she was out-voted and they all went to look at a litter of Old English Sheep Dogs advertised in the paper. Needless to say, they were the most adorable puppies they had ever seen. The littlest one kept going to Will, trying to get a hold of his shoelaces. That one would become a part of the family; the vote was unanimous.

With all that hair Sasha was to be an outside dog during the day when everyone was gone and a kitchen-back-hall dog when everyone was home. She would only be allowed to go downstairs when she was properly trained.

This time Will was a big help building the doghouse. Robert went to a lot of expense to have a cement slab poured on half the pen and gravel on the other half. He bought a strong fence. Sasha turned out to be a wonderful dog, but Ilse was right, she was the one who ended up walking her most of the time. In order to train Sasha, she was the one who took her to obedience class.

Robert got along with most of the neighbors at the beginning. As time went on if they disagreed with him or confronted him about anything, he would become defiant and nasty, retaliating in unusual ways.

In Clarkston, he was insistent that the neighbor next door put in a drainage pipe to route the water away from their yard. When the neighbor lady questioned the need for the work, Robert proceeded to dig a ditch across the front of the neighbor's yard. Then, to aggravate them more, he began to shovel their dog poop from the driveway and dump it on their porch, in front of their door. Ilse would apologize for his behavior and tried to remain friends. She begged Robert to just tell them kindly that they should keep their dogs tied, but he wouldn't budge. Ilse was embarrassed and her own anger smoldered, building like a volcano, smoking at the brim but seldom erupting. *She often thought about confronting him but knew the inevitable fight wasn't worth the destruction to the family. To a fault, Ilse wanted peace and harmony within her own family, particularly with Robert.*

165

It became more and more routine for Robert to have conflicts with the neighbors and Ilse continued to try to smooth things over. On the cul-de-sac where there were only seven homes, Robert managed to have an argument with four of the neighbors. He had 'words' with the osteopathic doctor belittling him by saying he made too much money after going to a mediocre medical school. *Ilse knew Robert was jealous that this young doctor made much more money than he did.*

He fought with another neighbor lady about her yard. She wanted to hire Will to mow her yard and at first, Robert thought it was a good idea. When she became dependent on Will, Robert refused to let him use the tractor, leaving her 'high and dry' when she was leaving on vacation. Ilse insisted that Will fulfill his obligation by using a small power mower to do the big yard.

It was the women that Robert tried to intimidate, more than the husbands. The osteopathic doctor was the exception. In spite of Robert's behavior, Ilse managed to make amends for her husband, trying to cover for his power plays and rudeness. *Ilse thought because Robert's confrontations were becoming more frequent and unreasonable it might be related to the stress of his job.*

Molly wanted to earn money. She was babysitting, but in high school she kept going back to the stores until a local druggist finally told her he'd give her a try. It worked for him and for her. She worked there all through high school, summer vacations, and breaks from college.

Since Robert didn't get to choose where he would go to college, he said Molly and Will could go wherever they wanted. Sight unseen, Molly decided to go to the University of Connecticut to study nursing, but not without trauma and tears. Robert had encouraged a nursing career suggesting Michigan State, but he was true to his word that she could go wherever she wanted.

Molly was a very pretty, strong, but feminine girl. Sometimes weight was a bit of a problem as she went through the normal growing stages. However, it was fortunate Molly didn't develop a severe eating disorder with Robert's comments about her weight beginning when she was a toddler, saying it was probably good she didn't like milk because of the calories. The pediatrician assured Ilse Molly's weight was in the normal range. In high school, she was afraid to eat ice cream or sweets in her father's presence, sometimes hiding in a closet or bathroom to eat, avoiding probable criticism.

She was always the picture of health with only a few childhood mishaps. One was when she ran through a glass storm door when she was four. Within minutes, there was blood everywhere, and the nurse next door was called over. Robert drove her to the Henry Ford Hospital, calling ahead so she would be properly taken care of. What a trooper! She hardly cried while a new surgical resident stitched her up, making the tiniest stitches. Robert sat with her the whole time, stressing how important it was to not have a big scar on her face. Robert said, "Her face is her meal ticket." *Of course, Ilse didn't want her to have scars on her face either, but a 'meal ticket?' Hardly.* Molly ended up with a small scar on the side of her face where her beautiful curly hair would always cover it.

Robert continued to be concerned about Molly's appearance. It was important that Molly wear braces. Her smile was part of her 'meal ticket.' Ilse was happy that they could afford to do that for her. It was the right thing to do for her self-esteem.

Robert had braces when he was a teenager, along with a few of the professors' daughters. He had perfect teeth and a beautiful smile. No one talked about braces in Ilse's family. Only the wealthier families had such a status symbol. For Ilse's family there was a lot of milk and an occasional visit to the dentist. Anyway, "pretty is as pretty does," her mother often said.

Will was a handsome young man who was not given the option to have braces. His teeth were not bad. The Kellys agreed that, although recommended by the orthodontist, it was more important to spend the money on a private education. They could have afforded both the braces and the school, but Robert didn't see it that way saying, "Will's forte' is not his looks, but his mind." Will's weight was never an issue. He was always on the slim side. Both children had good minds but the 'meal ticket' for the daughter was more important.

During the summer before Molly left for college, Steve's son, Kurt, came to live with their family. He was a fantastic student at Iowa State. Robert had convinced him to work at the hospital for the summer. He could get him a job. Robert was always better with children when they were older. He encouraged them to pursue their interests focusing on careers and he seemed to have their best interests at heart. He was especially proud of his sister's one son, Ilse's nephews, and his own son.

Will went to a private high school because Robert thought it would give him an edge when choosing a college. Molly was left in the local public school. She was also very bright, but he thought that, being a girl, it wasn't as important to groom her for an Ivy League school. Besides that, he was convinced, although smart, she didn't have the ability Will did. Ilse pointed out numerous times that it wasn't fair to compare the children. They both had strengths, were different from each other, but most important they both were developing into wonderful young people.

With her persistence in looking for a job, Ilse knew Molly had some qualities that would serve her well. She was very persistent, much more so than most of her friends. She just needed to learn how to study and focus on a goal. Nursing seemed to be a perfect career choice for her. Will was good in every subject, especially math and the sciences.

On a warm summer night when everyone was at home, the family relaxed in the cool recreation room downstairs that they all enjoyed so much. Ilse's nephew Kurt, Will, Molly and two other friends were watching a movie. They were engrossed in the movie with their popcorn and cokes while Ilse was stenciling the poolroom. She had cut her own stencils to match some fabric. She had already stenciled the larger room and it was looking nice, all coordinated and new. It was comforting to have Robert nearby when she was working on a project and she usually was nearby to help him when he was working on something. This time Robert was shooting some pool by himself next to where Ilse was working. Ilse had complained about an odor in the downstairs area but hadn't been able to pinpoint the problem. The dog hadn't left any messes and the cat's litter box was cleaned regularly, housed under the stairwell. This night, as she was stenciling, Blondie, their long-time pet that had come back several years before, backed up to the wall. She was urinating between the baseboard and carpeting.

"That has to be the odor I've noticed," Ilse said. "Blondie must be getting too old. We're going to have to talk about what we should do."

Robert replied, "It will only cost a quarter." Ilse didn't know what he was talking about, and after cleaning up the wet spot, went on with the stenciling project.

The movie came to a halt as everyone downstairs heard a 'pop-pop.' They looked at one another in disbelief. Then they realized what they were hearing. Gunshots! Molly, Will and Ilse flew up the stairs with Sasha the dog right behind them. Robert came in with his gun saying, "Like I said, it only cost a quarter, actually fifty cents because I had to shoot her twice."

Ilse was furious and felt sick! The kids were crying and trying to shield their dog, thinking their dad would hurt her too. The nephew downstairs was calling his parents. It was heartbreaking. Not only did the cruelty of the incident bother Ilse, but the look of triumph when Robert told them what he had done was incomprehensible. He had a proud smile on his face. They all knew what he had done when they heard the 'pop-pop.' *Why would he be so smug when he had done such a merciless thing?* Ilse found herself gagging, sick to her stomach, running to the bathroom *feeling not only sick but sad, mad and confused. Did she know this man she was married to she wondered. What kind of a father was he?*

When they first moved to this house, there was a pretty neighbor who would often ask Robert to help with a problem at her house. New to the area, before his dark side showed, he had a reputation for being able to come to any neighbors' rescue when something was amiss. If he was home, they would call him about a plumbing problem, to take down a tree, or in the middle of the night to help if someone was locked out. In most cases, he was resourceful and willing to help whenever he was around. Ilse was proud that he could do most anything at home. If he didn't know how to do something, he would work at it until he figured it out. He organized the neighbors for clean-ups...always a leader whether at work or at home. In fact, in the little village where the family lived next to Clarkston, he was soon on the town council and then mayor pro-tem. Whenever he became involved with an organization, if he was interested, he started to work his way to the top.

When Robert killed Blondie, *Ilse thought about another cat that Robert had killed under very different circumstances.* The neighbor came over crying that she had accidentally hit their cat on the road out in front of her house. The cat was still alive. Robert immediately got his gun and put the cat out of its misery. *That had seemed the right thing to do, but this time, to kill their pet that was old and confused seemed very wrong. Why couldn't she have been peacefully put to sleep?*

When the same neighbor had a mouse problem in the house her son, Will's good friend, said, "Whatever you do, don't call Mr. Kelly. He'll shoot it!" Some of the adults found it amusing, but Ilse was troubled by it.

To say it was wrong was all Ilse could or would do. Robert reminded her about how his high school friends went 'cat hunting.' Ilse well remembered the way they shot stray cats along the roadside because they could spot their eyes like lights at night. Robert wasn't a farm boy, but he joined in the 'sport.' *It seemed like a sick game they were playing. Wondering how Robert played such a 'sport' sickened her.*

Blondie had made them all laugh and feel good so many times. One night after a walk, when the family arrived back to the front door Blondie was there with one of her 'gifts.' This night it was a mouse. Thinking it was dead, Ilse opened the door. As the mouse came to life, it scooted into the house. The cat ran after the mouse. The kids ran back outside, Robert ran after the cat and the mouse until Blondie finally cornered the mouse again. Ilse had jumped up on the sofa. Remember, Ilse didn't 'do mice' dead or alive.

After Blondie was gone, Molly, Will and Ilse became protective of Sasha, spoiling her but especially making sure she didn't do anything out of line. Everyone was on their good behavior. None of them wanted to annoy Robert because he was hard to live with when he got angry. It was like walking on eggshells much of the time.

When she was a high school sophomore, Molly reeked of smoke one night when they picked her up from the skating rink. As soon as they got home, Robert demanded the cigarettes from her purse. When she ignored the request, he emptied the purse on the bed. Robert lost control and was furious. He roughly threw Molly over his knee to spank her without any consideration for her age, physical maturity or modesty. Ilse tried to stop him, not believing what he was doing and how utterly crude he was treating his teenage daughter.

No one had spanked Molly that hard when she was a little girl. *Why would he try to humble her in this way now? He had to show her HE was in charge and he was not to be defied.* No smoking. Period. *Verbal abuse was bad enough. Molly could be reasoned with if given the chance. This was the most disgusting thing he could do to her, to humiliate her in this way. He was only thinking of himself.* Ilse told him she would not tolerate physical abuse. Ilse was trying as best she knew how to protect her 'cubs,' however, when a big man decides he wants to use his physical strength to intimidate, there isn't much you can do. Physically, Ilse was no match for him.

There were other major conflicts about the parties where there was drinking. It was not allowed, period. It was illegal and that was reason enough, not to mention possible

173

accidents. Ilse didn't want to be as strict as her mother had been, but now she understood, and she remained firm, but Robert might flip-flop. *After the teenage spanking, Ilse was reluctant to involve Robert for fear of another uncontrolled act of discipline.*

Will seemed to be easier. He wasn't as obvious about any of his escapades as Molly had been. He went back in the woods with his two friends. They had built a mysterious fort far enough back that they could drink beer uninterrupted and didn't risk the combination of drinking and driving. They might have smoked but he never smelled like it. There was one time when Robert shoved him around when he obviously had been drinking, but it was nothing like his discipline of Molly. When the local cop told Robert a neighbor had said something about the boys' beer cans in the woods, Robert gave them a garbage bag and told them to clean up their mess.

If either Molly or Will tried drugs, Robert or Ilse were never aware of it. Probably they did, but it was never an obvious problem. Compared to many of their friends' children, the issues with Molly and Will were insignificant.

Life went on. One more trip to the beach, then Ilse took Molly to Connecticut for college orientation. Will was to stay home with his dad, continue mowing yards, babysit for two little neighbor boys, and care for Sasha, now full grown. Getting the dog was a bribe for the children when they moved away from the old neighborhood into the country. Robert thought it would help them to readjust to the new locale, but after Blondie, they weren't sure.

Ilse and Molly were off to Connecticut for college orientation. Ilse liked having some time with Molly, just the two of them. There hadn't been much one-on-one time. Molly was a free spirit, which Ilse approved of, but sometimes the direction she took made her want to reel her daughter in.

Ilse wanted the trip to Connecticut for college orientation to be a bonding experience. They were doing fine until they arrived at the area where the University of Connecticut is located. Molly looked around and said almost in a panic, "Where's the town?" Molly was used to the charming shops and upscale malls in the Detroit area.

Why had they skipped a college visitation before the final decision was made? It had been easier then, but now Ilse wondered at their foolishness. They should have insisted and both should have taken her there...certainly one of them. It was a bad decision, but here they were for orientation. Molly checked into the dorm and received a schedule. Ilse left the campus, not without trepidation. She drove to visit friends with the understanding that she would be back after the two- day orientation. She got back to the campus early and Molly was more than ready to leave, waiting on the curb. Ilse tried to find just a hint of interest, taking her to a nice restaurant by the ocean. But Molly was annoyed and anxious to get on the road back home. Ilse drove half the night, trying to understand what was going on in Molly's mind. Ilse was being treated with the 'silent treatment', which she remembered using on her mother more than once growing up. She knew that Molly was not happy. The university she had chosen sight unseen was not what she thought it would be. To make matters worse, she was headed there alone. She would know no one when she arrived on campus in about three weeks.

Before Molly went off to college, a week at the beach with Tom and Pam's family was perfectly glorious with wonderful weather, relaxing walks, games, and a feeling of togetherness for everyone. It was always this way because of years of vacationing together.

The last day there, after coming off the beach to get cleaned up to go out for supper, Robert sat down beside Molly on the sofa and put his arm around her. He was comfortable showing his affection to her, often hugging her. He asked her, "Well, how do you feel now that you're all set to go off to college?"

Molly hesitated, as if deciding whether to speak her mind. "Actually, I want to go to San Diego!"

Robert went crazy, yelling at her. Embarrassed, their friends left the condo as Robert began to rant about already paying the first semester tuition. He said, "You're going, and that's that."

Without saying another word Molly looked at him, went in the bedroom, got her purse, walked out the door and down the street making Robert more furious than ever.

This is so wrong, Ilse thought. It is our fault that we are at this point because we didn't help her with the decision and make a college visit.

For once, she spoke up to Robert, "Sit down and shut up." She had never talked to him like that, and she was surprised it worked. Then she called Molly back and they had a civil discussion with Ilse in charge for a change. It was necessary to assert herself. They talked about options. Although calmer, Robert was adamant that the tuition already paid was an important part of the equation. Molly relented, saying she would go to Connecticut as planned. However, the incident left scars. Not only was Molly hurt, but Ilse felt she had let her daughter down when she needed her most.

Robert went along to take Molly to school. It was to be one of the saddest days of Ilse's life. When they arrived, not many other students had arrived, including Molly's roommate. Robert made sure Molly took the best bed and desk. Robert kept saying he never had the opportunity to choose where he went to school. It had been dictated by his father. *In the end, this choice was dictated by Molly's father, Ilse thought.* He again pointed out that Molly was lucky he was willing to pay out-of-state tuition when she could get an equally good education at Michigan State. They left with Ilse crying, giving stoic Molly hugs and kisses. Molly's firm resolve made Ilse even sadder.

When Molly first said that she wanted to go to Connecticut, Robert told her he would only fly her home once during the school year and that would be for Christmas. Molly was agreeable until the first weekend after a week of classes. She called every day begging to come home. It was heartbreaking. She wrote a beautiful letter saying how much she loved them, that she was wrong about going away, that she wanted to come home and go to a school closer.

It seemed all the students went home on the weekends leaving Molly alone.

In all fairness to Robert, he tried to encourage her; he said he would fly her home for Thanksgiving break if she would agree to finish the first semester. *Ilse thought that was a good solution.*

"Good or bad, we often have to live by our decisions," Ilse said. However, by the time Molly came home for Thanksgiving, she had met a girl in the neighboring dorm room whose father had an administrative position at the university. Her family befriended Molly, taking her home on weekends along with their own daughter. Both girls had roommates that weren't working out, so they switched roommates, and college life took on a whole new feeling. She loved her new life, her independence and freedom. Plus, she was learning to study and was earning good grades.

The first two summers, Molly came back to the old job at the drugstore in town. She reconnected with her hometown friends. Her parents believed she was now mature enough to make good choices.

In the spring after her freshman year of college, Molly agreed to help with Robert's parents who were coming to Detroit for his mother to have total hip surgery. Ilse would still be teaching and Will was finishing his junior year of high school. The family had it worked out so that it would be comfortable for Robert's parents.

Will moved to the guest room to give Granddad the front bedroom upstairs. One of the twin beds in Will's room was moved downstairs to the dining room so Grandmother would have a light room with a nice view out the front windows. They made it into a beautiful haven for her recovery, shoving the table against the wall, putting a comfortable chair in the room for Robert's father.

Before Grandmother had to check in to the hospital, Ilse and the children planned a party for them, which was to be a combination welcome for both and birthday party for Granddad. It was hard to buy gifts for him, but he liked to exercise so they bought him navy sweats, thinking he could use the outfit for walks in the nearby park.

Robert felt somewhat responsible for his mother's health and happiness. He knew his father was difficult and his mother's life had not been easy although she had all the material things that she wanted. The two times his father had tried to commit suicide, Robert shuddered and stayed to help as little as possible, putting Ilse in his place. He didn't like his father. In fact, he said more than once that he hated him. He even told friends he hated him if the conversation revolved around his background and family. *It seemed pretty harsh to Ilse, but she didn't know the many things that probably happened as he was growing up. He had his own pent up anger.*

Along with all sorts of strange behavior, Dr. Kelly wore the sweats to the hospital to visit, which embarrassed Robert. Actually, Dr. Kelly had accidentally mixed up the sweats for Will's long ski underwear from the closet shelf. Robert relinquished the responsibility of his father to the rest of the family, asking Ilse to bring him to the hospital for visits after she got home from work every day. On Saturdays, he used mowing the lawn as an excuse not to be with his parents. It was a repeat of how it was when the family went to Nebraska to visit. He would disappear and expect Ilse and the children to socialize and take care of his parents.

When Grandmother Kelly was in the hospital, often sedated, she complained about the way Dr. Kelly treated her at home. She told how he often lost his temper. Not only did he yell at her, he sometimes hit and shoved her. Several times, he threw her onto the bed. When Robert suggested that it was not too late in life to divorce him she said, "No. I could never leave him after all these years. He has changed. He wasn't like that when I married him."

With the elder Kellys living with them, the family was juggling schedules to get everything accomplished...hospital visits, meals, work, cleaning, laundry, Molly's drugstore job, and end of school year activities for Will and Ilse.

When Ilse cleaned the bath that Granddad used, there were always little brown specks on the white surface that streaked when she rubbed her sponge across the counter. She couldn't figure it out until one Saturday morning she asked Robert if he would like coffee. He always liked instant Sanka. When he said yes, Granddad got up and left the room. Ilse turned her back to put on the water to boil while Granddad reappeared and put the Sanka back on the shelf. He had been using the coffee, in powder form by the spoonful, to wake up in the morning. What an awful taste it must have been! Everyone acted as if they didn't know he'd taken the coffee.

When Mrs. Kelly was ready to come home, Ilse was the one to get her, help her in, and make her comfortable. It was a Saturday, but Robert shirked his responsibility by saying he had to go in to work. Molly and Will couldn't get through the hallway without Grandmother hollering out to them for something. Ilse relied on Molly to hold down the fort until she and Will were out of school and Molly did a fine job, but was growing weary, especially with Granddad. He lurked around. He didn't like Sasha, often kicking her aside. It was very uncomfortable for everyone to be around him.

Granddad spent a lot of time reading. Robert told him he'd bring home The Wall Street Journal for him everyday, which he did. When she made his bed and cleaned his room, Ilse saw the neat pile of newspapers growing and growing. Toward the end of their rehabilitation visit, Robert looked out the window early one morning, as he got ready to leave for work. He said, "Here comes 'the old man' and he has the paper. He must go to the park to read it."

A few days later, the same thing happened with Robert saying, "Here comes the old man. He has the paper under his arm again." Ten minutes later they saw Dr. Kelly sitting in the big chair they had put next to Grandmother's bed reading the paper.

Robert said, "I see you're reading the paper."

"Uh huh," was the reply.

"That's today's paper."

"Uh huh," was again the reply.

"Where did you get today's paper?" Robert asked.

His father replied, "I picked it up along the way."

Robert said, "that's stealing you know.'

His dad again said, "Uh huh" and continued to read the paper.

They determined that Granddad had seen a "Wall Street Journal" delivery box several miles away when he went for his walks. Robert told Ilse she should stop by the house, apologize for his dad and offer to pay for the papers he had stolen. She refused saying that was his job. Robert never stopped there either, too embarrassed by his dad's strange behavior. Mrs. Kelly said he had been taking small items from stores now and then, nothing big.

Did that make it okay, wondered Ilse.

Amy, Robert's sister, told them that Granddad had been cited by the police for riding his adult tricycle down the middle of the busy four-lane highway at home. He ignored the honking and yells to move to the side of the road as though he was the lone person on the highway. His tricycle was his answer to go where he wanted after his driver's license and car were taken away.

When it was time for the Kellys to go home, Ilse was the one to take them to the airport. Granddad insisted that he should have a wheel chair with a special escort onto the airplane. Even though he was capable of walking miles, he said pointing to Grandmother, "I want the same attention that she gets!"

"No way!" Ilse told him. She'd 'had it' with his selfish behavior.

A year later, when Robert's parents again came to visit, Will was getting ready to graduate from high school, with many awards and honors. He was on the golf team, having the opportunity to play and practice at the country club where the family belonged. His other main interest was Outdoor Leadership, a special program that was just as the name implies. The select group of students in the program had special outings, learning survival skills. Each student did a four-day solo as part of a week in rough terrain and frigid weather. Ilse worried about Will because he was always on the small side, wrestling at the ninety-five pound weight when he was a freshman. Before that, he was pretty good at soccer, but had to give it up the last season because of a growth on his ankle. It was a scare but he was one of the lucky ones. The surgeon removed the nonmalignant tumor and there were no lingering problems. By the time he was ready to graduate from high school, it seemed he was going to be tall like his father, but would have his mothers' very straight hair and 'aristocratic' nose. In fact, his personality and sense of humor were more like Ilse's. Robert would say his intelligence came from his side of the family, after all, his father was brilliant. Ilse would pipe up and say that her father was also brilliant. *She would at the same time be thinking that her father was also even- tempered, well adjusted too, and very sane!*

Will went through the college selection process while Molly was away at college. An amazing student, he applied to Ivy League schools. He hoped to get in to Princeton, but was turned down. It was a big disappointment for him, but he was accepted to other good schools including Duke and Yale. This time there were college visitations before the final decision was made. The family all visited Duke on the way to the beach, but Yale was his choice, a good choice that Will said later was for the best because he was not a good match for Princeton.

Robert was continually advancing his career. While the children were teenagers planning their futures, Robert was planning his own. He worked extremely hard, long hours and was committed to producing results at work that would benefit the hospital...but also benefit him. He had returned to the Detroit area to be an Assistant Administrator. He had his eye on the Chief Operating Officer position held by a long time co-worker and friend. Robert would do what was necessary to win.

He was ruthless, even if it involved friends. When he was named COO, he participated in demoting the CFO. Once he fired someone, he simply would not speak to him or her again. It seemed to be relatively easy to discipline and/or fire his associates. However, there was one person that he had hired to whom he remained loyal. It was Joe Hawk. Joe still worked for him not vice versa.

Joe Hawk had become a very good friend, a confidant and a huge influence on Robert's private and public lives. Joe and his wife tapped Robert's need to relax and have fun, taking them to have a nice dinner, dance and frequent the bars. Whatever Joe suggested was fine with

Robert, unusual because Robert usually called the shots at work and at home.

Joe was willing to spend $800 on a well-tailored suit. Robert began to do the same. He wouldn't spend as much, but he became more particular about the fit and quality of what he was wearing so he would look successful. He always took Ilse along for her opinion. She willingly spent hours on shopping trips exclusively for him. Ilse was still making many of her own clothes, but Robert agreeably let her begin buying more expensive fabrics and shoes.

During this time, Joe bought his wife a beautiful fur coat. Not to be outdone, Robert bought Ilse an even prettier long mink coat. He couldn't let someone that worked for him outshine him. Ilse's fur was a mahogany colored mink with a large shawl collar, which looked good with Ilse's dark brown hair. Admittedly, for the very cold Michigan winter, Ilse could put the coat to good use. She even wore it to walk the dog. Robert was proud of her and liked to point out his generosity when they were out socially. Giving Ilse showy gifts seemed to be a status symbol, along with the country club and job title. He also said he was proud of the way Ilse dressed. Whenever she received a compliment, he bragged that she had fashioned her dresses herself.

20
The Fatal Move: 1986-1990

The CEO of the hospital was getting ready to retire, so Robert became focused on landing the job. He told Ilse about all the political maneuvering because he thought he was going to get the top position. He was in favor with the board members, the existing CEO, and seemed to be in the driver's seat. He was energized by the opportunity to cap his career with this prestigious job. His friend Joe Hawk had gone elsewhere but Robert had hired him back. He had major players in place. Suddenly there was a glitch in the smooth transition to the top job. The board decided to hire a doctor from the East to come in as an interim CEO. Robert still thought he would get the job, but he was very nervous and expressed both concern and anger about it.

To be proactive Robert said he was going to begin looking for another job, but would not move until Will was through high school. *That consideration was one of the nicest things he did for his family.* Molly was settled in at the University of Connecticut and did not need to be a major factor in the decision to move again. Of the many moves, Ilse was the happiest in this beautiful home they had built in the country. Her job was wonderful. She liked the faculty immensely and had established a bond with several friends. She was close to the neighbors and loved "junking" on the weekends, refinishing furniture finds, and collecting other bargains. Summers were perfect because of trips and special times with the family. *To move again would not be her choice, but she would do whatever it took to help her husband and support his choices.*

Robert became depressed as it looked like the new interim doctor was posing more and more of a dilemma for him. The new doctor/administrator was well liked, a bit older and he could relate better to the physicians on the staff. He was also well heeled, having married into a wealthy family so he could better influence hospital fund raising efforts. Ilse had seen Robert angry many times, but he was always the one that could wield the power. Now he was frustrated to the point of tears. He sat in their large bedroom behind his executive desk, which fit into one side of the room. Ilse had purchased the desk for him when he was promoted to Chief Operating Officer of the hospital. When he left one job and moved to another, he was traditionally given a University Chair. He sat in it, with his head in his hands, hurt that he was probably not going to get the CEO position. Ilse had never seen him so beaten. He could not be consoled. Putting an arm around him, he shoved her away. He wanted to be left alone, seeming to be

188

embarrassed that he might be showing some weakness. Ilse ached for him.

It became official. The interim doctor would be named the CEO and Robert would remain the COO. That was a wonderful position, but it wasn't the highest so Robert began the hunt with a headhunter. With his background and experience, it didn't take long for him to zero in on several jobs. He went to interview and was offered more than one position, but he thought the Summit offer appeared to be the best. He knew Ilse was reluctant to move but, always willing to help him succeed, she threw her complete support behind him.

He took Ilse along for the second interview, and they were treated like royalty. The hospital board put them up in a 'Bed and Breakfast' downtown and took them to special dinners. While Robert was being interviewed by different people, board members, administrative people, department heads, Ilse was taken to lunch or shown around town. They were also interviewing her, it seemed, to make sure she would fit in. The auxiliary ladies were setting up for their big yearly fundraiser called May Fair. Feeling comfortable, Ilse pitched in and helped set up some tables and displays even though she was dressed in her best pink suede suit, which she had made for the trip.

The morning when they were about to make an offer, Robert came flying back in because he couldn't get his car out of the small parking area. He was shaking, mad, thinking he was going to be late. Louise, the Bed and Breakfast owner, had to pull the car out for him.

Later she commented on how unreasonably angry he was. That was the only glitch in the whole interview weekend. They loved Robert, offered him the job, gave him more money than he had been paid before, and treated him with awe as well as respect. That night he took Ilse into the hospital lobby. He started right in by tearing down "tacky" paper signs that people had put on doors or walls, which he thought were unprofessional. He couldn't wait to get there and "turn the place around."

"They won't know what hit them," he said.

Before leaving, they drove around to the different areas to see what the housing market was like. They had lived in an ideal location outside of Clarkston, which would be hard to duplicate. Robert, anxious for Ilse to be happy, promised the moon. *She knew she would be happy. She had a philosophy that if you choose to, you can be happy wherever you live.*

Even though committed to a new job and the upcoming move, they needed to focus their energy on Will's preparation for college and Molly's summer job. During this time, Robert's parents decided to come for a visit while Ilse still had her end of school activities to contend with. Robert's work at Henry Ford Hospital continued to require much of his time. To add to the chaos there were numerous good-bye parties and the sale of the home.

It only took one trip back to Summit to find a beautiful old home. Even though it needed a great deal of work, it could become a dream house. Ilse looked forward to the project.

Everything fell into place. Yale was a good match for Will. He adjusted readily to college life and his classes. He stayed in the dorm a year and then joined a fraternity, which was more academic than social. Robert made a special effort to always be at the father-son fraternity events for Will and enjoyed their 'secret' meetings. Ilse liked the special treatment they gave the mothers...a rose, an escort, and a special luncheon while the men had their get-together. They were very proud of Will. He was a physics major, with a chemistry minor focusing on pre-med.

A problem surfaced when Will was still a senior in high school. He had developed a twitch. He would jerk his head to the side. It became annoying to him and hurt his neck. They took him to the family doctor who said he couldn't find anything wrong, so Will was living with the problem.

Robert said, "You can stop that. It is just a bad habit you've developed." The annoying twitch wasn't given much attention until Will complained that he had a difficult time in college chemistry lab. Because of jerking his head, he was losing data from his experiments. The problem seemed to be related to studying and stress.

In the meantime, Molly was ready to graduate from college. She had joined a sorority and finished a five-year nursing program in four years because her father said he would only pay for four years. She had reestablished her friendship with the young man in San Diego.

The family all headed for Connecticut to celebrate Molly's achievements, thrilled that she was so happy. Robert intervened so she would be able to begin work at University Hospitals back in Michigan. Will brought a girlfriend along and Molly's boyfriend drove out with his truck to move all the belongings she had accumulated in four years. She found an apartment and was ready to start a new phase in her life.

The final days before the move from Clarkston to Summit were marked with sadness and many tears as Ilse said her goodbyes. Then they embarked on the next stage of their life. Not aware that in four years her life would drastically change, Ilse began to adapt to the new locale.

Work on the old house, the new friends, entertaining, and volunteering at the hospital filled the void. In fact, Ilse was so busy that there was no 'empty nest' syndrome. She thought she had it all: two smart adult children, a successful husband she admired, loved, and adored, a beautiful home, many friends, good health and a full productive life.

Molly, after graduating, was back working in Detroit Children's Hospital where she went on to become certified both as a neonatal and pediatric nurse practitioner. She also became engaged to marry. Will had changed his major to pre-med.

During the past few years, Will had more problems with his head jerking. It was annoying and painful for him. Robert made an appointment for him with a neurologist who said he thought he needed to quit playing golf because it was irritating him. Robert didn't think the diagnosis was correct and began to do research which all pointed to Tourette

Syndrome. He also researched the leading centers for diagnosis and found the Detroit Clinic was at the top of the list. He used his influence to coordinate an appointment with the time the family would be together for Molly's wedding.

Wedding plans became a major focus for Molly and Ilse. It was such fun to plan a storybook wedding. Robert was generous with the budget. He was proud of his beautiful daughter and wanted her to have the wedding of her dreams. He even went to one of the gown fittings. Ilse went to New York City numerous times to find just the right laces, ribbon, and fabric for the bridesmaids' dresses, which she made for the six attendants. Friends helped make heart shaped wedding boxes covered with taffeta and French lace, which another friend filled with fresh flowers the day of the wedding. Wreathes filled with baby's breath and satin ribbon roses hung in all the church windows. Molly was to wear the Mikimoto pearls that Robert had given Ilse. The detailed preparations for Molly's "fairytale" wedding gave Ilse immense joy.

Robert made arrangements for the reception to be at the country club where they had been members before moving to Summit. He even went along to meet with the manager to plan the menu and bar. Molly and her fiancé Ed enjoyed a steady stream of wedding showers and parties.

A few days before the wedding, the whole family went together to the Detroit Clinic for Will's appointment. Even his sister was there to support him. The diagnosis was clear. The jerking was Tourette Syndrome. He had a choice to either take medication that would dull his senses or live with it. He chose to live with it. He was to begin medical school in New York City and didn't want to risk the side effects of medication. Robert asked Ilse if there was someone in her family who had it, since it was an inherited trait. "It must be from your side of the family,' he said. "There was none in my family."

Ilse knew the children had inherited her nose, but couldn't think of anyone with Tourette Syndrome. *She didn't say anything about it, never wanting to place blame, but when Robert was stressed, his eye twitched noticeably, also the side of his mouth.* For Will, it was the right decision to live with the problem. He grew out of it and rarely relapsed. *For Robert, his undiagnosed Tourette symptoms became more obvious later in life.*

The rehearsal dinner was held at the groom's home, and all of the out of town guests were invited. It was a wonderful dinner party complete with a band. The groomsmen from California and Will were all staying at the groom's home. The adult cousins were riding with their parents. Many couples had come from Summit including Robert's administrative assistant and her husband who was a paraplegic. After the dinner, Robert's sister and brother-in-law from Nebraska took their parents back to the hotel. Ilse's parents, Grandpa and Granny Mueller, were not well enough to make the trip from California, but her brothers and their families were there.

The young people were sitting around a huge round table on the deck, laughing and

telling stories. Most of their parents and other
guests were leaning against the railing or talking
in groups. A few couples were dancing. After
dinner was over, the young people started doing
shots. When Robert saw this, he lost control. He
was like day and night. He flipped from being
congenial to screaming at the young people,
grabbing two half-gallon liquor bottles, throwing
them against a tree in the woods, breaking the
bottles. He was yelling for them to look at the
paraplegic (who had been hit by a drunk driver)
in the wheel chair. Even though none of them
was going to be driving anywhere, he yelled as he
pointed,

"Someone else will end up like that if you
drink and drive!"

Molly, the bride, looked at him aghast.
She wanted to crawl under the table. Will,
pretending to do the shots, shrugged as if to say,
"That's my dad." Kurt was remembering when
Robert shot the cat.

Everyone just looked at him,
dumbfounded and embarrassed by his behavior.
But guess what...no one reprimanded
him...especially not his wife. The friends from
Summit and Clarkston witnessed first hand his
uncontrolled outburst. They knew him as a man
always logical and disciplined. In just moments,
Robert acted as if nothing unusual had happened
and everyone else tried to act the same. He had
managed to put an unforgettable damper on the
wedding festivities.

Very early the next morning Robert's
parents rang from their motel room with
numerous problems. Exhausted, Ilse hoped to
sleep, but Robert said he wasn't going to deal

with them. She would have to. He was going back to sleep. But first, he called Amy, his sister, to have her help take care of the problems. She didn't want to deal with them either. Her husband and Ilse ended up taking care of their in-laws' problems by taking them to breakfast.

At breakfast, Dr. Kelly was asking about the troublesome granddaughter that Amy and George had adopted. He said to George, "Don't you just wish she'd kill herself? Your life would be so much easier."

George and Ilse, the two in-laws, couldn't believe what he was saying. *Why were they always the ones that had to deal with this* strange *man?* Granddad offered to leave the tip for breakfast putting a handful of pennies on the table.

All day George ran errands, hauling bridesmaids' dresses to the church, taking care of the grandparents needs, and acting as a buffer so they wouldn't disturb the special day.

The wedding ceremony was beautiful. Perfect. At the wedding reception, Robert had another outburst and conflict with Molly, but the guests for the most part were unaware of it. He danced with Molly and Ilse. The band was great and Robert was a good dancer. The guests had a wonderful time.

Granddad, the doctor, decided the wedding reception was a good time to try to talk Will out of going to medical school. "You definitely should not go to an Ivy League School," he chided. "A state school would be just as good," he said, "and much less expensive."

He wanted to talk about medical school with Will and the stock market with Robert. He had already given his opinion to George about his granddaughter. He didn't try to corner Ilse or Molly. Talking about mundane things was his way of handling a social situation that was foreign to him. Grandmother, thrilled to be there, was disappointed when Granddad wanted to go back to the hotel before the cake was cut. Ilse would have told him to sit down and wait, but Robert still "danced to his tune," so George chauffeured them back. Grandmother kept the peace by doing whatever Grandfather wanted...*just like she did with their son, Ilse thought...and just like I am doing.*

Part III: 1986-1994

21
Questions: 1986-1990

Along with her regular activities, the wedding kept Ilse busy for almost a year. She had also kept busy with renovations and decorating the house. She enjoyed doing all the painting and papering herself. When he had time, Robert pitched in with the painting. He bought a folding ladder so she could wallpaper the high master bathroom, making a scaffold.

Ilse liked things done properly, but she was drawing the line when it came to stripping every bit of paint from another house. Robert worked diligently stripping the old paint from the exterior shake shingles. The house was stone and shake with a slate roof, very New England. Ilse refused to strip outdoor siding paint. She had done that with him on a house when the children were small, and it seemed a futile project for such excessive effort. Besides, it was dangerous to be up on the high ladders. Robert was a perfectionist; if he got an idea, he carried out the execution in every detail.

When Robert was stripping the paint shortly after moving in, the man in charge of the hospital fundraising stopped by to introduce himself. Robert barely said, "Hello" before he added, "I'm busy. I'll talk to you at work."

"Okay. I just wanted to say welcome to Summit."

Ilse witnessed his quick retreat and said to Robert, "Why would you be so rude to someone you'll be working with?"

"He works for me. I don't work for him. It's none of your business."

Robert was turning fifty, just four years after this incident. He would turn fifty the same spring Will would finish undergraduate work. He was beginning to make a big deal of it, saying he was feeling old. Ilse saw her glass half full, not half-empty as Robert did. She was going to turn fifty too, but it didn't seem different from any other birthday to her. She was thankful for another healthy, happy year.

A year before Robert turned fifty, he was made the CEO of the huge hospital complex, including the parent company. Before Robert's promotion to the top position, he reported to the President of Health I, who according to rumor was a womanizer. A young Administrative Resident named Carrie worked for Health I.

A few times at night, Robert wanted to drive over to the Health I building to check on the President...to see whose cars were there. In other words, he wanted to detect with whom his boss might be having his current affair. *Was he suspicious that it might be Carrie? Was exposing his boss's indiscretions part of his plan to claim the top job?*

In the beginning, Robert told Ilse about the bright young administrative resident. He said he didn't like her. *Ilse remembered that when he first met Joe Hawk he didn't like him either, but there had been a full turn-around with that relationship.* It was unusual for Robert to comment on other women, the way they looked, or their personality. Once Robert was made CEO of the entire system, Carrie worked directly for him. His attitude toward her changed. *What had she done to cause this attitude change?*

Carrie and her husband were now included in the administrative parties so Ilse got to know her. In fact, they were invited to the 'chili & cheer' party at Ilse and Robert's home before Christmas when they all exchanged 'white elephant' gifts. Most everyone brought something nonsensical, but Carrie brought a nice wooden bowl that Ilse won in the drawing. Carrie and her husband were rather quiet, perhaps a little uncomfortable with the other administrative people and their spouses. Ilse's forte was to make everyone feel welcome and at ease so they could enjoy themselves, and she did.

Robert had told her that Carrie was great with her work but, like him, she didn't like social events. For Robert, the social interaction was part of the package, part of the job. For Ilse, it was the most fun. Ilse especially liked going to gala affairs where she could get all dressed up, dance, socialize. She was a buffer for Robert, quietly feeding the names of people so he could act as if he remembered everyone. He actually remembered the 'important' people.

Ilse's exercise pattern included her walks in the nearby park. Often on weekends, Robert went with her so they could have the time to talk and catch up. With the entertaining or social events occurring almost every weekend, Robert struggled to keep his weight under control. The extra pounds had been an ongoing problem for years. Robert blamed Ilse for them because of the meals she served him, so every now and then he would go on a diet, asking Ilse to help. *She knew the pattern. Take the blame for the weight gain, prepare special meals, but take verbal abuse when a special diet didn't help.* He still wanted to have his cocktails before dinner, a full dinner and wine. He expected special treatment when they went out. In a word, he was spoiled. His mother waited on him and when he married, Ilse followed suit. The family always ate together, usually late. When the children were young, they often had a large snack meal when they came home from school, and then a big dinner with their father when he came home

All the years they were married, Robert ran for exercise. He enjoyed it. It was a way of getting rid of some of the built up stress. He had been on track teams in high school and college. With his lanky stature and strong legs, he was a good long distance runner. Robert was running more and more frequently again. Dressing in old sweats, he would head out to run in the neighborhood or in the nearby park where there were miles of paved trails. He'd usually be gone for about an hour. At social functions, neighbors would comment that they saw him out running in his sweats and headband. They were used to seeing him dressed in a suit or at least khaki's. He never wore jeans. His mother had always said he didn't have the right shape to wear jeans and as an adult, he had trouble finding a pair that fit comfortably because of large, strong hips. It was one of his 'hang ups.' Since people saw him out jogging, they seemed to see him as more approachable...just a regular, friendly guy. It was easier for the women to talk with him about his jogging than about hospital work. He didn't like 'small talk' and wasn't good at it.

Recently he had criticized Ilse for giving a description of the beautiful flower arrangements at a wedding they had attended. He intervened saying, "no one is interested in such a mundane subject, such small talk." Actually, the ladies were very interested, but Ilse, embarrassed, cut her explanation short. The looks of surprise when he criticized her did not go unnoticed. In the past, he might reprimand Ilse in private about something she said, but it was unusual for him to criticize her in front of friends.

Back in an exercise mode to try to take off some weight, Robert was running almost every day. He went out to jog at night and always on the weekends, coming home, totally wet from sweating, with a red face while he bent over to catch his breath. Ilse thought he was overdoing it. After all, he was no longer in high school and he couldn't push his body the same way. It was great that he was getting exercise and curbing his eating to slim down, but Ilse was worried.

One day, Ilse became concerned when he was gone much too long. *Maybe something had happened to him she thought* as she got in the car to find him. Only a few blocks away, she spotted him across from the park at a pay phone, deep in conversation. He was annoyed that Ilse had come looking for him. His annoyance and the look on his face when Ilse pulled the car up beside the pay phone told Ilse volumes. He motioned her on as he returned to his phone conversation, but he looked like he was being caught with his hand in the cookie jar. Ilse drove the few blocks home and waited for him to return, ready to question him.

"How dare you check up on me?" he said. There was a problem at work and he had to call Carrie. Ilse told him he could have come home to call. He was only minutes away. *Why did he just happen to have money along to use the pay phone? How long had he been talking on the phone, not jogging? AND how often had he been making similar calls?*

About a month later, Robert and Ilse went to the beach. They had their new Lexus with an open sunroof to catch the late fall weather. It looked sunny, but was rather cool, a perfect day for a run for Robert while Ilse walked the beach. Clouds began to form in the sky so Ilse hurried back to the condo. *When the storm erupted, Ilse remembered how angry he was the last time she looked for him, so she decided he would seek shelter somewhere and come back after the storm.* Instead, he came flying in soaking wet, through the lightning and thunder, yelling about the car keys and demanding to know why Ilse hadn't come to get him. The condo and landing shook with his weight as he rushed up the stairs. Because he had left the sunroof open, the inside of the new car was getting drenched. Ilse let him fume. *She wondered how she was supposed to read his mind.*

A few years before moving to Summit, they had purchased with Steve and his wife a condo right on the water. The couples had made several trips there together to enjoy it. Ilse went there separately with lady friends to redecorate and put up wall paper. The ladies all pitched in to work on the condo, but found time to shop at Myrtle Beach, sun themselves and walk.

Going to the beach with some of her friends was the one thing that Ilse did alone. She never went out in the evenings with friends except for an occasional bridal or baby shower. When they moved to Summit, Robert suggested Ilse actively volunteer two evenings a week, but she would be home in time for Robert since he usually worked until six, sometimes later. It was working out well. He didn't like her to be gone when he was home; she rarely was.

Fixing up the condo with Steve and Liz had been a joint effort. Most of the work they could do themselves. Steve was in charge of the painting. Robert had helped with some of the extra cleaning along with Liz. Ilse hung all the wallpaper and was given the responsibility of keeping accurate books and paying the bills.

When the two couples were together at the beach, they enjoyed evenings filled with card games, Trivial Pursuit, reading, and watching TV. It was totally relaxing. Hours were also spent on the beach, browsing in the shops or having dinner at the local seafood restaurants. It had become Ilse's favorite haven. Trivial Pursuit was often the game of choice as long as Robert could team up with Liz. Robert said he wasn't about to team with Ilse because he wanted to be a winner. Liz, full of trivia, usually helped her partner win. Steve knew all the sports questions but Liz did too. In all fairness, Ilse got her share of the answers right, but Robert wasn't thinking of her as the 'whiz kid.' He'd laugh about it and Ilse would laugh too.

Back at work, Robert kept saying things about Carrie. Many comments were made on her brilliance. He wanted her to feel more comfortable at work. One day he called Ilse in the middle of the day to ask directions for the place he bought his suits. They had women's executive clothing as well as men's. Another day, not long after, he called to get the private number for his tailor. He was going to send Carrie to him. *Again, Ilse was thinking it was unusual for him to be concerned about a woman employee in such a personal way. In fact, he never before had asked for favors for female colleagues. The topping on the cake was when he told Ilse that the chair of the department of dermatology had suggested to Carrie that he could help her with her bad acne problem and her face was clearing up. Pygmalion. He was getting her "fixed up" in accord with what he found attractive. Ilse knew he thought Carrie was special, but she also felt it was against his principles to become involved with another woman.*

Robert explained his behavior away: Carrie was brilliant and needed the extra help to be more presentable. He was mentoring her and promoting her, making her an administrative assistant. No longer was she a resident. She learned quickly. She was motivated to move up the ladder in the same way he was.

Robert said that Carrie and her husband were looking at a row house in downtown Summit to renovate, decorate and then market. They thought it would be a good idea if Ilse would team up with Carrie's husband for a joint project. Robert said it would supplement their income since her husband was JUST a teacher. Ilse would be the perfect person to team up with him. Ilse was already busier than she wanted to be and didn't encourage the idea, letting it ride. Nothing more was said until a few months later when Ilse asked about it. Robert said that Carrie and her husband were getting an amicable divorce. Their own row house was on the market.

It was during this time that Robert wanted to purchase a jewelry gift for Carrie in appreciation for all her help leading up to his promotion. *Ilse knew there was a problem*, but the denial from Robert was firm.

That same spring, Will graduated from college with honors. The newlyweds, Molly and Ed had come to the graduation ceremonies from Detroit. Proud to be present for Will's graduation, they found themselves browsing the shops. Ilse began looking at purses in a fine leather shop. Robert offered to buy one for Ilse.

"Which one do you like the best?" he asked.

Ilse told him she'd go to the outlet stores where she could get the same purse for much less. Even though they now had the money, she was still thrifty, but Robert pressed her, "Which one do you like the best?" Ilse pointed out a stylish navy Dooney & Bourke bag, thinking perhaps he'd surprise her with a nice gift. He didn't. The surprise was to see Carrie accessorized with the bag when she ran into her a month later.

Ilse thought about what she should do to make Robert's recent promotion special for him. He had everything he wanted. He had the top job, a beautiful home, a family that loved and supported him, When he was named CEO of the whole health organization in town, the family had gone together to the clock shop downtown to buy a large grandfather clock for him. Ilse had bought several clocks for him throughout his career as he was promoted, plus the huge desk in the corner of the large living room. They took Robert along so he could select the one he liked the best. They were all proud of his work successes. The clock was delivered and set up in the large foyer of their attractive home. Complete with a plaque on the inside of the door, Robert wound the clock faithfully every Sunday evening.

Robert seemed to work well with most of the men at the hospital but he was nasty in the way he treated some of the women, *except Carrie.* If the men seemed unimportant politically outside of the hospital setting, Robert didn't pay attention to them. This attitude surfaced more dramatically after the merger of the two Summit hospitals.

He easily fired a Director of Nursing at the hospital. There was nothing she could do to be reinstated, but her husband, a long time influential Summit resident, tried to intervene to no avail. He 'got even' however when Robert tried to rejoin the Rotary Club. Robert had taken a leave of absence from the Rotary saying that he was too busy to make the luncheon meetings. When he tried to rejoin, he was blackballed by the former Director of Nursing's husband, even though his name had been resubmitted by a hospital board member.

Another woman had been a volunteer as the Director of Patient Services. Her husband was also influential in the community and Sharon had volunteered her time as the director for several years. Robert decided she should be replaced by a salaried employee. There was an argument about the 'firing,' but Robert insisted she knew too many personal things about too many people and it wasn't appropriate to have her in that position. Many people were supportive of Sharon and were angered by Robert's action in dismissing her.

He had conflicts with other women. It seemed if their husbands were not hospital employees, physicians, or on the hospital board and influential in the community, Robert would do what he could to 'put down' the wives. Sometimes it was an argument with them at a cocktail party. He would tell them they didn't know what they were talking about, making them angry. *It was his way to 'Lord it over' the women. There was an obvious lack of respect for women. Did he respect his own mother for letting his father degrade her? More important, did he lose respect for Ilse when he was able to degrade her time and again? What was it about Carrie that made him think she should escape his venom?*

A hospital auxiliary member, with whom Ilse became good friends, was married to a long-time Summit resident with a successful business in town. Kay was a beautiful lady, past president of the hospital auxiliary and still a very active person in the auxiliary. She was also on the Board of Associates for the hospital. Ilse couldn't believe Robert would be rude to her and her husband, but he was when he was invited to their home for dinner. *He is already involved with Carrie Ilse thought, as he arrived late, didn't smile, wasn't appreciative of the lovely dinner, and then rudely left. Robert was showing a side that he had not often shown publicly, Ilse thought. Was he more stressed now? Did he feel he was so important that he could do whatever he wanted, even when influential people were involved? Was Carrie on his mind?*

Ilse recalled his comments about the one woman on the hospital board who had kindly invited them to return often to the local church after their initial visit there. Her husband was also successful in his business. Robert wasn't overtly rude to her, but he told Ilse that he didn't think she should be on the board. She wasn't very smart, he said. *Ilse thought she was VERY smart, well heeled and an excellent board member, who was tuned in to the hospital and the community.*

When Ilse tried to make positive comments and defend the women, Robert would get annoyed saying, "Why do you always have to contradict me? You don't know anything."

Interesting. He was kind and friendly to doctors' wives, board members' wives, and even the lady on the board. Behind their backs, he wasn't always so nice. When they were women more distanced from the hospital but married to wealthy or important people in the community, he was unrelenting in his methods to show his superiority.

Not only was Ilse embarrassed for her husband, but also she was embarrassed for

212

herself. The women didn't seem to harbor any resentment toward Ilse, but would sometimes make comments, letting Ilse know that they didn't think she was married to a very fair, compassionate man. *It hurt Ilse to know that people didn't see Robert as the 'prince' Ilse saw when she married him. Ilse carried with her a seed of anger and resentment whenever Robert showed such male chauvinist traits. It was as though he was a bad weed taking deep root in a garden as he became more important.*

22
Turning Fifty: 1990

For Robert's birthday, Ilse decided to surprise him with a video created from family movies from his childhood and movies they had of their own family growing up. She didn't want his dreaded birthday to be a roadblock for him, but a new lease on life. Ilse solicited help from his parents and brother-in-law George to put the pictures in sequence. She rented a projector spending many hours in the basement getting it organized. Ilse was excited about the gift. To go with it, she had gone to the travel agency and made arrangements for a trip to Ireland, a country he said he always wanted to visit. Since his ancestry was Scotch/Irish, Ilse thought it would be the perfect gift. Before she finalized the plans, she called Robert's Administrative Assistant to make sure it would work with his calendar, asking her not to schedule anything for the few weeks they would be gone.

During the family birthday celebration, Ilse was excited, hoping that he would be pleased with the video and trip. What a disappointment!

He said, "That's nice," when he opened the video but, "I can't get away to take a trip like this. I'm too busy." Ilse said that was too bad because it had already been paid for and his calendar had been cleared. In the end, he reluctantly went on the trip.

It was not the dream Ilse hoped it would be. Robert was withdrawn much of the time. Ilse would go to the lounge to hear the Irish music while he stayed in the room and read. He was short with Ilse over little things. For example, he got angry when she asked him to hold her purse while she went to the restroom. They kissed the blarney stone and toured the diverse countryside in a rented car because Robert was interested in the country's history. Pictures show a smiling couple, but under the surface, there was friction. *Robert was annoyed because he didn't want to be on this trip with his wife. Ilse was annoyed because she knew he was not pleased with her gift. She wondered if Carrie's birthday gift to him was sexual favors.*

They celebrated their 28th wedding anniversary in Cork and Blarney. At the Blarney house castle, they went up and down the 'wishing steps' backwards, making their private wishes. At the woolen mills, Robert reluctantly purchased a Lladro as an anniversary gift to add to their collection. Ilse asked to have it as a special memento from the trip. *She was thinking of their 25th anniversary when he had given her roses (the only other time he gave her roses was when Molly was born).*

Then he had planned a weekend getaway to Williamsburg. There was a hospital auxiliary luncheon before they left when he proudly announced before his speech that it was their 25th anniversary. He had adorned her with a sapphire and diamond necklace to mark the occasion. *He was proud of her then, but now, three years later, he was only tolerating her. Try as she did to ignore the feeling, she knew he had Carrie on his mind.*

The last night of the trip, Ilse arranged for them to stay in the beautiful Dromoland castle, near Shannon. It could have been a storybook ending to the trip, but it was not as Ilse planned. During dinner in the gorgeous dining room, the waiter brought Robert the phone. It was the president of the hospital board. Instead of going to another area, he took the call at the table speaking loudly so all the *other patrons would know how important he was. It was rude* and Ilse was embarrassed. One of his questions for the caller was, "How is Carrie doing?" He didn't ask about anyone else. One day they shopped for 'worry stones' to take back for all his management team at the hospital. *Ilse noted that Carrie was among the count when he was deciding how many he needed. Ilse thought she'd better take some extra worry stones back for herself. She had plenty to worry about!*

A few times on the trip, Ilse tried to approach Robert about the problems that had begun to surface. He said that he shouldn't be away on such a trip when he had so much responsibility at home. Sexually he was not interested, even in the romantic castle. Ilse had tried her best to make his fiftieth birthday a happy one, but knew she was unsuccessful.

Shortly after arriving home, there was a big picnic for all the May Fair auxiliary men and women who had chaired the various tents for their major auxiliary fundraiser. Ilse was in charge of the craft tent the previous year, arranging for all the vendors and setting up the tent. It was one of the more popular tents. This spring Ilse co-chaired the entire event with Mary, who was married to one of the department head doctors. They had become good friends, sharing lunches, working on the Arts Advisory Committee together, helping each other with entertaining or home projects. Mary could outwork anyone, even Ilse. She had become a confidant. With a new swimming pool to complement their guesthouse and their century-old home, Mary and her husband hosted the event. It was a beautiful summer day. As soon as they arrived, Robert and Ilse were surrounded by people asking about their trip to Ireland. Robert soon gravitated to the men to begin discussions about work. Later Ilse found out that there was speculation from a few of the men about Robert having an affair. These men never approached Robert, not being a part of his inner circle, only auxiliary member's husbands. *Suspecting it herself, she pondered how they knew it, probably by the way he was treating her.*

Ilse's fiftieth birthday followed shortly. Robert made a few comments about her body, which made Ilse look more critically at herself. *She thought she still looked good in spite of the years.* He went over the top with a birthday gift, buying her a second set of silver in the same pattern as Molly's wedding gift. Cost was no longer an issue to him. He was generous, and Ilse was pleased but not thrilled. *It was just 'stuff.' She just wanted to be loved. A simple, unpretentious gift, joyfully given, would have made her happier.* Molly and Ed came back from Detroit and Will was home for the summer. They were all together which gave her the most pleasure for her birthday.

Later in the summer, it was agreed that Robert, Ilse and Will would go to Michigan to help Molly and Ed move into their first home. They loaded up an extra refrigerator on a trailer loaned to them by one of the doctors. When they arrived, they would buy Molly and Ed a washer and dryer to help them get started. Ed's parents also came to help. It was fun for everyone to see the house and help them get settled. Robert suggested that Ilse should stay to begin the painting and papering. He said she could take the Greyhound bus back home and he would pick her up at the bus station. After working for about two weeks, Ilse had made progress on the house. Robert was calling regularly to see how everything was going.

Not having been on a bus for a long time, Ilse wasn't prepared for the experience. *In retrospect, perhaps it prepared her for the experience she was to have a year later when she was committed to the mental hospital.* It was scary to ride even a few miles with the people who were traveling with her. The 'regulars' hollered at the bus driver until he stopped the bus. When the bus finally got in to the station, it was dark and late. Robert was not in sight...certainly not waiting at the gate for her. When he finally found her, he was angry saying "Don't ever ask me to pick you up again. You're not where you said you'd be." *Wait a minute. Ilse would have preferred to fly. It was HIS idea that she was on a bus. Did he think she enjoyed it?*

The ride back to Summit was filled with a negative boding of what the future held. There was no welcome home hug or any indication that Ilse had been missed. Throughout their married life, it had always been hard for them to be separated, but now it didn't seem to matter to Robert. In spite of the cool welcome, Ilse was glad to be home. She still wanted to work on these negative feelings, get the marriage back on track.

While she was working at Molly's, Ilse had time to try to decide on a constructive approach. *The trip to Ireland together was not helpful, nor the separation while she was at Molly's. She would again suggest that they should get some counseling. Robert was reluctant to discuss any possible problem. He would say there was no problem. It was all Ilse's imagination. When she brought up Carrie, he just walked away and said she was crazy...and stupid to even think like that. She ought to know after all these years and all they had been through together that he wasn't the type to have an affair. He was right. He wasn't the type. What is the type? Ilse wondered.*

Will was soon to start medical school in nearby New York City. It had been nice having him home for the summer. It gave Ilse a buffer, someone to laugh and do extra things with. Hospital events were numerous, but in-between, Ilse and Will, sometimes Robert, had long walks in the park. There were father/son golf outings; Ilse played golf with her ladies' league. Will was sensitive to the feelings vibrating between Robert

220

and Ilse, but the dissention was never discussed. Will would be home for Thanksgiving and go with them to Molly's to celebrate Christmas.

Before Thanksgiving, Robert told Ilse that he had offered their house for the Christmas house tour. It would mean a lot of work, but it would also be fun and occupy her time by allowing her to do what she liked most, decorating and entertaining. Robert's recent rejection of her was the only thing that made Ilse hesitate, but he had already committed to it.

Getting ready for family holidays was always fun. Food preparation included the traditional turkey and all the family favorites. Ilse prepared as much as possible ahead so she could be with the family.

After Thanksgiving dinner, the family went together to Lookout Mountain to hike and enjoy the beautiful clear fall day, afterwards picking out a Christmas tree. Their foyer would hold a tall tree; the family room would hold another large tree and they would buy a third smaller one to have for their sand dollar tree decorated from their beach treasures. It had become a family tradition. Robert was willing to spend more than usual on trees and roping because of the house tour. Ilse went to work making bows, putting up the greenery, and decorating every nook and corner of the old home, including the bedrooms. People would be allowed to tour even the upstairs bedroom suites. Ilse arranged to have friends take shifts to be hostesses throughout the house. Robert was working very late these nights. Ilse was busy with her decorating, but still keeping her regular schedule of volunteering and entertaining. They would have their usual party for all the administrative people and a larger party for the board and the department heads.

For the tour, Ilse greeted everyone at the door in a pretty Herman Geist outfit she had purchased in a size 6. Losing weight over the past few months, she was buying more clothes to keep up with her changing size.

The home tour, although a lot of work, was a great success. *She asked herself why she was doing all this work for Robert's benefit when he was treating her so shabbily.* She tried to do it with a joyful spirit as a gift to him. Robert didn't usually come home until 9:30 pm when the work was all done, wondering why his chicken was tough. Didn't Ilse know he wanted to have a drink before he ate? Coming home late and complaining about a cold meal was becoming a pattern. She had no proof and only denials from Robert. *Ilse knew he didn't have late meetings except of his own making with a young woman named Carrie. He must have thought Ilse was so stupid she would believe he was working.*

Weeks earlier at an auxiliary luncheon, Ilse was seated next to Lisa, a good friend with medical connections. Ilse's demeanor had changed. She was quiet; when she asked questions about Lisa's large family, she had tears in her eyes. At the end of the luncheon, Lisa told Ilse she wanted to drop by; she would meet her at Ilse's house. As soon as Ilse met her at the door Lisa said, "Okay, let's have it. What is hurting you so much? I know there is something wrong." Ilse told her what her suspicions were and they talked until they heard

Robert coming in the door. He often stopped by the house during the day when he was traveling from one hospital complex to another. Lisa said, "wipe your eyes" and just kept talking about something totally unrelated. Robert said 'hi' to her, looked through the mail, and left. Ilse continued to tell Lisa what was troubling her. Lisa was sympathetic, but said she thought it probably wasn't what Ilse thought. None of the doctors had mentioned any gossip of an affair between Robert and Carrie. She would have heard it. There must be something else causing his behavior. He did, after all, have a very stressful job. An affair with someone he worked so closely with would not go unnoticed by other coworkers. She'd ask her husband what he thought, but she was sure it was not possible.

Ilse thought, No one will believe me, but I know there can be no other explanation for his rejection of me physically, emotionally and intellectually. Is there anything else that could make me feel so bad? After all these years and all we've had together, I'm at a loss about what to think or do.

For Christmas, it was agreed that the family would all go to Molly and Ed's new home to celebrate with them. Molly would fix her first turkey and Ed's mom and Ilse would be there to help with the other main dishes and trimmings. Will was home for a long winter break, so he rode with Robert and Ilse leaving several days early. *For the first time in their marriage, Ilse had not sent Christmas cards. Her heart wasn't in it. What could she say...that Robert no longer loved her? He said he didn't have a girl friend? He just didn't like Ilse anymore? Maybe she could simply sign their names? She always wrote a personal note and the card list was large since they moved so much. Why make excuses? She would send cards this year to only a few people such as her parents who must not know because it would break their hearts.*

Always in charge of the gifts, she had already sent gifts for Robert's and her parents. Usually at Christmas, Robert shopped for her, a piece of nice jewelry or an outfit. He was always generous. He also would help shop for the main gifts for Molly and Will. She doubted he would do that this year.

Before leaving for Molly's, Ilse asked Robert to go along one evening to the jewelry store to buy Molly a gold bracelet. Will was home from medical school and would go with them. Robert got home late on the agreed upon shopping night and Ilse was anxious to go. Robert was mixing a drink and said he wasn't going. Will told him, "We need to go right away. It's our only opportunity. We've already scouted out the gift, so it won't take long." He did cave in and go along to the jewelry store, but only at Will's urging.

Ilse told Robert, in the heat of the argument, "You had time to take me along to buy a gold necklace and bracelet for an employee, but you don't have an hour to buy a bracelet for your own daughter." With that comment, Molly got her bracelet. When they got to the jewelry store, Ilse knew why Robert didn't want to go there with her. *She thought he had been shopping there for a gift for Carrie from the way the clerk was treating him. When she didn't*

224

receive a jewelry gift on Christmas day, she knew her suspicions were probably correct.

On Christmas morning, there were huge packages for Ilse, four of them, all beautifully gift-wrapped. Will had gone with his dad to select a gift. Ilse loved the beautiful French luggage he gave her. It was suede and tapestry, in soft pinks, blues and beige. *She thought he was saying to the grown children, look how nice I am to your mother, and to others, look how generous I am to my wife. Why would he give her such beautiful luggage when for months he'd been so mean? Ilse thought the message was, Take a hike! Get away from me! Or maybe he was trying to make amends.* It was confusing but Ilse accepted the gift graciously, quite happy that he took the time to shop for her.

For New Year's Eve, the whole family was back in Summit to serve punch, coffee, and cookies in the hospital lobby to people coming to visit. Robert's idea the first year they were there, it had become a tradition the community and hospital staff appreciated. Until this year, the family was portrayed as what it had been: loving, loyal and supportive of each other. *This year it seemed like a dishonest portrayal even though it looked good for Robert to show he cared.*

23
The Most Difficult Years: 1990-1994

After the holidays, Ilse became more insistent that they seek counseling. She had suggested it many times because *it didn't make sense not to at least try to work on an obvious problem after so many, mostly happy, years.*

Still sharing a bed, but rarely intimate, Ilse tried to show compassion for Robert by always being there for him, giving him the space he seemed to want, supporting him, and still loving him regardless of how she was being treated in return. On the rare occasions when he wanted sex, he was not always, but sometimes impotent. Ilse encouraged him to get a physical and talk with a urologist. She tried to encourage him to seek help by saying she thought it was a common problem for many men as they got older, especially if they were under a lot of stress. *She was also thinking that if there was another woman (Carrie), guilt might play a role in his sexual performance. It was something they could talk about with a marriage counselor.*

With Robert's go-ahead to find a counselor, Ilse checked with Dr. Frank to get

227

some names and numbers. Robert said it wouldn't help, but if it would get Ilse "off his back," he'd go. They kept a late afternoon appointment with a lady psychologist whose office was close to their home. Robert wanted to be assured no one would know he was going. When Ilse made the appointment, she voiced Robert's concern. The psychologist said she would make sure it was totally private, that no one would be in the office besides her.

Ilse liked Dr. Wren, but Robert was cool, almost rude. It was predictable behavior when he was doing something he didn't want to do and he had no reason to impress. Dr. Wren stressed the importance of being honest, totally truthful. Robert said that was no problem. *He prided himself on his reputation of honesty and integrity.*

With Robert there to hear what she said, Ilse told the psychologist how upset she had been since he had rejected her, physically and emotionally. She said she was sure he was having an affair. She didn't tell her whom she thought he was involved with. Robert made a face, laughed, then looked at her with disgust, interrupting to say, "she's crazy." When it was his turn to talk, Robert told about the tremendous stress he was under with his job. Furthermore, he said, he couldn't be having an affair because he was impotent. The infidelity idea was just "off the wall," he said. Although he said the idea that he was having an affair was insane, he portrayed Ilse as a woman scorned when she told about the jewelry gifts he had purchased for another woman.

One thing that Robert said made sense. He said that Ilse was depressed. He said he was depressed too with her constant nagging about another woman and the need for counseling.

Dr. Wren suggested that they both might benefit from taking medication for depression, probably Prozac. She would contact Dr. Frank to write a prescription. Robert said he'd take it, but the prescription had to be in Ilse's name. He wanted to protect his image. He told the doctor it would be unacceptable for anyone to know he was on medication. Within days, Robert gave Ilse Dr. Frank's prescription to fill, but he also said he would find it difficult to continue appointments with Dr. Wren. He didn't think she could help, certainly not him. Ilse was the one who needed help.

One hour a week was all Ilse was asking of him. *After twenty eight years of marriage, he owed it to them, to Ilse.* He reluctantly went a few more times, but Ilse recognized lie after lie coming from this husband who used to pride himself on high moral standards. The trust established over all those years was beginning to crumble. She scarcely recognized the soul of this man.

Dr. Wren suggested that they see a psychologist in Princeton. It would literally distance them from the possibility of running into anyone they knew.

"You should keep seeing Dr. Wren," Robert said to Ilse. He'd think about Princeton. *It was just as well Ilse thought. When he talked, he was not truthful because he twisted things around. Whatever he said, however, was firm and convincing. She suspected he rehearsed his answers over and over in his mind.* For example, he'd say, "I can't be having an affair. I'm impotent."

Ilse also began crying at the few sessions with Robert. He turned that against her too. In the end, Ilse continued to go to the local psychologist and both she and Robert took the Prozac. The one thing, above all else, that Dr. Wren said was that they MUST talk with each other. They had to communicate.

"Can you talk and listen to each other more?"

"Absolutely! Trust me. I'll go along with that," Robert said. *Of course Ilse was* agreeable and *thought maybe here was a window of opportunity.*

Years before they had gone on a 'marriage encounter' weekend where they attended sessions, then went back to their room to write each other letters, then exchanged the letters and discussed what they had written. Ilse suggested that they try that again but Robert said, "You've got to be kidding. You just don't get it. I'm too busy." *What Ilse got was that he didn't care enough about the marriage to put in any time or effort.*

Even on the Prozac, the relationship continued to deteriorate. The Prozac seemed to have no lifting effect on Ilse's emotions. It couldn't cover the pain.

All the years of their marriage Ilse and Robert slept in the same room, in the same bed. Robert would go to sleep after Ilse rubbed his back, with his arm around her waist. It had been like that for years, comforting for both of them. They would almost always retire together. That had not changed. What had changed was there was no arm around Ilse's waist. Ilse no longer could look forward to intimacy in any way, shape or form. She missed the affection.

Robert began telling Ilse he couldn't sleep because the neighbor's outdoor light bothered him. He told Ilse to go and tell them to turn it off at night. Ilse refused saying, "If you want it off, YOU tell them. It doesn't bother me." *She no longer was going to have conflicts with neighbors on his behalf.*

Robert had already told another neighbor that he was going to have their children arrested and press charges because they hurled eggs at him when he was on the back deck.

Robert lowered the boom one night as soon as the lights were out. He angrily said; "You snore, I can't sleep in the same room with you. I have to get a good night's sleep. Go into the guest suite." *Did she just begin snoring? She knew it wasn't something new as she began to cry*, heading for the hallway. The first night in another room was a very sad night for Ilse. She had already been having trouble sleeping, haunted continually by this mess of a marriage. So as not to disturb Robert, she had often left the bed after Robert went to sleep, gone downstairs to the sofa to try to sleep and listen to music. She had borrowed earphones and tapes of ocean surf sounds. She had never been asked to leave before.

This night, in her heart, Ilse knew there was another woman. She still had no real proof but if he didn't want her in the same bed, then he was sharing a bed with Carrie. There was no other logical explanation. Thinking about it in the lonely bed, she cried most of the night and her body began to quiver. *Did Robert sleep better without her snoring? She didn't think so.*

The following day Ilse fixed his coffee. He went off to work as if nothing had happened the night before. Ilse continued to think of what she should do. *She decided to push the snoring issue by seeing a nose and throat specialist. There was* the *possibility she had a deviated septum or some other problem.* Without mentioning it to Robert, she made an appointment.

The nose specialist could not see any physical cause for excessive snoring, but he suggested she check with Dr. Blue about possible sleep apnea and the sleep rhythm cycle, so she made the next appointment. After that visit, she told Robert she had been to both doctors (who were both on the staff at his hospital*). She knew he wouldn't be pleased that she was trying to remedy a problem that didn't exist. He was furious. His reaction told the truth. The snoring was just an excuse to get her out of the bed and she was trying to corner him by seeing the doctors. It was as though she was trying to make him more angry. She did.*

Robert's warped code of ethics wouldn't allow him to share a bed with more than one woman. Ilse remembered that when they were soon to be married his old girlfriend resurfaced, trying to convince him to sleep with her. He told Ilse immediately, afraid that she would find out about it. *It happened a long time ago, but Ilse remembered he wanted her to know he was loyal to her. Now was Ilse like the old girlfriend while he had to show his loyalty to the new girlfriend, Carrie? It was an upsetting thought.*

Yes, Ilse thought, not only was he admiring Carrie's brilliant mind and getting involved with her emotionally, but he was also sleeping with her or he wouldn't have pushed Ilse out of the bed they had shared for years.

The more Ilse internalized what was happening, the less she slept and ate, and the more she cried. Insult had been added to injury. Truly heartbroken and beginning to feel hopeless, she continued to work to be a good wife. She was making meals, taking care of the home and laundry, entertaining and supporting Robert in his career.

Ilse also continued to see the psychologist and made an appointment for both of them to go to Princeton on a Saturday. The Prozac wasn't helping at all, not for Ilse anyway.

After a whole year, Ilse started confiding in many friends, especially an older lady with whom she had bonded early after their move to Summit.

Ilse liked Alexis and Alexis liked her, literally taking her under her wing as though she was one of her chickens. She lived in the country with her husband in a gorgeous white and stone century old home on a large estate. A huge barn plus other outbuildings could be seen not far off the road. Alexis' husband was an executive for a company in town and a former chairman of the hospital board. Petite, dynamic, and strong-willed, Alexis was also fun. She and her husband were philanthropists, involved with the community and especially the hospital. They gave large donations to support new programs, but they gave of their time as well. Ilse went for lunch or coffee with other board member's wives, but the person she became closest to was Alexis.

Alexis invited Ilse to her country home to see where she lived and meet her animals not long after Ilse's arrival in town. On her first visit there, Ilse was overwhelmed by the beautiful home. Alexis met her with a big smile and the energy of a twenty year old. Ilse had only seen her at hospital functions and Alexis was always perfectly dressed. Now she was in her casual work clothes, jeans and a sweatshirt. Ilse was immediately at ease.

Grapes were growing over an arbor on the walkway to the back door and gorgeous flowers bloomed with abandon. Alexis proudly showed her the huge garden and the two started to pull a few weeds before Alexis said, "Hop on," as she jumped on the tractor. Ilse couldn't believe this fine lady was so down to earth and so much fun. They rode all over the farm, bouncing along, Alexis showing flower beds in unexpected places. Next, they went to the chicken coop. Calling each one by name, Alexis introduced the chickens as though they were her best friends. She collected some fresh eggs for lunch.

A pony, goats, and sheep, each with names, Ilse couldn't believe what she was seeing. Alexis' dog followed her everywhere, running to keep up when they took off on the tractor. Here was a woman who had grown up in New York City, obviously wealthy now, who was also the most down to earth, unassuming person Ilse had ever met, doing her own chores at five each morning.

Driving up to the house Ilse admired the huge red barn with Dutch doors trimmed in white. It looked like Kentucky Downs. Alexis kept miniature horses. Her daughter kept full sized horses on the neighboring farm. Going through the side door of the barn, Ilse saw what seemed like an Olympic size swimming pool inside the barn. Ilse was astounded!

Ilse was having such fun with this amazing, totally unpretentious lady. *She thought, Wow, what a breath of fresh air!* Inside the house, the friendly kitchen was the heart of the home. Ilse was given a tour, then they settled in for the delicious fresh egg salad sandwiches. Alexis talked about their three children and Ilse told her about her family. This first get-together at Alexis' country estate was the beginning of a deep friendship. Ilse was grateful for the acceptance shown her by this incredible woman who cared deeply for people's feelings.

The first few years in town, Ilse went out to the farm to visit Alexis only occasionally. They met for lunch now and then, sometimes with Alexis's daughter. They saw each other at the big hospital functions. Alexis attended parties with her husband, Jim, at Ilse's home. Robert was also in awe of this man who was so successful and was giving back to the community through his time on the hospital board, his expertise, and monetary gifts.

Shortly after Ilse began to see the marriage counselor alone, Alexis had surgery. Ilse told Robert she was going to visit her when she got home from the hospital. Robert thought that was a good idea, still wanting to keep up the appearance of the perfect marriage. When Ilse arrived for the visit, Jim greeted her. After almost fifty years, Alexis was still his sweetheart and best friend. It was heartening. Ilse's parents' marriage was the same way, but she saw little warmth in her in-laws' relationship.

Jim had a fire burning in the living room. Alexis was sitting on a couch. Always before they had sat at the kitchen table, but this time Jim brought in tea and placed it on an antique table before he left them alone. Alexis told Ilse she didn't seem herself. *What a perceptive lady! Considering whether she should say anything that might make Robert look bad, she decided to be frank and honest as Alexis had always been with her.* Ilse was sitting on the floor next to the coffee table. As tears came, Alexis got off the sofa, knelt beside Ilse and wrapped her arms around her. She was not much younger than her own mother was and Ilse knew she cared. Alexis didn't suggest that it was Ilse's imagination. She was a sympathetic listener, but she was not judgmental of Ilse or Robert.

"I will help you through this," she said.

It was late when Robert finally got home that night, but he was anxious to know how Ilse's visit went. He hadn't been interested in anything she did for some time, but he was curious about this visit. She told Robert that Jim was there, they'd had tea and Alexis was happy she'd visited. *Ilse knew Robert thought she would never say anything about their marriage, especially since Jim was there and he was on the Board of Directors for the hospital. Alexis was the only person, other than her Clarkston friends who seemed to believe her.*

Early one morning, as Ilse was getting ready to leave for her walk, the phone rang. It was a sister-in-law calling from California telling her that their parents needed to move to a retirement care facility. Since Ilse was the only girl, she said it was her responsibility to get to California and convince them it was time to make the move. After her parents moved back to California when Ilse was in college, she had visited them once a year, and in spite of the distance, Ilse felt she had kept close contact with letters and phone calls. She often felt they should visit more frequently, especially after they moved to the East coast. Daddy had commented that they couldn't move any further away. But they also knew that where Robert's career took him was Ilse's first concern.

After the conversation with her sister-in-law, Ilse asked for Robert's approval and was soon headed for California. He was happy she'd be gone for a few weeks, and he promised to take care of the dog. But knowing he wasn't especially fond of animals, Ilse made arrangements to leave Sasha at the kennel. *She didn't want to find out after the fact he had given the dog away as he had the other dog and kitten years ago.*

In California, no one was aware that Ilse was having marriage problems. Being away from the situation, and with the help of the Prozac, she carried off the deceit. Busy with the problem at hand the only thing people noticed was Ilse's weight loss. She was able to focus on reassuring her parents that a move was necessary and concern herself with detailed arrangements. She packed many of the belongings under her mother's direction...what her parents would take, what they'd leave, and what they would give away.

They had moved from a large house overlooking the Santa Cruz Bay to one side of the duplex they owned, so they had already downsized and the packing wasn't an impossible task. Ilse's mother had her pack a couple of large crates to ship home. The twins had found a suitable retirement facility not far away and they all met with the administrator and staff. After hard work and many decisions, Ilse was comfortable going home leaving her brothers in charge of the actual move. She couldn't bear to tell her parents about her problems at home. She knew they would be devastated if the marriage failed.

The year before Molly was married, Ilse sent Molly and Will to spend time with Granny and Grandpa, uncles, and cousins in California. Summers past, they had all met to camp in a National Park. It was a special time for them to be together without their parents. In spite of distance, the Mueller family kept close contact with each other. Ilse and Robert's children were now aware their own parents were having problems, but Ilse didn't want the rest of her family to know. It was a matter of pride, her belief in the institution of marriage, and her commitment to her marriage vows. At this point she was still trying to put things back together, to put things right. Robert was still denying that he was having an affair and he said he didn't want a divorce. With such a flimsy explanation, it would confuse her family as much as it did her.

Back in their east coast home, Robert was agreeable to taking the two-hour trip to Princeton to talk with the psychologist recommended by Dr. Frank. The winter weather was horrible, but Robert wouldn't cancel an appointment, even in a bad storm. It showed a new commitment to try to work out their problems. *Ilse was still hopeful, thinking maybe the California separation had given him a chance to readjust his thinking.*

Dr. Rule was ready for the challenge. The first meeting with Dr. Rule was a joint session, but Robert said he wanted to have a time to give his point of view alone, and then they could have the remainder of the session together. He laid the ground rules. It was his way or no way. Dr. Rule was agreeable. Ilse didn't object because at least Robert was going for counseling.

Ilse was not privy to what Robert was telling the doctor in his separate session, but Dr. Rule came back to the joint session to say Robert was NOT having an affair. Robert had 'honestly' told Dr. Rule that. He pointed out that working at the hospital, "There must be numerous attractive nurses and other personnel that would, with his good looks and important job, find him attractive." Robert obviously wasn't the type to be swayed. *How Robert was so convincing to Dr. Rule, Ilse couldn't imagine. He must have looked Dr. Rule in the eye when he'd talked with him, but now he couldn't look Ilse in the eye.*

Before they came back for the joint meeting, Ilse had to wait in the waiting room for her turn to join the session. Other patients told Ilse, when they saw she was tearful, she could wait in the car. When it was her turn to join them, the time was minimal. Dr. Rule had spent most of the hour with Robert. *Since he was willing to take the long ride to Princeton, Ilse knew he was relating better to this doctor than to the woman psychologist.*

The final session was terminated by Dr. Rule. He said he didn't see how he could help them anymore. He said Ilse was not willing to face reality. At the final session, seated in chairs side by side, Robert reached over and took Ilse's hand, a show of affection missing for months. It made Ilse cry because she became even more confused. Dr. Rule said he understood that Ilse would have a hard time keeping up with the intricacies of Robert's job. He also said, as the last psychologist had, they needed to communicate better.

On the way home, Ilse tried to ask Robert about his work. He used to talk about it. He replied that he didn't want to talk about work, besides she wouldn't understand. "Furthermore" he said, "you want to grill me about Carrie. Dr. Rule believed me. Why can't you? I'm not having an affair. Your insistence that I am just shows how crazy you are." In front of Dr. Rule, he had moments ago taken her hand as if he cared about her, but already he had turned on her. In front of the doctor it was an act, carefully calculated. His real feelings surfaced on the way home.

Days later, Ilse was on the back deck. Robert came out at about the same time the neighbor across the street, who was on the hospital board, walked over with an envelope. The bill from Dr. Rule was inadvertently put in

240

the neighbor's mail drop. Robert took the envelope, saw where it was from, and appeared embarrassed. He made the conversation short. When Ilse went back in the house, he lashed out as though it were Ilse's fault the mail went to the neighbors. He said, "I told you I can't have people, especially board members, knowing I'm seeing a "shrink."

It was always her fault, no matter what happened, Ilse thought.

She noticed a hospital flyer advertising a free clinic on recognizing depression. Ilse decided she should sign up. It was risky to cross Robert, but Ilse was going to do whatever she could to help herself get back on track. Robert again got angry with her for going.

She was beginning not to care what he thought because she now knew he didn't want her to shed her depression and return to feeling more normal.

24
Physical Abuse and Robert Leaves

Problems escalated with the couple still existing in the same house. Robert expected dinner to be prepared and waiting for him, no matter how late he came home. With every verbal lashing, Ilse began to cry. Sometimes she'd cry just from his body language, which expressed repugnance and annoyance.

She was beginning to wait for him in the family room, often sitting on the floor with Sasha's head on her lap. One late evening, when she wasn't at the door to greet him, Robert headed to the bar in the family room. Before dinner, he needed a drink. It was almost time to go to bed, but she would wait for him to have dinner and clean up the kitchen. All she said was that she'd like to tell him about the auxiliary luncheon. He said he didn't want to hear about it. He'd been working until just moments ago, and he was tired. He was in another late meeting.

Ilse knew where he'd been. They didn't have that many late meetings.

Robert mixed his drink. She no longer did it for him and that in itself annoyed him. Ilse was sitting on the floor, leaning against his recliner with the dog next to her, when suddenly Robert began kicking her with his heavy size thirteen wing-tipped shoes.

"Get up! Get up!" he screamed at her. "Act like an adult! Don't be so stupid. Can't you get it that I don't want to talk with you about work?"

Ilse got up and ran from the room. He was twice her size and *she knew her thigh and hip would be black and blue.* Sasha ran with her up the stairs as she cried uncontrollably, locking the guest room door behind her.

Ilse, think about what is happening. What was it Dr. Rule said? He said it was understandable and quite okay that Ilse couldn't keep up with Robert intellectually. *This also wasn't fair. She didn't pretend to know how to run a hospital, but she knew she wasn't stupid.* She had heard hospital talk for years, beginning with the time Robert was in graduate school and she typed all his papers. *She knew more about his work than Dr. Rule thought.*

Ilse was thinking that Jim treated Alexis so differently. He showed adoration and respect for her. They had married young. Jim didn't expect her to know how to run his business, but he could talk with her about it. Robert was unfairly comparing her to Carrie who was trained in hospital management.

Almost two years earlier, when things were still normal, Joe Hawk had called to say he wanted to drive from Detroit to see them. The two men hugged; Joe, always charming and

244

gracious, hugged Ilse too. The three sat down in the family room. Joe said he "wanted to clear the air" about the rumor that he was having an affair which wasn't true. He told them he was leaving his wife. The truth was that he felt Marilyn wasn't intellectually stimulating enough. He had grown beyond her. As well as Robert knew Joe, he didn't question him, knowing full well he was lying about the affair. *Years before Joe and Robert had joked in the presence of their wives about how they'd have to turn in their wives for some young chicks with great jobs. When they were ready to retire, the wives could keep working to bring in an income while they played golf.*

Not long after Joe's visit, Robert made a weekend trip to Detroit for Joe's wedding to the young, executive-type hospital employee.

Ilse, after being cruelly kicked, thought about Joe's visit and his 'intellectually deficient' wife. Then there was Dr. Rule's comment that it was okay that Ilse couldn't keep up with Robert intellectually. It was bad enough that Robert had been emotionally abusive. She had tolerated it however, but being physically abused would put the final nail in her coffin. It was barbaric. She wouldn't tolerate it.

Life was better for a few weeks. Robert did not apologize or even talk about what he had done, but he was more civil, and he backed off with his criticism. Ilse continued her long morning walks with Jackie and Joyce, withdrawn but with the usual tears. She did not tell them that Robert had kicked her.

Both counselors had told them they must communicate. It was central to solving any problems. Both had agreed, so Ilse decided to be insistent.

There was more physical abuse. When Robert came home again very late, he fixed a drink and said he was going upstairs to change. She should serve his dinner in about twenty minutes. *He was treating her like a servant* and suddenly she decided to confront him. Before he had a chance to head upstairs with his drink, Ilse requested some time to talk.

"I'm not talking to you. I've had a long enough day without getting grilled by you."

Seeing red, Ilse followed behind him up the stairs, down the hall, and into the master bedroom they no longer shared. As he turned, Ilse got directly in his face as he tried to put his billfold and martini on top of his chest of drawers.

"You've got to quit ignoring me. You're going to talk with me, just like the counselors suggested." *As she said the words, Ilse saw the surprise, and then* the *fury take over* as he swung back his huge right fist, landing a blow on her left jaw as she tried to turn her head away. He knocked her down, not out, but almost, as her head was swirling. She was dizzy. He didn't try to kick her or hit her again as she staggered to her feet, shaken. She went back down the stairs to the kitchen and reached for the desk phone. With the phone in her hand, trying to clear her head enough to dial 911, Robert came up behind her and grabbed the phone.

"What do you think you're doing?" he asked.

"You will never hit me again," Ilse said. "I'm calling 911."

"Oh no you're not. If you call the police it will be all over the news in the morning." He wrestled the phone from her hands and then removed the phone from the jack.

Ilse's jaw hurt. *She thought he must have chipped a bone* since his fist had hit so hard. She had seen his fist winding up, *but why didn't she predict the rage coming in his fist?*

Quickly he took Ilse by the hand, led her to the couch in the adjoining family room, and after he sat down, drew her onto his lap.

"I barely tapped you," he said. "It couldn't hurt that much." Ilse kept her hand over the spot waiting for a welt to form. Although it was very sore for weeks, there never was a bump and it never turned black and blue. *She would not tell anyone, but if she did, they wouldn't have believed her because she didn't have a bruise to corroborate her story.*

Ilse got up and went to her bedroom, locking the door behind her, giving up on the 911 call. In fact, she didn't mention the incident even to her psychiatrist at the mental hospital later on. *It was too humiliating that she had allowed it to happen.* She never told any of her friends either.

Things calmed. Robert softened and Ilse went off to the beach with Will over his Spring Break. Will took a roommate along. The boys had their golf clubs and played every day, only going out on the beach a few times. *It seemed many of* the *days were dreary, perhaps reflecting Ilse's mood*, but she found the sound of the ocean comforting. Every day she walked the beach, barefoot, for endless hours. In the evenings they went out for dinner and a few times Ilse cooked, wanting to give Will and his friend some home cooked meals.

The time at the beach was good. They worked puzzles, read, watched TV and played games at night. It was nice for Ilse to have the company. The week was drawing to a close when Robert called. He said that when they got home, he would be moved. He was leaving. Ilse was not surprised, maybe relieved, but still sad. Will put his arm around her and said it would be okay.

When they arrived home, Robert's garage door was open. He was still there. When Will and Ilse drove into one garage area, Robert left from the other side, driving down the alley so they wouldn't see him go. *It was spooky that after all those years he would sneak away. He's a coward, Ilse thought.* When Ilse called the next day, Robert said he didn't take much, a quilt from Will's bed, some sheets, pillows, towels and his clothes. Looking in the closets Ilse saw he left many suits, sport coats and even new shoes. Ilse made him angry right away by telling him she had made the quilt for Will and she wanted him to return it. She would give him another blanket. *Feeling guilty that she wanted the quilt back, when he had taken so little, Ilse put together all sorts of things he might need.* She asked where he was living and he said he wasn't ready to tell her yet. She could call him at work. He never did tell her.

Ilse had been taking a silver jewelry class for several years. Most of the students and the teacher were hospital auxiliary members. Ilse required special help to solder because her hands shook so much. Gossip was rampant. Ilse didn't say much, but soon everyone knew that Robert had left her. She told them there was another woman. With Ilse in the class, they thought they could get a first hand report. One of the women asked where Robert was living. Ilse sadly said he hadn't told her. She didn't know. They seemed surprised. Then someone in the class said she knew where he lived. Ilse asked how she knew. Someone else had seen him leave his new apartment to go jogging.

Will came home the next weekend bringing a friend to clean the high copper gutters on the old house for Ilse. Ilse talked him into going to the apartment complex where his dad was supposedly living. Not wanting to go at all, Will was anxious they not be seen. They saw Robert's car, which confirmed the tip, and they quickly left. That was the beginning of Ilse's own private investigation.

She worked at the gift shop and on the cancer floor once a week. She called a May Fair meeting with the respective chairpersons and asked two women to co-chair. May Fair would be the following Spring and the groundwork entailed hours of hard work and many meetings. Chairperson responsibilities would be much more involved than chairing a craft tent.

Two years before, Ilse had been invited to be honorary chair for the golf fundraiser for breast cancer. It was an important event. She had to speak in front of the large luncheon group after the tournament. Even though the Public Relations department had prepared the speech for her, Ilse was nervous speaking in front of a large group, so different from teaching a class where she was confident.

Recently, Ilse had heard Carrie speak at an auxiliary luncheon. Ilse had to admit Carrie was confident as she spoke, even knowing Ilse was listening to her. *Maybe she was particularly up to the challenge that day. Ilse hated hearing others praising Carrie for her presentation. Ilse felt when people were impressed, it was confirmation of how brilliant she was.* Robert had once said to Ilse, "I do all the work and you get all the glory," *seeming to be jealous of her popularity. Now she wondered how he would eventually feel about Carrie's 'glory' if he had to share the limelight with her.*

After Robert moved, he came often to the house, usually during the day. He seemed more at ease and sometimes even congenial since he was out of the house. He would use the garage door opener, and pull his car into the second garage, closing the door behind him. On a few occasions, he had asked Ilse to attend a function with him. At one recent gala, *Ilse felt like a phony as Robert tried to act like he was still a faithful, caring husband.*

About a month before he left their home , there was a management dinner dance. Ilse had selected an outfit to wear that she thought was becoming on her. It was new since she had lost so much weight. She knew that Carrie would be there. Robert came home and said, "We have to hurry, and why are you wearing something so dowdy and matronly?" It was too late to change to suit him. Anyway, she knew it was an appropriate choice, but he had done the damage by dampening her confidence.

When they got to the dance, Bob, head of Family Practice, immediately complimented her

250

on how great she looked and how much he liked her outfit. Others complimented her too. *Ilse knew Robert was trying to break her spirit* and she was appreciative of all the friends' compliments. Robert, always a good dancer, danced with Ilse only once. Carrie was watching.

In the Spring, after Robert had moved, he called Ilse telling her he wanted her to go with him to the Masters golf tournament in Augusta, Georgia. They had been invited the previous year, flown down in a private plane by one of the doctors. They had gone and had a wonderful time. This time when Robert was insistent that she go, Ilse said, "No."

He said "No? Why would you say no?" He tried to convince her to join him. She told him she refused to go and to pretend she was a happy wife when he no longer lived with her.

"I won't play this game," she said. It made him angry and he became more mean.

In the late Fall, the usual spaghetti dinner sponsored by the auxiliary, was served by the administrative staff and their wives. This year, Ilse wouldn't be helping as she had in the past, but she would attend with some of the other auxiliary ladies to support the group.

When they got to the cafeteria, they chose a table in the corner where Ilse could watch Robert, who was there. Carrie wasn't in sight and someone said she was seeing the eye doctor. After eating, suddenly Ilse told her friends she was going to talk to Robert because when she called him, he would say, "I don't have to talk you. You're crazy," and then he would hang up, *but in front of all these people, with their eyes focused on him, he would have to talk to her.*

Ilse's friends said she should sit down. They didn't want a scene. Robert tried to walk away when he saw her coming, but Ilse wouldn't let him escape. The first thing he said was, "You shouldn't be here!"

She told him she was still active in the auxiliary and wanted to support their efforts to help the hospital. She reached up and gave him a kiss on the cheek for everyone to see. He was trying to keep control as his face reddened and he looked up to see if Carrie was watching. She had arrived late and was watching. Ilse told Robert that both their children were coming for Thanksgiving and she wanted to invite him to join them. He started to hesitate and Ilse pushed him saying, "What can be more important than your children?"

He said, 'okay.'

Feeling bold and somewhat successful in her efforts to corner Robert, Ilse headed over to Carrie. Everyone was watching. Ilse smiled at Carrie, and asked, "A speck in your eye? That must hurt." She smiled brightly and turned away. There were no tears, but when she got back to the table, she began to tremble slightly.

Robert called and suggested the family go to New York City together to the Macy's parade before Thanksgiving dinner. A very pregnant Molly and Ed would be coming from Michigan. Will would be home with his girlfriend. Robert would borrow a van and drive them in to the city, then they would return for Thanksgiving dinner. He'd bring the wine. Ilse thought it was a good idea. They'd never gone to the Macys' parade before and it would be nice.

The trip into the city went well; Ilse sat in the back with Molly. Will and his girlfriend sat in the far back of the van. Ed sat next to Robert, shot gun. It was cold standing outside watching the parade, but such fun to be part of the excitement. Robert held Ilse's hand going back to the car. *Ilse knew his mood could quickly switch. Since he had kicked and hit her, it was nice to be shown some consideration, confusing as it was.* From the far back seat, Will's girlfriend was talking non-stop which annoyed Robert. It made Ilse nervous because she wanted the 'family' outing to be a success.

Robert returned the borrowed van and drove his car to their house, parking in the alley. Back at the house, dinner was soon on the table. Ilse had put the two ovens on auto time. Carefully planned, the table was set with good china, sterling and crystal. Robert waited for the rest of the family to put the finishing touches on dinner while he watched the football games in his navy leather chair. Dinner was good with Robert's gift of fine wine.

After a pleasant dinner, Molly and Ed left to drive back to Michigan. Will and his girlfriend were in the kitchen. Ilse and Robert were sitting on stools at the big butcher-block island and Robert was asking Will about med school. His girl friend, not intimidated by anyone, including Will's father, told Robert that Will should have some allowance. He didn't have enough money to do anything but study. Robert took a checkbook out of his pocket, asking how much he needed, ready to write a check.

It didn't occur to Ilse that her leaning over to see the name of the bank would anger him. He had left their regular account for her use, but had a new account of his own. *He never told her, but she knew he was putting money in an account she couldn't monitor.*

He lashed out at Ilse as he wrote the check saying she had no business knowing what he did. He earned the money and he'd spend it however he wanted. He threw the check at Will, got up from the stool, and headed out the back entrance to his car. Ilse followed him out. As he pulled out he almost ran over her and she kicked his car, *hoping she put a dent in his Acura*, the one that matched Carrie's. *He was still denying that there was an affair with Carrie or anyone else for that matter. He was telling everyone now that Ilse was crazy.*

When Ilse went back in the house, Will met her in the kitchen. Now he was angry. He had seen her go through so much already. He was thinking of the day when his father had called at the beach to say he was moving out. He said, "Mom! Don't let Dad treat you like that. He's treating you like a child and a stupid one at that!" *That comment from her son never left her mind.* Originally, the family Thanksgiving seemed to be going well, but it ended in disaster.

Soon after the Thanksgiving fiasco, Robert called to tell Ilse that he was going to Philadelphia to see a urologist about his impotency. *Strange that he would tell her this. When they were still living together, she had suggested this, but the suggestion had landed on deaf ears.* Now Ilse offered to go along, but he said he didn't want her there. He was going to

254

Philadelphia where no one would know him. *After the initial call, he called again, this time to tell Ilse he was impotent and could not possibly have a sexual affair. Ilse was not convinced. In fact, Ilse thought he never had an appointment. Perhaps it was all part of his plan to convince Ilse and everyone else that he wasn't having an affair.*

Months later, Robert called again about the impotency problem. He was now going for a scan, this time at his hospital, and this time he wanted Ilse to go along. She waited with him while he had the scan. Other patients would wait for the radiologist to read the scan, but they called Ilse and Robert in to see the photo right away. The radiologist pointed out a growth on the pituitary gland. A side effect was impotency. *It was like "gotcha!" He couldn't possibly be having an affair. Why was he going to all this trouble to try to convince Ilse?* He could have surgery or take medication. He began taking medication.

She had been unrelenting in her insistence about the affair, and now Ilse knew she had been set up to convince everyone she was wrong. Too bad, Ilse sarcastically thought, if sex was a big problem for him and Carrie. He wasn't about to do anything about it when he was with her.

Before the Thanksgiving get together, Robert called to talk, not the usual curt, brief call, but this time he wanted to tell her about a board meeting. He was proud and smug as he told her that a special meeting of the hospital board had been called for the specific purpose of bringing to rest the many rumors that were circulating. He said that Ilse had caused the rumors by telling people he was having an affair with Ms. Shearer.

That is probably true, Ilse thought because certainly no one else thought he was unfaithful to her, even though he had moved out.

The special board meeting was at Robert's request. He wanted to set the record straight, as rumors were detrimental to his image and work. They were causing Ms. Shearer considerable concern since they caused a blemish on her fine reputation. Robert told Ilse that the board asked him to leave the session for a private discussion. Then they called him back and asked him point blank, "Are you having an affair with Carrie Shearer?"

He said emphatically "No!" Afterwards he said that all the board members came to him, shook his hand, said they supported him and were sorry that Ilse was unhappy.

The special meeting of the board exonerated Robert. *Ilse didn't want to hear it, but she let him ramble on, confident now that he could continue working without this uncomfortable question in people's minds.*

Another Christmas came. Ilse didn't decorate like she did the previous year when she had lavishly prepared for the Christmas house tour. *Whom would she decorate for?* Will would drive with her to Molly and Ed's who had sold their first home with a nice profit and moved into a new house. Will and Ilse would stay at Molly's. Robert said he'd drive by himself and stay at a motel.

Ilse sent no Christmas cards again. *What was she going to say? Now Robert had moved out of the house? He was sick of her? She was crazy?*

She had failed as a wife? He had turned mean? Ilse kept accusing Robert of an affair, but even the hospital board believed it wasn't so? He was impotent, so he couldn't be having an affair? No, she wouldn't write a card.

Christmas was sad. This year there wasn't a gift for Ilse. Everyone focused on the upcoming birth of Molly and Ed's new baby. Ilse and Will stayed to wallpaper Molly's master suite, bath, and the nursery.

Shortly after Molly was married, Ilse thought it would be appropriate to tell Molly and Ed that she had been menopausal at an early age. If Molly was planning to wait a long time to get pregnant, she should consider that early menopause might be hereditary. It did change their plans to begin a family sooner.

When Ilse quit having periods at age thirty-two, she told Robert she needed to see her obstetrician. He had had a vasectomy several years back after Will was born. Right away when she told him she hadn't had a period, he lashed out, "If you're pregnant it's not mine." *She had always been faithful and was hurt at the time that he would start placing blame.* Never had she given him reason to believe she would ever be involved with someone else.

Anyway, now Molly was pregnant and the entire family was happy about it. She would make a wonderful mother. Ilse would have a diversion...a perfect new life to focus on.

Back in the beautiful old, now empty home after Christmas, Ilse tried to keep busy working on a quilt for the new baby. *Maybe Robert would reevaluate their relationship in the New Year and maybe she should try to believe him.*

257

Everyone said he was innocent of her accusations. Maybe she should be more positive and not place blame. She had no proof, only ideas she had pieced together from things he said and from things he did. Did she want to live again with a man who called her stupid and crazy and no longer had any respect for her? Could she live with anyone who would probably hit her again? Why would she want to be with anyone who didn't love her? The events of the two previous years had erased twenty-eight good ones.

Ilse continued to cry and shake every time she thought about her dilemma. *The problem was there was no way to divert her attention from this ongoing situation. Staying involved with other things just wasn't enough.*

Before Christmas, she gathered gifts for everyone. Along with quilting lessons, she went to jewelry class every week. She hosted luncheons and wedding showers. She kept volunteering. She shopped, buying more than she needed, hoping it would lift her spirits. Daily walks in the nearby park continued, no matter how cold it was. She brushed the long hair on Sasha. Keeping busy was Ilse's way of running away from the dark feelings that plagued her. But everything she did was not enough to sidetrack her depression. *Trust and love were broken, along with her heart.*

25

Coping with the Unbelievable

Early in the new year Robert dropped in and invited Ilse to lunch. It was unusual, but *Ilse thought that maybe he was finally going to come straight, ask for a divorce, and start the New Year right. Then he could get on with his life.*

Even though he was inviting Ilse to lunch, he stopped at the pantry cupboard, nervously rummaging for something to eat. *There was something wrong, Ilse thought.* His eyes were glazed as though he was tired, yet he seemed anxious and exhilarated at the same time. His eye was twitching which was always a signal of his nervousness. He didn't look directly at her. Instead, he focused his attention on the cupboard and the possibility of finding a snack. Unsuccessful in finding anything he wanted to eat, Robert roamed into the front hall, then into the living room where he checked something in his desk. *It was hard to tell what he was up to.*

Ilse went to the front hall closet while Robert rummaged in his desk. She pulled out her burgundy Geiger coat preparing to go for lunch. She had dressed carefully that morning, as she always did.

Instead of getting ready to leave, Robert headed back to the family room; Ilse followed behind carrying her coat. He was taking a break from work and Ilse didn't want to keep him waiting long if they were going out for lunch.

Sunlight filtered through the windows in the family room. The country curtains were tied back at either side of the paned windows that framed the fireplace. It was a comfortable, homey room.

Why is he so nervous? Ilse wondered. Why did he have such an odd look on his face? Was it disgust? Was it hate? What would explain that look? He looked mean. He seemed hesitant at first, yet firm in his resolve to talk to her.

Robert sat down, patting his hand on the sofa next to him, inviting Ilse to sit down beside him. *She was anxious to hear what was on his mind.* She threw her coat over the back of a chair and sat down next to him.

He began to talk. After all this time of not wanting to talk with her, she was again confused but ready to hear what he had to say. He became increasingly nervous and chatty.

Obviously, they wouldn't be going for lunch Ilse thought. She wasn't hungry anyway. She continued to note the firm, hard look on his face. She knew from the look that he was ready to make some sort of announcement, a prepared speech, probably lower the boom and finally ask for the divorce. He couldn't look at her, but she saw his eyes shifting. *She was ready for whatever he was about* to say. *She thought she was ready* but nothing could have prepared her for what he said.

He began, and it was not what Ilse expected, "You ARE crazy and I'm sorry about that. I can tell you feel awful all the time. Do you really want to live like this? It has been so long; it doesn't look like you will get better." As they sat on the sofa together, Ilse began crying, her body soon racking with sobs. He took hold of her hand.

"Do you want to live like this?" he repeated as he put his arm around her shoulder. Then he said without flinching, "Do you ever think about killing yourself and getting it over with? Don't do it like Elaine did. It was really a mess to clean up. Anyway, I took the guns so that won't work. My Dad tried to OD on pills twice. That didn't work for him."

Then he said without any regret, as Ilse looked at him in disbelief, tears streaming down her face, "The best way is to take the car. If you're driving fast enough, you could run into a tree. It would be quick and painless and it would all be over. Don't use the Lexus. Take Will's car. It's small and not as expensive. I'm sorry you've gotten so bad." He actually laughed, a sick, demented laugh. *This was his idea of a joke?*

She remembered how he looked and laughed when he killed Blondie, their pet cat. Only this time he wouldn't do the killing. He was trying to get Ilse to kill herself so he wouldn't have to do the dirty work.

Suddenly Robert realized he had said what he wanted to say. A look of triumph crossed his face. He dropped Ilse's hand, jumped to his feet, laughed his deep throaty laugh again, turned and headed for the back door.

Unbelievable! Ilse lay on the sofa, her head hanging over onto Sasha's soft head, sobbing uncontrollably. *She would put his suggestion from her mind she thought. She had to if she was to survive. This was the man she had loved all these years. Shaking as though she would shatter into a hundred pieces, Ilse felt a desolation and wave of sadness that she had never felt before. A sharp pain was in her chest. A lump was in her throat. Tears wouldn't stop. Her heart had broken along with any thread of trust she tried to salvage for the only man she had ever loved.*

All her anger and now another secret was bottled up inside. If she told anyone what he had just suggested, they'd never believe it. They didn't believe her about the affair. Why would they believe her about his suicide suggestion? She needed to get the negativity out of her head. It wouldn't help to dwell on Robert's suggestion.

Was it possible she was mistaken about the affair? Any possibility at all? Before the trouble started, Ilse had been good friends with Robert's Administrative Assistant, bringing her gifts from European trips, having her for dinner, and even shopping with her. *She'd try to ask her about Carrie and Robert, how they acted at work, and if they stayed late for work together?* Totally professional, Lori wouldn't tell Ilse anything. *Now that he was aggressively suggesting suicide, Ilse decided to go to his office and confront Lori.*

Putting on a nice suit and taking care to look her best, Ilse made the short drive to the hospital. Everyone still went out of their way to treat her kindly when she went in to volunteer or

262

go to a meeting. It was mid afternoon when Ilse arrived at Lori's outer office. The door to Robert's office was open. Large floral watercolors Ilse had painted framed the outer office, and Robert's office showed off her best scenes.

It was good that Robert wasn't around, Ilse thought, as she tried to question Lori about his schedule. Lori wasn't cooperating; she didn't know anything. She was protecting her boss, but she didn't know how to be firm and kind at the same time. In the future, she would scarcely talk to Ilse; caught in the middle, she needed her job.

Ilse told the secretary who shared the outer office with Lori that she was going to check Robert's calendar. Unfortunately, she couldn't find any appointments that would tie Carrie to her husband after hours. Getting any solid proof that he was having an affair was not working. *Whatever he was doing, he was being very careful, except with the things he said to her. He was using his power to treat Ilse like an idiot, a fool. All Robert's human decency had broken down just as he tried to break Ilse down.*

In spite of everything Robert had said and done, Ilse wasn't prepared for being committed to a mental hospital. She was disturbed that Robert would put her in such a place after he suggested the most vile way to end the marriage. *Now, prepared to make the best of the situation so she could get out, she needed to decide what she would do when she did get out.*

In the hospital, the daily sessions with Dr. Morrison were sometimes uneventful and even pleasant as she looked back on her growing up years, but it was disturbing when she talked about the way Robert treated her.

Dr. Morrison didn't probe into Ilse's sex life like one might expect, thinking that could be the root of the problem. However, right away Ilse told her that Robert said he was impotent and couldn't be having an affair.

"I don't know why he's making it such a big deal."

"Let me tell you it is REALLY a big deal to a man," Dr. Morrison replied.

To Ilse the big deal was that he was having sex with another woman when she had never turned him down, complained of a headache, or made other excuses. She had done everything she knew to do to please him.

Thinking about their sex life, Ilse wondered if perhaps she carried an underlying resentment and anger because of her disappointment on their honeymoon and every sexual encounter thereafter. She never got the romance, warmth and satisfaction she expected from the relationship. Robert had been cold, only concerned about his personal satisfaction and pleasure, never hers. He was selfish. Now he was romancing a young woman, and why should Carrie be the recipient of what he had never given her? It was part of a slow burning anger that may have been simmering for thirty years.

Since Dr. Morrison didn't ask for details, Ilse didn't offer any. Their sex life remained a private matter except for his claim of impotency. It wasn't something Ilse discussed with girlfriends, and since Dr. Morrison wasn't asking, she wasn't about to discuss it with her.

Was there another woman or wasn't there?
Was Ilse right or was she wrong? She had no idea
what Dr. Morrison thought. She never said
much, but prodded Ilse to talk, talk, talk. Ilse
continued the crying and shaking every time she
talked about Robert. She always felt horrible,
destroyed every time she thought about him.

In the group sessions, they said she
needed to learn to be more assertive, but not
aggressive. Dr. Morrison told her the shaking
was because she kept all her anger inside of her.
The tears and shaking were angry emotions
coming out. She had continued to be nice and
controlled whenever she talked with Robert or to
anyone else. She had been taught early in life to
be kind, no exceptions.

Ilse realized Robert's hint that she might
need shock treatment was another attempt to put
her over the edge. He knew it would scare her. It
was not something that would actually happen Ilse
decided, and she relaxed somewhat. Very quickly,
the psychiatrist took her off "watch," and she
soon realized bed checks were routine.

One night, several attendants came in the
room with their flashlights, looking in the
drawers in Ilse and Nanci's nightstands and
checking inside the toilet tank. Nanci was in her
bed. After they left, Nanci turned on her light
and showed Ilse that her bed was all bloody. She
had hypodermic needles to hurt herself. *Ilse*
knew she had to tattle and that's probably what
Nanci wanted when she showed her the bloody
bed. Down the hall, she found aides who ran
back to remove Nanci from the room.

There were things on Ilse's mind that she
needed to take care of. She wouldn't be able to

carry out her chairmanship of the big May Fair fundraiser. It would be impossible to continue her leadership, so she decided to call her co-chair and resign. She felt guilty, but she didn't think she had a choice.

A major goal in the mental hospital was to 'socialize' the patients, to prepare them to go home and be able to adjust. *"How could you adjust if you returned to the same problems?" Ilse wondered. She decided she would readily go along with activities hoping they would help.*

One day the aides asked who wanted to go bowling. Ilse said she didn't have any money, so she couldn't go.

"You can go. You don't need money," they said as they loaded two vans with patients. Ilse was uncomfortable because she didn't know the others. She saw Frank and his psychedelic shoelaces. She debated whether she wanted to go if he was along, but she climbed in the van along with the other patients. They had the clinic name written out in big letters on the van.

Is this really me? she thought. She put her head down, hoping she didn't look too crazy to the curious on-lookers. The outsiders who seemed afraid of what could happen watched the 'inmates.'

The bowling team from the 'cracker factory' was a diverse group. *Ilse thought she didn't fit in, but here she was.* Being a part of the bowling group made Ilse nervous, aware of who she was and aware that she was being watched and judged by 'normal' people. She was more aware than ever of how she must look. It made her sad to be in this situation. *Did she look odd or crazy to these observers even though she wasn't crying or shaking? Could these onlookers see the pain and hurt hidden under her eyes? Could they feel anything that she was feeling, just by looking at her?*

It wasn't her choice of a social group. She bowled poorly in the dark alley, her eyes and attention straying to the regular bowlers that kept looking over at the hospital team. She wanted to stick her tongue out and wave her fingers from her ears. Instead, she tried to act normal, bowl, get back in the clearly labeled van and chalk it up to experience. *She didn't think it would help her readjustment to real life when she got out of this place, but she'd go along with whatever they planned at the clinic.*

The only good thing was that Frank, with his bright green shoelaces, attracted the onlookers' attention more than any of the weird patients. Speaking of Frank, Ilse had him on her 'get even' list. She was still mad at him for going through her lingerie with such glee when she was admitted to the hospital.

Since Robert had told friends that she was suicidal and committed herself, they had started to call. Two doctor's wives that she was closest to said they were coming to visit Wednesday night after she had been at the clinic for almost two weeks. They asked if there was anything Ilse wanted and she told them to bring some of her old mascara, still trying to make her eyes look better after all the tears.

Excited to see friends who had been supportive, even though they didn't believe her accusations about Robert, Ilse stood in the lobby with some of the patients she knew, anxiously waiting. There were only a few hours allowed

267

and her friends were late. While waiting, Peter, who was in Group III with her, said it would be fun to have her go to her room. He'd greet them and tell them, "Sorry, they had to put Ilse in the locked, padded room." Ilse went along with it and it was fun to come out and see their look of relief. *It made her feel like she wasn't as disturbed as everyone thought she was.*

Frank was in the group waiting for Ilse's visitors, so as she introduced her friends to the inmates she said, "This is Meg. She's a patient. This is Peter. He's a patient. This is Gretta. She's a patient. And this is Frank. He's a patient."

Scruffier than usual, Frank began to holler, "I'm staff! I'm staff! You have to believe me, I'm staff!"

Ilse said with a big smile on her face, "You know how it is here. Everyone's disturbed. Don't listen to him. He's a patient. You can tell by the way he's acting."

"I'm staff! I'm staff!" he yelled louder and louder as all the 'real' patients laughed, enjoying Ilse's joke as much as she did. It was worth it, even though he was furious and stayed angry at her for the duration of her stay.

One weekend Robert arrived with Molly, who had come from Michigan, and Will with his girlfriend from New York City...a family outing. They all seemed happy to see Ilse. She got hugs from all, Robert too. The kids had brought a gift. They thought she should start painting again. They gave her watercolor paper, watercolors, and brushes. She was touched. It was such a thoughtful gift. She'd give it a try. It had been years since she had painted. They

268

played some board games and included another lonely patient who didn't have any visitors. They appeared to be a happy, loyal, loving family. *Ilse knew better. Robert didn't belong in the loving picture. Why would Robert now treat her well? Ilse wondered what he had been telling Molly and Will about her, probably that she was suicidal and his kindness to her now was an act.*

After they left, Ilse tried out the paints. What she did was tight and ugly, *just the way she felt.* She used to be able to paint flowing seascapes, duck scenes and flowers effortlessly. She couldn't anymore, not yet anyway. *Ugly! Ugly! Ugly!*

Molly made another trip to see Ilse. Robert flew her to Summit from Detroit and she drove down to the hospital for an afternoon visit. To Ilse's delight, she brought Sasha along. It was a wonderful, thoughtful surprise. It made Ilse feel good to look in Sasha's understanding eyes. Sasha had witnessed Robert's brutal behavior and she understood what Ilse was going through. Molly sat on a bench with Ilse while Sasha put her head in Ilse's lap. Ilse hugged Sasha closely, closing her eyes, taking all the comfort and warmth from her dog.

Having Molly close was also a comfort, but she clearly did not see the situation like Sasha did. Molly had written a card to Ilse. "Mom, you have always been there for me. Now it is my turn. I am here for you."

Ilse knew that Molly was supportive of her. She knew it was a big sacrifice to take off work and make the trip for a short hour visit. They didn't talk about the hospital or why she was there, just pleasant small talk about friends and the baby that would be arriving soon.

She doesn't know that her own father is wishing her mother dead, Ilse thought. It would be wrong to tell her what her father has suggested.

The days were passing quickly with sessions with Dr. Morrison, group III, and some activities. *Some of the activities were by choice and Ilse thought they were good diversions.* She signed up to go gardening. It was too cold to work outside, so they potted plants inside. When she went to the craft class, she ended up teaching it, doing her projects along with the other patients. She painted a wooden goose blue and made white ribbon roses to loop around its neck. *Pretty cute.* She taught some of the ladies how to make the roses. None of the men went to crafts. Since she ended up taking over the teacher's responsibilities, she was able to abscond with a huge piece of butcher paper and a black magic marker. She was well enough to get into a little mischief.

Back in her room, Ilse made a big sign. Ilse had applied to have a day outing to be with two friends who were going to visit her. By now, they trusted her. Dr. Morrison approved the form she filled out for her friends to take responsibility for Ilse before she could leave. When Ilse thought her friends would be arriving, Ilse walked to the driveway. If she went around the curve, the staff wouldn't notice her as she held her sign saying, "Take me out of here. I'm being held against my will." They laughed when they saw Ilse, heartened that she could find some humor in her situation.

The friends had to meet Dr. Morrison before Ilse could sign out. They headed to the shopping mall to help her reenter the 'real' world. The first stop was at the money machine since Robert had taken all her cash but left her card. They tried and tried her card, but he had blocked her bank use. Ilse got frustrated and then angry. Before this, she still had use of charge cards and the money machine card. Now penniless, her friends said "no problem." They had money and cards, but the damage was done.

She decided she might as well make the best of the day. Ilse thought maybe escape was something she should consider after all, but they weren't agreeable. Ilse only joked about it because *she thought she'd soon be discharged.* Ilse didn't want to borrow money from her friends. They treated her for lunch, but she still didn't feel like eating much. Before the shopping day was over, Ilse was exhausted. Back at the hospital, Ilse went to her room and tried to skip dinner. She was tired and wanted to go to sleep early, but knew she had to go to the lounge. They'd be checking.

After a month of therapy in the hospital and changes in medication, Dr. Morrison said she thought Ilse was ready to go home if she would return for weekly sessions. Robert would pick her up the following Saturday morning. Ilse packed her bag, including all those panty hose that Frank had overlooked.

She thought of telling Dr. Morrison what fools they were. She could have hung herself with panty hose because they're so strong. She could have given some to patients that really wanted to kill themselves. Since killing herself wasn't part

271

of her agenda and she wanted to go home, she decided she wouldn't say anything.

Robert was there on schedule. His body language was hard to read. He had called her on the phone about two times a week and visited three times. He had picked Sasha up from the kennel and the dog would be waiting, *a comforting thought.*

Robert said he wanted to take her for lunch. She needed to readjust. Her self-esteem had been destroyed. There was a time when Ilse had plenty of self-confidence, but she had been broken and brainwashed. She was nervous about going out with Robert, but was *glad he wasn't embarrassed to be with her,* knowing there had to be rumors about them.

They went for lunch and Robert gave her a pretty gold link necklace because Valentines Day was that week. *She knew it didn't mean anything.* He had told people only what he wanted them to hear. In most cases, if he was questioned, he would say she was suicidal and he did what he had to do to keep her safe. *She knew better but people still trusted him...except Alexis*

Then she made a major error asking, "Did you buy a Valentine gift for Carrie too?" In the restaurant, he kept his anger under control. *He's a phony, Ilse thought. She didn't trust him. Giving her a lovely gift in front of some people was smart.* He didn't deny giving a Valentine gift to Carrie.

Being back home in her own bed with Sasha was nice, only she still wasn't able to sleep. She had moved back in to the master bedroom. She began to walk and go for lunch with friends and got back to a routine with jewelry class.

Back home, Ilse realized she was never alone, except at night. Friends were with her every day. Once, she went to the couch with the dog and a blanket while they were trying to force her to eat the lunch they had brought.

When Ilse got up from the sofa and started upstairs to take a shower, they were on her heels, "Where are you going? What are you doing?"

"Leave me alone," Ilse said, "I just want to take a shower."

Robert made the friends feel responsible for her care and they were, in turn, scared.

Dr. Morrison called her to come in for a visit. Robert had called her to report, that in his opinion, Ilse was suicidal again. To Ilse's knowledge, Robert's call to Dr. Morrison at the hospital was all it took to recommit her. Robert said he was going to take her back to the hospital. She packed her own bag and Robert left work to take her. Later friends told her he had called a 'conference' and tried to get them to drive her to the hospital, but they said it was his job. He drove her, but this time didn't visit her.

This time when Ilse went in the hospital, Frank didn't check her suitcase. They didn't even check what she brought. She knew better than to take any ties or belts. The strange thing was that they took her to the same room and assigned her to the same bed. Nanci was back in her same bed after a time at home as well. Nanci showed Ilse her arms to explain why she was back. Self inflicted cigarette burns were all over her arms. *Ilse wondered if this would be a life-long pattern for her.*

273

They had a third roommate, a beautiful young blond girl named Sarah. One afternoon, shortly after Ilse's return, Sarah was screaming, trying to hide under her bed. Ilse watched as three men came in to get her out. One wore boots, which frightened Sarah even more. She had hidden under a bed after she had been viciously raped. The intruder had worn boots.

Ilse cowered on her bed watching the horrible ordeal, *feeling Sarah's terror and pain. Ilse's problems seemed insignificant compared with what Sarah and Nanci dealt with.*

Ilse wasn't there more than a half hour when a big, dark haired male patient came into the room and told Ilse he was assigned to her bed. *What did he think he was doing? He didn't scare Ilse.*

"Get out of our room! I told you to GET OUT! Get out NOW!" She shoved him toward the door.

"I'm going. I'm going!"

Why can I stand up to this big man and not stand up to my husband? Ilse thought.

Again trying to be cooperative so she could get out, Ilse followed the routine. Dr. Morrison continued to be her psychiatrist. Ilse talked and talked and a new medication was prescribed, this time Zoloft. She had been on the maximum dosage of Prozac. It might have dulled her senses, but Ilse continued to cry and shake violently when she talked about Robert and what her alternatives were. *If he didn't want to live with her even if he wasn't having an affair, why not divorce her after all this time?*

During this second stay at the clinic, Robert's good friend Joe Hawk called her. He told her he knew how she felt. He had to have psychiatric help when he left his wife. *Ilse thought after the conversation that whatever Joe did, Robert thought he could do too, including leaving his wife.*

Soon after Joe's call, Janice, who was one of the hospital lawyers and also a friend, visited Ilse. Ilse was surprised to see her because they weren't that close. She brought a huge box of chocolates, which was shared with everyone. Janice tried to get information about Robert. It was no secret what Ilse thought and there was no reason to protect him. Ilse told her about Joe Hawk's phone call.

Janice said she had met him at a meeting in Texas. Joe told her they had a mutual friend, Robert. *Then she said something that surprised Ilse.* She said she didn't think too highly of Joe Hawk, but she didn't elaborate. Months later Ilse found out why. The little kitten, Noel, was not taken to the police station as Robert said. Joe told Janice that he had a private joke with Robert about it. Ilse had never guessed that Robert had shot the cat, but that was what he did.

While she was hospitalized, she received a phone call and flowers from Alexis. No one else sent flowers.

Ilse wrote to friends this time to tell them she was in the hospital, but she didn't tell them why. She called her twin brothers in California and did the same. No reason was given, but they speculated with their wives. She asked them not to tell her parents or oldest brother. Robert had already called the other brother Steve, telling him that Ilse was suicidal.

One day Dr. Morrison said a psychiatrist from a nearby college who was noted for group session therapy was coming to conduct a session. He was a drama teacher. Ilse wasn't happy about going to another group, but her doctor said she'd only have to go once.

She hadn't participated in such a group when she was a patient the first time, nor had she heard anything about the psychiatrist then. Now only six patients had to go to the session and Ilse didn't know any of them. They met in a little room with metal chairs facing a small stage. The room was quite light with windows along one side. Ilse sat down in the back, quiet, not quite sure what to expect. *She would simply watch, she thought.* The psychiatrist was about fifty, short, with a full beard. With glasses in one hand, the other hand on his chin, he said, "We'll be play acting."

Not me, Ilse thought. She had never liked drama class, being too self-conscious.

While Ilse was wondering what they would be acting out, the psychiatrist-teacher was talking about the word 'protagonist.' Ilse had no idea what that meant. Then he said to one of the patients, "Get up there and be the protagonist." He asked the man some questions and in response, the man acted out. Ilse didn't remember what his little biographical play was all about.

I wonder   why they're doing this, she thought.   It seemed like a waste of time.

The doctor looked at Ilse next and asked her name. Ilse said her name and quietly told the doctor she couldn't act. He told her that was fine. "Just get up on the stage and answer a few

276

questions." Reluctantly, Ilse slowly went to the front and stepped onto the stage.

Then the doctor asked her what her husband's name was. She said, "Robert, but I can't act."

"That's okay," the doctor said. He said that for just a few moments she wasn't going to be Ilse, she was going to be Robert. He put a metal chair beside her and told her that the chair was Ilse. Then the doctor set the scene, with his hand thoughtfully on his chin.

"Talk to Ilse." he said. She began talking as though she were Robert. Soon she was screaming at the chair, then knocking it over, kicking and yelling, "Get up! Get up! Get up and act like an adult!"

Then he said, "Now you're Ilse," and she began to shake and sob. She couldn't stop. Next he said, "You're Robert again. I'm Ilse now," as he stepped onto the stage with her. Robert tried to strike him while he said, "I don't have to talk to you. You're crazy." He dodged aside and said, "Now you're Ilse."

She was on the floor crying and shaking and trying to get up while she said, "You're never going to hit me again!"

Finally, the doctor let her go. He said it's over, and helped her back to a seat while she cried uncontrollably. *They had what they wanted out of her. She had never told Dr. Morrison about Robert's physical abuse, only the emotional.* The others in the group smothered her with hugs, but she wanted to be left alone. She wanted to go back to her room, the safe haven of her bed and to sleep. She was totally drained. One of the patients in the group took her hand and walked back with her. She was allowed to beg off from lunch. *How the doctor got her to expose herself like that was a mystery to her. She wasn't happy about it. They were supposed to help her, not upset her.* Shaking and crying again she went to sleep, and no one disturbed her for the Group III session.

At her session with Dr. Morrison the next day, Ilse brought up the protagonist skit. Dr. Morrison already knew about it. The fact she had done it would be helpful to her Dr. Morrison said. It would help get rid of the pent up anger. She had been internalizing everything.

Three weeks after he took Ilse to the hospital Robert finally called her and said, "You have exactly one week to get well." The insurance would no longer pay. When she talked with the doctors about getting out, they said they couldn't release her unless Robert agreed to counseling sessions with her, because he was the problem.

It was not long after the protagonist session that Robert came to meet with the psychologist to get Ilse out. He wasn't about to pay for days or weeks not covered by insurance. He told Ms. Loren, the psychologist, that he wanted Ilse released, and she said that it seemed he was part of the problem. He would need to agree to go again for counseling. He got angry, saying he wasn't going to have some 'young snip' tell him what to do. *Ilse was watching all this wondering if the psychologist would relent in her demands.*

Instead, she told him, if that was his attitude, then they couldn't release Ilse. She pressed him further. The appointment had to be made. He finally said he'd go to a counselor in Philadelphia and they made an appointment. Ilse was released. They went to one session in Philadelphia and then Robert refused to go another time.

After Ilse got out of the institution the second time she got progressively better. Robert backed off. He rarely called and she rarely called him because she knew he would say, "I don't need to talk to you. You're crazy."

Soon after her release she helped with May Fair and attended hospital functions. Although she still thought Robert and Carrie were having an affair, she quit pressing the issue. Jackie, her walking buddy and neighbor, came over one day saying they had had Robert for dinner. He told them he was sorry that he had depended on her so much when Ilse was sick. He even brought a house gift. She said to Ilse, "I know you don't believe it, but it's just not so. He's definitely innocent of your accusations."

Ilse started to back off from everyone about her suspicions even though *she knew she was right.* Robert didn't make any more suggestions that she take her own life and she didn't tell anyone about it. *It was too over the top. Even Dr. Morrison didn't know and the 'protagonist doctor' didn't get her to play-act that incident.* She still shook and cried, but not as much.

Alexis called and invited Ilse to come to the farm. She had been cleaning out some old things and said Ilse could help her with a tag sale. Pitching in and doing 'real' work relieved Ilse's anxiety. Ilse told Alexis about the clinic because she was one of the few people who believed Ilse's thoughts about the affair theory.

Ilse had her checkbook back, so she bought some of Alexis's treasures: an antique doll bed, and some serving pieces. Alexis gave her a long white scarf, which Jim had brought from Ireland.

Molly and Ed's baby was soon to arrive. It was agreed that they would call when Molly went into labor and Ilse would drive to Michigan. Ilse wanted to find a special gift for Molly. She called Robert to ask him that if she found a beautiful large Waterford vase, would he order a dozen roses to fill the vase? It could be given to Molly from both of them.

"Great idea," he said.

Ilse bought the vase, wrapped it, and signed the card, "Love from Mom and Dad."

Robert signed the flower card, "Love, Dad."

Ilse drove herself the thirteen hours on a stormy winter day when their first grandchild was born. What a perfect baby! Ilse was happy for Molly and Ed. Robert arrived not long after Ilse and they left the hospital together, heading for separate cars. Somehow, somewhere going toward the cars in the icy parking lot, Robert started yelling at her. She didn't know what it was about, but heads were turning. *She began to yell back not believing they would make a public scene, but remembering that she was supposed to be more assertive.* To make matters worse, the Lexus security siren went off. Frustrated, she got in the car, stalled the engine, and when she finally got going, skidded on an icy patch. She spent the night at Molly's and Robert went to a motel. She was in tears again. Fortunately, she was home alone. They were going to meet the next day at the hospital with Ed's parents to take their grandchild home.

The next morning, just as nice as he could be, Robert called and said, "How about putting on a cup of coffee for me and we'll go to the hospital together?" He walked in the door ten minutes later. In a dither, she forgot she had already put water in the pot. Coffee ran all over the counter and this day Robert was calm and kind, unperturbed with her error. Ilse was angry with herself for letting him make her so nervous. Ilse stayed a week to help with the new baby while Robert went back to work.

26
Facing the Inevitable

It was time to get her ducks in order. *She was not going to be the one to ask for a divorce, but the damage to the marriage was irreparable. She needed to find a lawyer so she would be prepared if and when Robert filed.* She began to ask for suggestions.

Money would be an issue. Ilse didn't know if she'd have enough to buy a loaf of bread. She was scared. Jackie said she knew a 'hot shot' woman lawyer in Philadelphia who would go after anyone. Her retainer was $10,000. When Ilse said she couldn't afford that, and Philadelphia was too far away anyway, they came up with another local woman, and Geiger, the best divorce lawyer in town. He charged $300 for the initial consultation fee and approximately $3000 for a retainer.

Where was she going to get the money? A friend suggested Ilse call the attorney her daughter worked for in the neighboring county who didn't charge a retainer fee. He usually got a good settlement.

Upset, and clearly not wanting to make the calls, Ilse called the three lawyers to set up initial consultations, the first step in her selection process. First, she would go to the local 'barracuda woman,' then Geiger the 'hot shot,' then the one who didn't charge a retainer, Mr. Donald. Nervous even making the appointments, she gave her name, told them she wanted to discuss a possible divorce and clarified the amount of the consultation fee.

The woman lawyer left her cold. She gave Ilse a tape to listen to, to calm her nerves. The tape was all about the power of women. She charged her $100, and Ilse knew immediately that she could never work with her.

A few days later, she found her way to Mr. Geiger's office. Now focused and in control, dressed in a business suit, Ilse was shown into a conference room. Before she had a chance to sit down, a very tall, large, but trim man came into the room. He shook her hand with a big smile on his face and said, "What do we have here? A divorce? A dime a dozen! No big deal!"

His nonchalance annoyed Ilse. She said, "It might not be a big deal to you, but it's a GREAT big deal to me." "I understand," he said as he handed her a yellow legal pad and pulled back a chair to seat her. He tossed his own yellow pad in front of him on the big conference table indicating the 'consultation' was to begin.

Ilse knew she should be forthright with information. Ilse began to frankly answer his questions, poised and knowledgeable. He wanted to know if she understood the couple's finances. Ilse had done much of the bookkeeping, and had always gone along to see the accountant at tax time.

"Do you know his net worth?" he asked. She knew, partly because from year to year, Robert would proudly call her to his desk to show her his charted figures as they grew year after year. She told him what the approximate net worth was three years before when the marital problems began.

She didn't tell him that she had been given cash and stocks for many years from her parents. Over the years, particularly the last ten, Robert would call Ilse to his desk to discuss the stock. "The money could be better invested and you should sell it and I'll reinvest it," he would say. She would sell and he would reinvest, co-mingling the funds. This happened over and over again.

"Another woman?" Mr. Geiger asked. Ilse said she was quite sure there was another woman although he had denied it for almost three years. She had no positive proof. She had to tell him that she had been hospitalized twice for depression.

After about forty-five minutes of questions and answers, Ilse said she was concerned with choosing a lawyer who wouldn't be intimidated by Robert's influence in the community. Mr. Geiger probably knew of him since his name was so often in the paper. Mr. Geiger said, "What's his name?" When Ilse told him, he frowned and said casually, "Oh, he's already been here. He hasn't retained me, but I can't represent you."

Ilse's composure immediately evaporated. She began to cry as she said, "Now what do I do?"

As Mr. Geiger said he'd write down the names of other lawyers, *she knew she had been set up. He knew who she was all along. He was using the opportunity to find out what she knew, especially about the family finances. He is unethical, she thought.*

Ilse told him that she had two other appointments scheduled and he pressed her for their names. She told him the name of the woman lawyer she had already seen and when she saw the amused expression on his face, she said she didn't remember the name of the other. An outright lie, but she wasn't about to tell him more than she already had, even the name of the other lawyer she was going to consult who was in the neighboring county. Then he told her it wasn't a good idea to go out of the county. It would "confuse the issue," he said.

He made some suggestions from the Yellow Pages he pulled out from a shelf behind the conference table. Ilse took the sheet on which he had written the names and numbers thinking, *Why would I take his suggestions? Wouldn't he recommend someone he could walk roughshod over?*

Ilse got up. *She'd had it with this 'ethical' lawyer* who charged a big fee to win a case for his clients. Mr. Geiger said, "You're still a young, attractive lady. If you're not married or at least going with someone in six months, I'll take you to dinner. I tell that to all my divorced clients."

No thanks Ilse thought, but what she said to Mr. Geiger was, "I'm not paying for this sham of a consultation. If you want to be paid, bill Robert Kelly for it."

When Ilse got to the car, other than the tears and frustration when Mr. Geiger told her Robert had already been there, Ilse was glad she responded the way she did. She didn't tell him she was seeing Mr. Donald the next day and she wasn't going to pay him, both good decisions. *Wasn't what he did a form of malpractice?*

When she told Dr. Morrison about it in her next session, she agreed. It was unethical to say the least. Everything she tried to do to move on with her life seemed to backfire. *At least a question had been answered for her. Robert had been saying he wasn't interested in a divorce, but in reality, he'd already talked to a divorce lawyer.*

The following day, Ilse rallied her courage and headed to the neighboring county to consult with Mr. Donald. The offices were smaller than Mr. Geiger's and the receptionist wasn't as business-like. She was friendly and offered Ilse coffee. It helped put Ilse at ease, since she was especially nervous after yesterday's lawyer visit. This was turning into a difficult matter.

Ilse was shown into Mr. Donald's office. He smiled, and got up from behind his desk, laden with paperwork. He extended his hand, then gestured to one of the two chairs facing his desk. Ilse asked him if he would be intimidated by Robert Kelly because he might lose out on some of the hospital's legal work. If he was, she didn't want him to waste his time.

He said he had been District DA and his life had been threatened more than once. Robert Kelly didn't scare him. Then, before any financial discussion, Ilse told him she thought Robert was having an affair, but she had no tangible proof. He replied, "99.9% of the time that's the case." *It wasn't what Ilse wanted to hear, but she knew that his comment was a good indication that he would be upfront with her.*

Next, she asked about the consultation and he reaffirmed the fact that the first visit was free. It was an opportunity for both of them to see if they could work together. Ilse thought they could after only a short visit. He was firm, confident, but kind. She told Mr. Donald that Robert had committed her, telling her she was crazy, stupid and suicidal. He said that Robert might try to use the supposed necessity to put her in the hospital against her, but added, "We'll show him how stupid and crazy you are! We can make these so called negatives work for you! He's set his own trap!"

When he told her that, she knew they could be team players. He agreed with Ilse that she didn't need to file, but they needed to begin the daunting task of 'discovery' and getting her financial information together. Ilse had no reservations. There would be no retainer fee. He would get his money in the end.

Ilse was relieved that she didn't have to come up with any money. Facing the fact that Robert might cut off funds, as he did the bank cash card, frightened her.

After a good lawyer was chosen, Ilse felt somewhat better. She wouldn't file. Robert would have to. He had done more than enough damage to her emotionally. She wasn't going to let him destroy her financially. *She knew what he must have been thinking when he tried to get*

her to do herself in. If she died, he would have
everything that was hers and his and what they
had accumulated together. He's not going to get it
all, she thought. She was stronger. She was going
to give him a fight.

Ilse spent hours during those sleepless
nights going through Robert's desk, through all
the records she could find, trying to piece
together the financial picture. It was
complicated. She went through all the back
checks, looking specifically for the cancelled
check for the proof of the necklace that was
purchased for Carrie at the jewelry store almost
three years before. Every other numbered check
was there but Robert had removed that one.

Other records were missing, which made
it even more difficult. He must have come to the
house and removed records from his desk the
two times she was hospitalized. It was time to
get some help, "bring in the troops, so to speak."
She would call her twin brothers in California
and come clean with them. She would tell them
why she had been depressed and put in the
mental institution. She would need to call Steve
and Liz too, although they already knew about
her inner turmoil and concerns for the marriage.

In the Spring, Ilse drove to the beach
where Steve and Liz were. Getting there late at
night after a twelve-hour drive by herself, she
told of her dilemma. Ilse lay on the love seat.
She couldn't stop talking. They looked at her,
saying very little, *probably not believing all she
said about Robert, what was happening, and her
stay at the institution.* They hadn't heard her
version of what happened until now. They
didn't know what to say, especially Liz who had

always liked Robert and got along well with him. Steve was great with finances and she solicited his help.

Next Ilse went to California. She needed to visit her parents anyway. It had been more than a year since she had encouraged them to move to a care facility and her brothers had moved them to a second one. Although Ilse had called them faithfully every Sunday, whether she was in the hospital or not, she still had no intention of telling them of her problems. It wouldn't be fair to have them worry about her. They would be upset, worrying about her and what was going on back east with her. With the medicine she was taking and a strong resolve, Ilse could retain her composure when she was around her parents. She would tell James and Jacob, not Walter. He'd find out sometime along the way, and he couldn't help her because he had enough problems of his own.

Summer was just around the corner and Ilse had been out of the institution for several months. She had managed to drive to the beach to be with Steve and Liz. She had driven herself to New York City several times to be with Will. She had driven to Detroit to be with the new grandson, her daughter and Ed. She had spent hours talking to Molly. Although verbally not judgmental, Molly looked at Ilse with doubt clearly written on her face. She believed her father's story. A lot of damage had been done over the past few years. Now, flying to California, Ilse knew she would get the support she needed from her twin brothers. She already had Steve's support.

Ilse's parents bodies were gradually shutting down, but their minds were sharp as tacks. Daddy would be ninety-three at the end of the summer. The visit went well. The California family spent a lot of time together away from their parents, giving Ilse a chance to confide in James and Jacob who did not have negative things to say about Robert, but they commented how he had been aloof and unusually temperamental. Their wives said they had never liked Robert, but Ilse already knew that.

Once Ilse returned home, her brothers went to work digging into financial records. They began the long process of reconstructing records of all the stock and cash their parents had given their children for the last thirty years. They had kept and retained impeccable records. Family loyalty was just what Ilse needed. Her lawyer was already motivated to get a fair settlement from Robert, but with the records of what came from her family, it made it somewhat easier. Regardless, it was very complicated. After returning home again, her brothers called her often giving her the support she so desperately needed.

After all of this time, Robert still wouldn't say where he was living, although Ilse got a clue of sorts from a friend. When she told him where she thought Robert was living, he said she was wrong but wouldn't tell her the correct address. He would only say that Robert had moved to another place many months before.

The method of contacting him was the same. She had to call him at work and he would return the call. His demeanor and response was also the same: "You're crazy. I don't have to talk to you," and then he'd hang up. It was predictable, a broken record. Ilse was used to it now and she was stronger, but it continued to be painful.

The quivering, then steady shaking, could still be set off by a comment from friends, sometimes when they were discussing happy times about their own families. Often it happened when Ilse was alone, which wasn't as embarrassing.

Will came home one weekend, and when he came up from the basement, after playing a game of pool, he said, "Mom, the table saw and belt sander are missing from the basement workroom. Dad must have taken them." Ilse used the saw as much as Robert did making her own picture frames. *How could he have room for a table saw and huge sander in a small apartment?*

Ilse decided she was going to figure out where Robert lived. She would follow him, but not with her car. He'd recognize it. She thought she could solicit help from her friends, but they weren't willing to get involved. He was still stopping by the house now and then for mail. Ilse had been checking the mail carefully looking for clues.

Finally, someone had seen him near where he lived. She decided to start there. *Were there any apartment complexes in that area?* Driving around and going through the phone book, she located the possibilities.

When she called each apartment office, she told them she was moving in from Connecticut and wanted to check on the size of the apartments. She needed a place big enough to hold large tools. The answer was always, "no, the apartments don't have that much storage space." *He must be using the tools elsewhere. Who loaned him a truck or trailer to move the tools? And who helped him lift them up the steep steps out of the basement?*

No answers. Finally, by phone she found an apartment at Evergreen. Using the same approach she did the first time, Ilse drove the twenty miles to see if his car was at Evergreen. It was. *He must be living here, or maybe Carrie is, she thought.*

Checking the mail carefully every day to glean any financial information, Ilse stumbled on a clue sent by an appliance store. It was sent to Mr. Robert Kelly and contained an invitation to a special sale for customers. It also said thank you for purchases already made. On a whim, Ilse decided to try to figure out what he bought, if anything. She immediately made the call and spoke to a pleasant man on the phone. Ilse told him, "This is Mrs. Robert Kelly. I'm trying to verify our accounts. I can't tell what was purchased there, or the exact date. Can you tell from your records?" He said he probably could, but he'd have to get back to her.

Ilse was disappointed, but she left her number and hung up the phone, *thinking, sure. He'll never call back. It's just another roadblock.*

Later the same day, the call came from the appliance store. Len said he had the information she needed right at his fingertips. Did she have a pen to write it down? Robert had purchased a Maytag stack washer/dryer.

"What was the price?" Ilse asked.

"$968 with tax," Len told her.

Wondering about the purchase and thinking she already knew where Robert lived, she asked Len as an afterthought, "Which of our properties was it delivered to?"

"It wasn't delivered," he said, "Mr. Kelly picked it up himself with his pickup."

Hmmm, Ilse thought to herself.

"That is such a big help to me with the bookkeeping. I have trouble keeping track of all the properties. Thank you! Thank you!" she said to Len. *Now she was a liar, but she finally got some information.*

She was feeling a little smug. She had sniffed out where he was living and she knew he made this purchase. Interesting choice, Ilse thought. When they put the addition onto the house, she had included a closet as part of the master suite/bathroom area and purchased a Maytag stack washer/dryer to fit in the area. As a part of their suite, it was great to get out of the whirlpool or shower and put towels right in the washer

Something told Ilse she needed to get back on the phone and call 'Evergreen' again. This time she pretended she was a single lady, coming to the area to work at the hospital. She said she was a nurse. She would be interested in looking at the apartments if there was hook up for washers and dryers. 'No,' she was told. There was a coin operated central laundry room. Ilse pushed. Were there any apartments in the area, even occupied ones that had space for a washer-dryer?

"No!"

"Thank you so much!" *He must have bought the washer/dryer for Carrie, Ilse thought.*

294

That rat! First the gold chains, then the Dooney & Bourke purse, and now the stack washer and dryer. There were probably many more items that he duplicated for Carrie that she would never know about.

Ilse was having periodic appointments with Mr. Donald, her attorney. They were putting together financial information. He gave her lengthy questionnaires to take home about her expenses, what her needs were, and what she was accustomed to having in recent years. He was always encouraging. *She couldn't have chosen a better lawyer.*

Somehow, even though he was in the neighboring county, he picked up the gossip that involved Robert. He had his ear to the ground. People told him things they wouldn't tell Ilse. Ilse wasn't sure what his sources of information were, but she didn't think they were always right. One time he said there was a rumor Robert had gotten one of the nurses pregnant. She was pretty sure that wasn't true, but she was told the same rumor by another lawyer a few years later. *Because of his earlier vasectomy, it was probably just another rumor. Besides, he was impotent. Remember?*

Mr. Donald's 'source' had not told him Robert was having an affair. Ilse told Mr. Donald everything she knew for sure and most of her suspicions. He always listened carefully. Sometimes Ilse would be crying before the conference ended. Ilse asked him about hiring a private investigator and he said it wasn't necessary.

Quite by accident, Ilse gleaned another precious bit of information that helped in her 'discovery' as the lawyers called it. She needed to call about her car insurance policy. When she did, the lady asked if the information she needed was for the Lexus or the new Toyota truck. Ilse pushed and got the news about a new, gray truck...*another deception Ilse thought, but she herself was getting more and more deceptive too.*

During the summer, the man in charge of fund raising at the hospital hosted a big party at his country home. A 'Garden Party,' you could dress accordingly if you wished. Ilse had made a long pale pink skirt and matching top years before. It was linen, trimmed with beautiful off-white French lace. She received an invitation, addressed just to her and decided to RSVP.

"Yes. She'd love to go. "She enjoyed getting dressed up. She put on the pearls Robert had given her and pearl drops from her diamond earrings. They were perfect with her dress...simple but elegant. *Maybe Robert would be there, maybe not. She didn't care. She was going to enjoy this gala evening.*

The weather was perfect. Tables laden with fantastic food and a string band were to be enjoyed. The board member who lived across the street was there and his wife had a similar dress including a wide-brimmed southern hat and gloves. Ilse felt good that she had dressed appropriately and she knew she looked nice. That was important to her.

Robert wasn't there, but Carrie arrived alone. As she talked intensely with some of the board members, Ilse decided to make a move. She entered the group making small talk with one of the wives. Alexis was there and quietly told Ilse, "Be good." Ilse was. Carrie looked at her.

It wasn't Ilse's imagination that she acted guilty, but she could still look Ilse in the eye. That was more than Robert could do. She said to Carrie, "I like your pearls; they're bigger than mine." Ilse gave her a huge smile and turned back to talk with Alexis. *How could anyone criticize her for so kindly complimenting Carrie? Ilse knew Robert had bought the pearls for Carrie. There was no question in her mind. He thought pearls would go with anything Carrie wore.*

When Molly was married, Ilse wanted Robert to buy pearls for his daughter, but he refused. *No, he had spent the money on another woman instead. Ilse had waited for many years before she received hers. Insult added to injury, Carrie's were bigger and all she had to do was "sleep with the boss."*

As spring progressed into summer, Ilse kept meeting friends to walk and go to Auxiliary meetings. She also decided to have a luncheon shower for Jackie's daughter, as feminine and fancy as possible. The food was all planned, shopping and the early preparation completed. The day before the shower, a call came from California from one of her twin brothers, James. He told Ilse Daddy was in the hospital. He just wanted her to know. Ilse asked if she needed to come and, because he thought she was so fragile, he said "no." As they continued to chat, he said Steve was there from Nebraska. Ilse knew she needed to be on the next flight possible when she found out Steve was already there.

After her conversation with James, she immediately called the airlines. Balking at the cost, she made a reservation. When she called Robert to tell him she was going, he kindly said he'd pay for the ticket. A friend came over to help her pack so she could finish preparations for the bridal shower. Robert never did pay for the ticket.

Friends agreed to clean up and lock the house, since Ilse would have to leave before the shower was over. Not wanting to ruin it for the guests, they decided not to put a damper on the celebration by telling anyone she was leaving because her father was gravely ill.

When she finally arrived at her parent's duplex in Santa Cruz where everyone was waiting, Ilse said, "How's Daddy?" They all told her as gently as possible that he had died while she was in the air. Ilse began to cry.

"I wanted to be here. I wanted to be with him. I needed to tell him one more time that I loved him." Jacob said that Daddy knew she was coming and that all of them had been with him shortly before he passed away.

The next morning Steve took Ilse to view the body and then left her to be with her mother. Mother was always strong and this was no exception.

After the funeral, the family went back to the duplex to try to get things divided up since they would be together for such a short time. With the help from her medication, Ilse again met the challenge, kept her composure, and still didn't tell her mother what she was going through on the east coast.

At the end of the summer, Ilse began to plan to use her home for a Christmas boutique. She had been doing a lot of quilting. It would be a good outlet for the many wall hangings she had made. She could decorate with Thanksgiving and Christmas wreaths and silk table arrangements, many of which she could make herself. It would be an opportunity to use her organizational and creative skills.

More important, *it would show she was positively moving forward….and show Robert that she was not stupid. It seemed he had given up on trying to get her to kill herself. Now he was focusing on how crazy and stupid she was. Ilse needed to prove to herself that she was really okay in spite of what she kept hearing from him.*

The house was perfect for a holiday boutique. The dining room had built-in cupboards across one whole wall. The dinette area, which used to be a study, had open shelves across the window wall. There were shelves on either side of the living room and family room fireplaces. She could decorate as she did for the house tour two years ago, only this time everything would be for sale. Contacting all the better crafters she knew from when she chaired the May Fair craft tent, she had overwhelming enthusiasm and support. There would be no junk. *It would get her mind off the marriage problems, keep her busy and she could earn some extra money. It would work. She knew it would.*

Ilse got busy. Getting ready involved packing away everything on all those shelves and using furniture pieces for display areas and putting up trees for the numerous ornaments that would be sold. Ilse organized her friends to take shifts as hostesses/salesladies. They all wanted to 'work' because they would get first crack at all the unique items. Ilse planned it so people could enter from the front door, circulate the living-dining rooms, then the back porch where they were served 'Holiday Harvest' tea. After sampling, they could buy bagged tea mix. The back porch featured hand-braided rugs, a tree with nature-like ornaments and wreaths. Back in the dinette area, the customers found pottery from a popular local potter and in the large kitchen, fresh baked goods and candy, with hand made baskets hanging from the beams overhead. There were four decorated trees, hand-made clothes, a wrought iron crafter, silver jewelry and stained glass and original paintings by two well-known area artists. Available for the children were home made dolls and teddy bears, even kaleidoscopes. Thirty-four crafters participated.

The business agreement Ilse made with them was simple. Everything they brought had to be marked and they were assigned a code number. They didn't need to be there for the boutique. Ilse's friends worked shifts and she fixed them an enticing lunch. After coming in the front door and picking up a basket to carry their purchases, the people would leave through the former maid's quarters where they would pay and drop off their shopping basket.

Ilse hired two children to take flyers all over, as far as they could walk. With mail drops in all the houses, it was ideal. Hospital friends took stacks of flyers to the hospital. The first morning of the sale, people were waiting in line all the way down the walkway and up the

300

sidewalk. It was such fun. Ilse was again in her element, entertaining in a different way. *It was also heartening. People might not believe what she was saying about Robert, but they had certainly gone all out to support her.*

At the end of the three-day sale, the crafters were thrilled with their checks and Ilse was more than satisfied with her 25% commission. It was a nice 'chunk of change,' but more important, *the tremendous success was good for Ilse's damaged ego and self esteem.*

Robert came by twice. The first time was when she was still setting up and he said, "Just what the heck do you think you're doing?" The second time he stopped by during the show and Ilse asked him if he wanted to buy something for Carrie. He glared at her and quickly left by the back gate.

The 'Holiday Harvest' worked so well that Ilse immediately began plans for a 'Spring Blossoming', which she would sponsor before Easter. She couldn't do it without the help of all those friends. Whether they believed her about Robert having an affair didn't matter. They were supporting her. It was amazing how many of the hospital people came: nurses, secretaries and other staff people. Ilse was so grateful.

This year Thanksgiving was a non-event. Will was home, but would be spending Christmas with his new girl friend's family. He had fallen head over heels in love. Ilse was happy for him. He had taken on an extra burden with his mother's emotional ups and downs, and was always sensitive to her moods, coming home more than he otherwise would have.

27
Ilse's Private Investigation Continues

The most important clue for continuing Ilse's private investigation came unexpectedly. The local flamboyant colo-rectal surgeon sent an invitation to Ilse for a holiday party. He had a huge home everyone called the 'Hemorrhoid Hilton,' a lovely wife and three beautiful daughters. It was his wife who bought a new Jag for herself one birthday. His party was always one of the best: great food in a beautiful home full of artifacts and interesting paintings, and off-color jokes. Everyone important would be there. Ilse decided to go. Ilse thought Robert had been pre-warned that she was going to be there. Two things happened that night that changed Ilse.

Always friendly with the wives of the physicians and board members, she joined one group for conversation, then another. Two of the wives said hello without a touch of friendliness and then turned their backs on her. It had never happened to her before. Ilse mentioned it to a single, attractive, widowed friend who said, "Get used to it Ilse. You're now single and you're a threat to them." She said it happened to her right after her husband died, and it was still the same with certain women. *Ilse was hurt. She wasn't like Carrie. She would never go after anyone else's husband. It was a slap in the face, but a warning for what was to come.*

Interestingly, some people asked her where Robert was. After all this time, they didn't know he had left her. She told them they were no longer together and they were shocked. Most knew, however. The men were nicer to her than the women were. Ilse didn't know what to make of that until Marie told her about her own experiences. It seems the women were afraid she'd 'hit' on their husbands.

At a table laden with appetizers a friend came up beside Ilse, leaned over and said, almost inaudibly, "Saul knows where they live." That's all she said. Ilse asked her to repeat, and she turned her head so only Ilse would hear, "Saul knows where they live."

Ilse asked "Together?" When the friend nodded yes, Ilse said, "He wouldn't be that stupid."

Several days later Ilse traveled to Molly's for Christmas. It was a long drive alone. For a break, Ilse stopped to see an old friend who now lived only two hours from Molly. They used to do craft shows together, Ilse making reproductions of colonial bandboxes and Lucy making baskets.

By the time they finished talking, it had started to snow, and Ilse hurried to get on the road. The plan was that she'd stop to see Molly, Ed and the baby and go on to spend the night

304

with other friends. Molly and Ed had plans and this time the plans didn't include Ilse. She felt Molly was shutting her out sometimes and was embarrassed if her mother started to cry or shake. Going through heavy snow, the trip took longer than it should.

Instead of a warm welcome, Molly said, "Where were you? You knew we were going out." They had their coats on and baby Kyle was all bundled. Ilse was looking for hugs and kisses. She hadn't seen them for months and her only grandchild was the light of her life. Ilse called Sue to tell her she was heading there. Dejected, rejected and disappointed, Ilse went to her car in the deep snow that was getting deeper by the moment. Molly, Ed and Kyle followed her out the door. They probably never realized how hurt she was by their impatience and annoyance.

After living in the area many years, Ilse was familiar with the roads but by now, they were treacherous with blowing snow filling the ditches on both sides of the road. The Lexus had snow tires, but didn't have front wheel drive. Ilse breathed a sigh of relief when she pulled into her friend's drive. Here there were hugs and kisses and the warmest welcome. After a few moments they knew Ilse had had a 'melt down' when she left Molly's. With a roaring fire in the family room, and a big warm blanket, they served her hot soup and freshly baked bread. She tried not to dwell on Molly's attitude. She would go back there early Christmas morning hoping it would be 'bygones be bygones.'

That night Ilse slept like a log, secure in the protective haven of friends. They had all but tucked her in. The next day the other 'sister friends' dropped by to exchange gifts and hugs. Ilse was off to Molly's early Christmas morning, in time for Santa Claus' visit to little Kyle. It was hard to believe he would be one in just a few months. Molly acted as if nothing negative had happened the few evenings before.

Ilse didn't know where Robert was spending Christmas. Perhaps Molly, Ed and Kyle were meeting Robert on the night Ilse arrived. It might have been a somewhat logical explanation for their hurry when she arrived, but she didn't ask. It was a typical Christmas morning with Kyle happily overwhelmed by too many gifts. Ilse helped with the big traditional dinner along with Ed's mother. She had hauled her own luggage upstairs and was given a nice room and bath. When the couple had been moving in she had helped them with some of the decorating choices. They wanted 'Row' tile like Ilse had in her kitchen and back halls, but couldn't afford it. Ilse had given them the money to do some extras. She didn't know if she'd have extra money in the future to help out since she didn't know how the divorce would work out.

Ilse spent the rest of the week with friends, having lunch, shopping and playing with Kyle. Looking for Molly's birthday gift, they had a pleasant day shopping together. It seemed everything was better between the two of them again.

Her old friends wanted Ilse for a few days. The group, minus Robert would see in the New Year together as they had several years before when there were four couples instead of the three plus a stray. Rene and Josh were like Sue and Stan, taking Ilse in as if she were a stranded waif. Again, a fire was burning and soup was brewing, but this day the big tree was being taken down. Rene decorated to the hilt, but quickly got tired of the decorations and would take them down early. Ilse could help and the two laughed about some of their teaching days together, talking for hours. Everyone pitched in and brought the food for New Year's Eve dinner. Jean brought the salad. She made the best dressing. It would be a relaxing but fun night being with these dear friends who believed her and believed <u>in</u> her and were supportive of her. Sue said over and over that they were sorry they didn't come and get her when she called begging for help from the institution.

For New Year's Eve, Ilse wore a long black velvet skirt and a cashmere sweater. She was always cold, probably from the weight loss. Now she wore a size four. Again, they bundled her up in a big chair in front of the fire and treated her like a princess. Jean's husband was an excellent conversationalist, asking her questions. He asked Ilse about her jewelry class and had her scurrying upstairs to bring down and show off some of the things she had made.

They all encouraged her about everything she was trying to do: the jewelry, the 'Holiday Harvest,' driving to Detroit and to New York City to see Will. They were so positive. Some of it had to rub off on Ilse. The men stayed up most of the night counseling her. *The 'sisters' didn't have a problem leaving her with their husbands when they went to bed.* That all night session was a significant turning point in Ilse's struggle to

recover from the deep depression. It did almost
as much good as all the counseling and further
visits with Dr. Morrison. They talked to Ilse and
gave some advice. *The best thing was they all
believed her. They didn't think she was crazy and
imagining things and they didn't think she was
stupid.*

The words kept repeating: "Saul knows
where *they* live!" Ever since she heard the words,
"Saul knows where they live," they ran over and
over in her mind like a broken record. Ilse's
first reaction had been that Robert would not
risk living with Carrie. Have an affair, yes, but
not live with her. The broken record wouldn't
stop, all the way to Molly's, all through the
holiday and all the way back home.

On the way home, Ilse made a decision:
she had to find a way to check it out. Saul was
an older man, emeritus on the hospital board,
and a leader in the community. Ilse had met his
wife numerous times for lunch or breakfast. Ilse
decided to solicit information from her. As soon
as she got home, Ilse called Sylvia who was
happy to go for breakfast.

Feeling guilty for being devious, Ilse
asked about the usual when they met for
breakfast. She asked about Sylvia's grown
children, grandchildren, Saul and what she'd
been doing. Then she zeroed in to try to get the
information she wanted. Sylvia said she was
angry at the hospital and didn't know anything.
Ilse remembered that Robert wouldn't hire their
son after he came to an interview in bright
yellow pants. It was a big mistake. It was the
beginning of Robert's conflicts with some of the
people in town.

Since Sylvia didn't know anything about Robert and Carrie, Ilse asked her if she'd check with Saul and get back to her. *Promises. Promises.* Ilse waited for a few days for Sylvia or Saul to call. When she didn't hear anything, she decided she'd better get up the courage and call them if she wanted any answers.

Sylvia told Ilse that she forgot to ask Saul, but she would put Saul on the phone. Nervous about involving board members with her investigation, she told Saul that other people said he knew where they lived. Saul said,

"Sure, they live on Acorn Street in Roudensack. If you don't believe me, ask Eric, Marc, Dr. Carothers or Paul Snyder. They wanted me to help hire a private investigator, but I'm not spending any money for that."

That was easy Ilse thought. She thanked him. As soon as she had hung up, she began to mull over the information he gave her. Ilse wasn't about to call anyone else. They were all important people in the community, and they all happened to recently be in conflict with Robert. She knew that Marc Green was now Chairman of the Board and Robert had not been getting along well with him.

It should be easy now to find where they lived and check it out. Ilse had never heard of Roudensack, but she knew once she looked at a map, she could find it. She decided to call Alexis. She'd lived in the area a long time and knew where most everything was. Alexis had never heard of Roudensack either, but said she'd check with her mailman when she saw him.

Very excited now to have an address, Ilse called some other friends. The group planned to go for dinner, and Ilse was to be the designated driver since she never drank. On the way back from dinner, Ilse asked if they knew where Roudensack was…No, but two gay friends who were part of the group said that when she found where Roudensack was, they'd go to the door and pretend to be Fuller Brush salesmen. Everyone laughed, *but Ilse thought they'd actually do it if she asked them to. They had been wonderful to her.*

Ilse looked at a map but couldn't find Roudensack anywhere. Marie, who was head of the hospital dialysis unit, had an idea. She would check the address with her realtor friend. She never told Ilse any hospital gossip, but had been supportive of Ilse, inviting her to Telluride, Colorado to the film festival the summer before. They spent a lot of time together. Sometimes Robert came by the house when her car was there. He seemed to disapprove of Ilse's friendship with Marie *perhaps thinking she knew too much and could cause him embarrassment. If she did hear gossip, she would never pass it on, Ilse thought.* The following weekend she called to say there was no Acorn Street.

Was she going to give up the search? Never. Alexis wasn't able to come up with a location, but said she'd go along to look if Ilse couldn't find where it was.

Planning to meet up with friends for lunch…*probably to end up crying and shaking like she usually did*, Ilse headed to the country to drive around the general area until she found Acorn Street. *It was no wonder she couldn't find the town or village she thought.* She saw only a sign for "Township of Roudensack." For two hours, Ilse drove around in her gray Lexus, up and down every street in the vicinity. There was no Acorn Street. *Dejected, she finally decided to give up.* Several miles toward home, Ilse was almost past a tiny Post Office when she decided on a hunch to ask about Acorn Street. There wasn't any other car in sight, so Ilse just backed up in the road and zoomed in, very excited.

Ilse jumped out of the car, energized again and walked inside the little country Post Office to ask, "Is there an Acorn Street in the area?"

The lady hollered to the back, "Maud, you deliver on Acorn. Come and tell this lady where it is." Ilse was feeling better already. Maud appeared, plain and rotund, with a friendly smile anxious to help. She started to give directions when Ilse asked if she knew which house was Carrie Shearer's.

"Sure," she said. "The reason you can't find it is because you first have to go on an unmarked gravel road before you can find Acorn." She drew a map for Ilse saying, "After you finally get to Acorn, you just keep going, past a gate that says 'private property' and 'no trespassing.' You'll see THEIR house." Ilse thanked her profusely, got back in the car and headed for Roudensack, then the unmarked gravel road, then Acorn past the 'no trespassing' and 'private property' signs to a dead end, to a desolate house in the woods. It was just as Maud said. Perfect directions!

All the windows were covered with sheets, even taped tight to the edges so no one could peek in, even on the garage window. It was a dead give-away that they wanted total privacy.

311

The house was all alone, surrounded by trees, without another house in sight.

There was a big turn around so Ilse repositioned the car, then got out. It was bitter cold, but a sunny bright day. All bundled up in her long burgundy Geiger coat, Ilse tried to lift the garage door since she couldn't see in the window. It was locked down. Walking on the shoveled walkway to the back of the house, Ilse saw a large grill. She knew Robert couldn't get along without a barbecue grill. There was a huge covered hot tub and then, to her surprise, a large sliding glass door.

With all their other top security, they forgot to pull the drapes that day, so Ilse tried the door. It was locked. *Which one of the brilliant pair forgot to pull the drapes that day, she wondered.* She peeked inside, hoping to see something of Robert's she recognized. Instead, she saw mounds of white semi-sheer fabric on a table along with a portable sewing machine. *Carrie was obviously going to cover the windows with sheer curtains. On closer inspection, Ilse could see through the neat kitchen to a hallway and there it was...the stack Maytag washer-dryer. This was certainly their place, found at last.* The hot tub looked over a small ravine leading into the woods.

With a skip in her step, being careful not to slip on the ice, Ilse headed back to her car, then headed back into town to meet her friends, all of whom thought a love nest was non-existent. This was the proof Ilse had been looking for. *She joined her friends in remarkable high spirits. They hadn't seen her like this for a long time. She was happy, laughing, calm and already more self-*

assured. She wasn't acting crazy. This was what she needed to confirm her suspicions all along. For three years, she had no confirmation and now, finally, there was no other explanation. Since not one of them had believed her before, Ilse decided not to tell her friends what she had just found.

This day was a great day! Ilse went home after lunch and called Alexis, asking if she could go to her house for tea after her appointment with Dr. Morrison later in the week. Ilse slept that night, *finally relieved to have some truth. She would keep it to herself for a few days, not tell anyone what she had found.*

On Friday, Ilse took the hour ride to see Dr. Morrison. It was another bitterly cold day, but sunny. *Ilse had a plan, but she wouldn't tell Dr. Morrison yet.* During the appointment, Ilse regaled her with the story of finding the love nest. Dr. Morrison was clearly amused, and Ilse was her most vivacious, happy self.

Dr. Morrison told her it was brave of her, but she cautioned Ilse not to go there again. In fact, she wanted Ilse to promise she wouldn't. There could be legal repercussions with private property signs, she said. Also, there would be negative publicity if she got caught and they wanted to press charges, causing her public embarrassment. Ilse said flippantly, "I promise," *knowing full well what she had in mind.* The trip back to meet Alexis went quickly.

Alexis met her at the door and Ilse told her she knew where 'they' lived. She had found it.

Alexis said, "Forget the tea. I'll turn off the tea pot." Alexis was excited too. "I'll drive. Do we need wigs?" Alexis asked.

"Oh no! They'll be at work," Ilse said laughingly. *Here was her seventy plus year old partner in crime...her only local friend who had believed her, and her husband was a member of the hospital board.*

Alexis pulled her gray truck around and Ilse hopped in, but not before she retrieved her camera from her car. *She wanted to take a photo of that hot tub overlooking the ravine and woods. She wasn't sure why.*

Both feeling mischievous, Alexis and Ilse were off. They discussed whether it was too late in the day to go to the hideaway. It was only four o'clock, but the sky had already darkened. Ilse said that Robert had stressed what long hours he worked when they had gone for counseling together.

Alexis got nervous when they went up the steep narrow road, wondering out loud what would happen if they met Robert. Ilse urged her to keep going and when they saw the house with its windows still draped in sheets, Ilse was anxious to jump out of the truck. She told Alexis she was going to walk around the front and side to get a snapshot view of the back.

Right after getting out of the truck, while Alexis began to turn the truck around, Ilse tried to lift the garage door, with Alexis signaling "no, no, no." It was locked, so Ilse walked around the front toward the ravine, and tried the side basement door, which was locked. Getting ready to take a snapshot, she noticed steam rising from the hot tub on the porch when it hit the cold air.

Damn; they're here, Ilse thought. Well, I'm here too. I may as well take a picture. As she lifted the camera to her eye to take her picture, Carrie stepped out of the sliding glass doorway. She had a pleasant look of anticipation as she looked the other way, and she was stark naked!

Her head turned toward Ilse as she snapped her picture, and quickly Carrie jumped backwards into the house. *She must have thought the car she heard turning around was Robert,* Ilse thought, calmly returning to the truck. She didn't hurry; she was enjoying her discovery. Totally calm, back in the truck she told Alexis about the hot tub and her candid picture of Carrie's naked body.

Alexis put the truck in gear, anxious for the get-away. Ilse removed the long white scarf she had wrapped around her head on this very cold winter day. She was glad she had worn her boots to walk around to the side of the house.

That rat! Ilse thought. If she had greeted Robert outside or inside totally nude on a cold day, or any day, he would have said she was crazy. Who is crazy now? Ilse and Alexis laughed, but Alexis became extremely nervous, saying her husband must never know about this. Ilse assured her that she would never tell who was with her on this risky adventure.

Then she asked Alexis to drive a few more miles out of the way to see if Robert's car was at the apartment he supposedly rented. Not only was his car there, but a gray Toyota truck like the one the insurance agent told her about was parked outside.

Next Ilse, in her excitement, made a major mistake. She asked Alexis to drive down

315

the dead end that went by the front of Robert's apartment. She didn't know which apartment was his, but they saw Robert looking out a window in his jockey briefs and white tee shirt with a drink in one hand and the phone to his ear in the other. He had come home from work early and must have been changing to go to 'the house.' He saw them drive by, and Ilse was sure since he was on the phone, Carrie had called him about her nude predicament. Robert always did think you could see out a window without someone looking in. *Wrong.* Alexis and Ilse could see him clearly. *They should have worn wigs.*

Alexis and Ilse drove back to have tea at Alexis's kitchen table, excited they had snaked out some truth. It had been fun but Alexis was afraid of getting into trouble, bad publicity, and her husband's disapproval. Ilse was concerned for her friend. She no longer cared if <u>she</u> got in trouble, but she didn't want Alexis to be in a predicament. *She was also tired of no one but Alexis believing her. She rejoiced in discovering evidence that proved she was right all along.*

It was dark when Ilse headed home. She decided to take the film to the drugstore close to home. *On the trip back, she decided that it was possible and maybe even probable that Robert would be looking for her camera and the picture.* When filling out the developing envelope, Ilse used an alias in case he tried to pick up the pictures. Ilse had taken the picture with a new camera. Her old camera was still in the cupboard above the desk and *she suspected Robert probably rushed to the house to check for the camera while she had tea with Alexis. Not knowing she had a new camera, he would be confused.*

Ilse thought it would not be wise to tell anyone about what she had done, except she needed to call Marie whose name she used to get the film developed. Marie rushed over, *confiscating the Geiger coat, the long white scarf Alexis had given Ilse, and the new camera. No clues were to be left behind to connect Ilse as the intruder in the 'love nest.'*

A phone call was expected from Robert. It would be like him to confront her, but he didn't call Friday night and the weekend went by undisturbed. *Obviously, the brilliant lovers thought long and hard about how to handle the situation.*

Monday morning the phone rang. Robert was ready to play the game. His attitude was a total turn around from most calls. *He was as nice as could be...a dead give-away. Ilse was expecting the call and for once felt in control.*

He said, "Ms. Shearer came to my office early this morning, very upset." Ilse said, "What is she upset about?"

"Carrie thinks you have been on her private property taking pictures."

Ilse had fun playing along. "Where does she live?"

"Oh, way out in the country."

Ilse asked, "Does she own a house there?"

"No, she rents one."

"Might it be for sale?" Ilse asked, toying with him.

"It might be," he said. He wasn't sure.

"Maybe the realtors are taking pictures for their listing."

"Ms. Shearer said she was sure it was you." Robert said.

"Why would I want to do that?" Ilse asked.

"Well, she is very disturbed about the incident." Robert said calmly.

"What 'incident' are you talking about? Why is she disturbed?"

"You know what I mean. You were at her house," he pressed.

"Maybe Carrie is seeing things now, hallucinating. Perhaps Carrie is the one that is 'crazy,' not me!"

He went on and on trying, to get Ilse to back down, but she kept playing her cards, one by one, making him more nervous by the moment. He never got mad, or raised his voice. He was completely controlled as though they planned all weekend what they should do about being cornered. *Since he was staying calm, Carrie was probably in the office coaching him. Maybe they had made notes to follow.*

Ilse knew they couldn't accuse her. Surely Carrie looked out the front window, peeking around her white sheet curtains and saw Alexis' truck. She probably wouldn't know the truck, but she might have noted the license plate. They could easily find whom the truck belonged to.

That was a problem for them. They could accuse Ilse, but they could never accuse Alexis, a prominent board member's wife. Alexis's presence threw them off their game. It raised questions in their minds. She surely wouldn't be involved with Ilse in this way, but if she were, they

318

had better tread lightly. Uncertain, they didn't know what to do. The worm was turning.

There was another phone call from Robert, only a few days later. It was pleasant. Robert was again unusually chatty. He wanted to keep Ilse informed about his plans to go to the board and offer to resign so they could replace him. He said he thought he could get them to agree to a 'golden parachute.' This was the first time Ilse heard about the plan. *Things are starting to close in, she thought. He must smell a rat trap and thinks it is time to get out.*

Ilse asked him if there was anything, anything at all, that would hold them back from making some sort of agreement, knowing full well they had a private investigator on him. He said, "No, nothing." He was totally confident that he could pull it off and wanted Ilse to know.

He knew she had been disturbed, (not crazy this time) and maybe it would relieve her anxiety to know that he was going to resign and move on...with the 'golden parachute' of course. *He's clueless, Ilse thought. She knew he was looking for the 'golden parachute' now, because he must be nearing the end of his game if Alexis was involved with Ilse.* He went on to tell Ilse he had had some minor outpatient rectal surgery. *Fitting, Ilse thought.* He said he had to soak in the tub and Ilse knew how he hated baths.

Thinking of the hot tub she had seen, she said, "you're welcome to come here and use the whirlpool."

"No thanks. I appreciate it, but I'll just sit in my tiny tub."

He still thinks I'm a gullible fool, Ilse thought...actually I'm a pain in his butt.

A day later Robert called, again pleasant. He had the appointment with the chairman of the board, who assured him that they thought he was doing a tremendous job.

"Please stay on. We can work out our differences," Marc Green, the board chairman, said.

Sure, Ilse thought. He fell for the trap and he's the fool.

On the way to see Dr. Morrison that week, Ilse thought about what she would tell her about the week's escapades. *It had been quite interesting to do her private investigating. She had not lied to Dr. Morrison until she promised not to go back to the 'secret' address. In the past, she had avoided telling her some things but had not directly lied.*

Today she would tell her of her adventure, she decided. Dr. Morrison listened with renewed interest, smiled, and did not reprimand her. She could see it did Ilse good to seek out the truth about Robert and Carrie. It amused Dr. Morrison to hear how Ilse handled his accusatory call...not really lies but not confessing to Carrie's accusations either...just toying with him. There were no tears. No shaking. It felt wonderful.

Ilse now had to wear a different coat. She had a long blue Geiger coat, and if Carrie said the coat she had on was just like it only burgundy, she'd tell her she must be colorblind too.

She never got the white scarf back, but she did have the photograph. Being twenty years younger, Ilse didn't think Carrie looked that good, even though she was bustier. You couldn't tell too much from the photo, but you could recognize who it was and that she forgot to put on her clothes when she headed out into the freezing cold. *It would have been even better if she could have captured Carrie's surprised expression as she waited for the clandestine arrival of her lover.*

January was almost gone. It had been almost a year since Ilse had been in the institution as a patient. She had gone back weekly to the hospital to see her doctor. She was better emotionally. *The best thing was KNOWING, finally, that her suspicions were correct. She was not crazy and she had a right to be depressed when Robert had lied, cheated and done every ugly thing he could do to her.*

Ilse could not deny any longer what kind of person he was. Knowing lifted some of the burden, but Ilse wondered when was he going to move on with his life with Carrie and let her move on with hers?

A formal letter arrived from a lawyer in town, one that Ilse had never heard of. As she opened it she laughed, but *she thought she'd better call Mr. Donald, her lawyer.* Carrie had her lawyer send a warning that Ilse stay off her property or there would be serious repercussions.

Ilse wondered if Carrie told her lawyer, when she asked him to threaten Ilse, that she had been involved in a plot to get Ilse to kill herself so she could happily continue her affair with Robert. Did she really think she could scare Ilse with a letter after all the unspeakable things they had done to her for three years? They might have enjoyed their ruse before now, but even if she was still shaking and crying, she wasn't going to let this woman help push her around anymore.

Robert and Carrie thought they were so smart. They had fooled almost everyone else, but Ilse knew they were having an affair the night Robert said she snored and he could no longer sleep with her. She had no proof until now.

It was unbelievable, (and still is) that someone that she had grown up with, loved, cherished, bore children with, and trusted would turn on her in this manner. The letter from Carrie's lawyer...hmm...she needed to call Mr. Donald, her lawyer and tell him it didn't scare her one bit. They were done pushing her around and she would do the pushing and manipulating from now on!

Mr. Donald asked if she had gone out 'investigating' and Ilse told him the story of finding where they lived. She told him someone went along but never told him who it was. Then he wanted to know if there were 'no trespassing' or 'private property' signs? He said not to worry. *Carrie and Robert shouldn't be pointing fingers after all they had done.* We'd just wait to see if they wanted to pursue it more. Mr. Donald thought they were just trying to scare her, just as Ilse thought.

28
Robert's Demise

There had been many changes at Robert's hospital since this fiasco began. Ilse thought some of it was according to Robert and Carrie's plan. Ilse was put in the hospital the first time with the cooperation of Dr. Frank.

Since she was stronger now, *Ilse would like to talk with him about it.* However, Dr. Frank had left the hospital as the Chairman of the Department of Psychiatry. He had taken a job out West and moved far away from the unethical collusion with Robert. *He probably didn't even realize he was being manipulated until it was too late.* When Ilse was discharged from the hospital the first time, Dr. Frank offered to help with her readjustment and Robert refused the offer. The second time she came home, Dr. Frank had accused Robert of the affair. Robert was mad enough that he told Ilse about both the offer of help and the accusation. *Could it be that Dr. Frank didn't like being manipulated and he knew too much? Ilse would never be sure, but the timing coordinated with the pressure he must have received from Robert to help put Ilse 'away.'*

Before Paul Snyder was made the hospital Chief Operating Officer, another man had been the COO for several years. Ilse had a good relationship with him and his wife. She even met him for lunch a few times when the problems first began. He was demoted and took another job in a neighboring state. *Another timely coincidence...getting rid or pushing out people that perhaps knew too much.*

Another casualty was the nurse, Marie, who headed the Dialysis Center for many years. She had grown up in the town, was established in the community, and was an asset to the hospital. Summit was her home. Whatever the reason, she resigned and took a position in Georgetown, South Carolina. *Ilse thought, she must be afraid for her job because of Robert. Why else would she give up benefits and her beautiful home after so many years of service?*

Now Robert had recently demoted Paul Snyder from the COO position, with the approval of the board, of course. Ilse knew that Robert had promoted Carrie from an Administrative Resident to a Vice President of the hospital and then to a SENIOR Vice President. Such quick advancement was unprecedented when Robert was in charge. He was supported by board members because she was so brilliant, and they had assigned her to projects that challenged even the best administrators.

When Robert demoted Paul Snyder, Ilse knew Robert was making the way to promote Carrie again, this time to Chief Operating Officer of the Hospital. No one else had said anything about it, but Ilse knew how he operated, and she was sure that promoting Carrie again was part of his overall plan. He would be number one and Carrie would be number two...the CEO the COO. What a plan! It would not be possible if they were married, so an affair was the appropriate path for them.

Ilse remembered how Robert had avoided the military twice, how he plotted and planned every aspect of his life. Ilse was able to help him at the beginning of his education and aspiring career. In the past three years, Carrie had been able to help him look good. Carrie had done whatever she needed to do to be promoted quickly up the corporate ladder, even when it meant sleeping with the boss and destroying a family.

The trap was set. Robert didn't know that he set it himself. His three-year effort to get Ilse to 'go away' had not worked. She didn't buckle even though he had clearly plotted every detail of her demise. There was no doubt in Ilse's mind that Carrie helped participate in the plan from the beginning. Ilse knew how Robert thought, and that he actually had fun deciding how to best manipulate the situation. He thought that he and Carrie were so clever they would never get caught. It was a power thing with them, a way to control.

Only three days had passed since Ilse received the threatening letter from Carrie's lawyer, telling her to stay off Carrie's private property. The day had started with the usual long walk in the park, Ilse now bundled in her long blue Geiger coat. It was a dreary day and snowy. Ilse then spent several hours trying to shovel off the snow from the flat roofs over the back porch and garage. The walks also had to be shoveled or the city would cite the homeowner. Keeping up the house and the property helped to pass the time for Ilse. After a long nap, Ilse began to work on her quilting project.

The phone rang. It was Alexis. Ilse had talked with her a couple of times since their adventure into the country. Without any greeting, Alexis said that she wanted Ilse to know that Robert had 'resigned' just about an hour before.

Ilse said, "Oh, that didn't happen. He went in to give his resignation and try to weasel a 'golden parachute,' but Marc Green told him, they would learn to work together and he was doing a good job."

"No. No." Alexis said. "Jim is in California on business and a fax came through saying that Robert is being dismissed for his affair with Carrie. They've called a management meeting for the staff to announce it, but are saying that he 'resigned for personal reasons.' I have to go. I shouldn't be telling you this. The fax came from another board member. I wanted to forewarn you. They showed him a private investigator's report and told him to move out of his office immediately."

Ilse sat thoughtfully in the black rocker next to the phone, one of the many University chairs he had received as gifts from the hospitals he had worked at throughout his career. After she finished talking with Alexis, Ilse mulled over many questions: *How did they call him in and confront him? Will everyone be told the reason for his resignation? How did he react?*

Continuing to work on her quilt, Ilse heard the phone ring again. It was Lisa, the wife of the Chairman of the Department of Medicine. She just wanted to forewarn Ilse that her husband had just called to tell her that Robert had 'resigned.' An impromptu meeting had been called of the medical and management staff and Marc Green, the Chairman of the Board had announced Robert's resignation.

Ilse told her she had already been called but didn't tell her who called. Lisa said, "It's not what you think. It has nothing to do with Carrie. I know that's the conclusion you'll draw. Ray said he was watching Carrie when they made the announcement and she was as surprised as anyone." Ilse thanked her for calling. As she hung up, she was again grateful to Alexis for her support. She expected that the next call would be from Robert, *that just out of a thread of respect for his wife he would tell her that he had 'resigned.'*

Robert never called. Instead, someone called to tell her to turn on the TV; his surprise resignation was on the local news. *Maybe he'll call before the ten o'clock news, Ilse thought.*

It was Will's birthday. Ilse was planning to call to say 'Happy Birthday' to her fine son. *Should she act like she forgot his birthday or just call and not tell him, or should she tell him? She decided to tell him before he heard the news from someone else. Since Robert wasn't calling her, it was doubtful that he would call Will. He probably didn't remember it was his birthday anyway. The birthday call was sad and brief, a hard call for Ilse to make and not a very nice birthday gift for Will. He deserved better. Ilse felt like SHE was the one letting her children down.*

Ten o'clock came and Ilse watched the news again. It was the same, short and to the point, with a photo of him.

"Big news at the hospital…Robert Kelly, the CEO has resigned for personal reasons. No other explanation has been given at this point. He has been at the hospital for seven years, first coming to run one hospital, then the merged hospitals, and then named CEO of the whole hospital complex." *She couldn't believe that Robert didn't have the decency to call her.* She stayed up until midnight, waiting and waiting.

Finally, Ilse took Sasha out for a long walk in the bitter cold. There were no tears over his job loss. *It was what he deserved. If he had been as smart as he thought he was, he wouldn't have forced a meeting of the board to deny his affair with Carrie. He was fired for lying to the board. If he would lie about that, he would lie about anything. That is what Alexis had told her with the initial call.*

An affair would have been tolerable, but the lie is what trapped him in the end. He'd been lying endlessly to Ilse and possibly to himself, and now people would know she had been right all along. It didn't change the hurt she had suffered, but maybe she would be exonerated with all these people that hadn't believed her before. For Robert to lose his job was a big price for him to pay. Ilse had no sympathy.

Bright and early the next morning, before Ilse left for her walk, Mr. Donald, her lawyer called.

He said, "I saw the ten o'clock news and read the paper this morning. Ilse, I think we have to move ahead."

Ilse answered, "He'll still have to be the one to file, but move ahead." She was glad that they had already had numerous meetings and were prepared, waiting for the boom to fall. *Her lawyer choice was the right one.*

Robert walked into the house, unannounced and without knocking. He never did...*still thinking he was king of his castle.* He didn't say 'hello' or anything at all to Ilse, walking right by her to his big mahogany desk in the living room. He pulled some papers out and started to head toward the back hallway to leave again.

Ilse said, "Just a minute. You owe me some explanations!"

Nothing had changed in his attitude toward Ilse. It was the same. "I don't have to talk to you. You ARE crazy and everyone knows it."

Ilse told him the same thing she told him at the beach when he was so furious with Molly. "Sit down and shut up!" she said. "Since you don't have to talk to me, I'll talk to you." He sat down and Ilse started in. She was going to say some of the things that she had bottled up inside the past three years.

Robert said that he had 'had it' at work and resigned.

"Quit lying! A board member's wife called me and told me the truth." *He still isn't going to tell me the truth Ilse thought.*

"It's not what you think!" he said.

Ilse continued to give him a piece of her mind about his ethics, his moral character, his dishonesty, and the illicit affair.

329

He jumped up. "I don't have to listen to this! I'm leaving!"

"Not until you tell me what happened!" Ilse said.

He replied, "Like I said, I'm leaving. What are you going to do about it?"

"Go ahead and leave," Ilse said. "I'm leaving too. I'm headed to the hospital to confront Carrie and make a scene! I'll blow her away."

That did it. A look of surprise and uncertainty replaced the smug look he was wearing. They were in the dining room in front of the big bay window. The sun was streaming in the window from the eastern exposure.

Robert sat down again and Ilse pulled out a chair for herself. *Then he thought he'd be more in charge if he stood up.* Suddenly he jumped to his feet. *He was still going to deny the affair.*

Robert said that Marc Green called him in to his office and another board member was there. They didn't say much. They showed him pictures that a private investigator took. They even had pictures of when he went home after having surgery. He accused Ilse of joining in the coup against him.

She didn't reply. *She'd never have to tell him and he could always wonder, she thought.*

He said the Chairman of the Board gave him a legal paper to sign, which they had prepared ahead. They agreed to say he was resigning for personal reasons. He signed it right away, without question, but asked that they change the financial agreement.

They were going to pay him his salary for six months. He asked them to spread the six months over a year's time, which in the end hurt Ilse because she got half of what she would have received. *He probably planned that too, just in case he was ever fired. He was good at firing people and making final deals.* Carrie was fired too, but was allowed to stay to finish a building project. They were going to provide an office for Robert in a neighboring town to use while he looked for another job.

Next Ilse asked about Carrie. She told him he was a fool for promoting Carrie so quickly.

Ilse said, "You gave her a huge salary for sleeping with you!"

"She's not like that! But she does earn over $100,000 a year," he said proudly. *He was defending her character. Ilse couldn't believe she was hearing Robert say,* "She <u>earned</u> her money." *I'll bet she did, Ilse thought* as Robert continued, "You! You only made $4500 a year! Look at you! You were JUST a teacher!"

"Just remember that I helped you for twenty-eight long years to get to the top of the corporate ladder. In three short years, Carrie helped you lose everything. $4500 was enough to put you through graduate school, put your career on the fast track to success and then save enough money to put the kids through college," Ilse replied. "At least I'm honest and can live with myself. After all of this you'll lose everyone's respect and that is what you've always said you care about."

Robert said, "Molly will still love me."

"Speaking of love, do you love Carrie?" Ilse prompted.

He said, "I do love her. We're soul mates. I NEVER loved you."

Ilse sadly said, "I hope she loves you. You can never trust her and she can never trust you."

"Trust me," he said. "She's not like that."

Ilse replied, "Trust you? Why would I ever trust you after what you have done to me?"

He tried to soften his comment about never loving her. He said again, "You can trust me. I've always cared about you. I'll always care for you. You think it's about the money. You can have it all."

She knew it WAS at least partially about money. If she had killed herself, he would have it all.

"What do you expect coming from the family I came from?" he said.

"Everyone is responsible for their own behavior. I expect that by the time you're fifty you can move beyond blaming other people for your behavior, using that for an excuse. It would be sad to think that your children might use your behavior for an excuse someday." Ilse said.

After Robert left Ilse cried again, *knowing he wasn't worth crying for. He had been fired, and that was what he deserved. That's not what she was crying about. The statement about never loving her hurt. She thought he had adored and loved her for many years, in spite of the way he had treated her for the last three.*

If Carrie and Robert were soul mates, maybe that would explain their collusion to destroy Ilse. Only two like-minded people with sick minds could join in a plan to try to get rid of Ilse, trying to convince her she didn't want to live.

They probably are soul mates, Ilse thought, and evil ones. They would have to be alike in their thinking to do what they had done together. One wasn't any better than the other. It was unspeakable, but it hadn't worked the way they planned.

The next week passed quickly. There were several calls from the local paper. The lady who wrote all the hospital news and many articles about Robert and his successes, was trying desperately to get the 'scoop' on what really happened with the 'resignation.' The initial press headlines read, "Prominent CEO of Summit's Hospital Resigns for Personal Reasons." Mr. Donald advised Ilse not to tell the news media anything.

There was a call from a hospital administrator whom they had known for years telling Ilse maybe he could help Robert find a new job. He called for Robert at the house so he obviously didn't know they were separated. Ilse told him that Robert lied to the Board about an affair he was having, and she was no longer willing to help him in any way because of the way he had treated her. That was the end of that. The call was quickly terminated and he didn't call Robert with his offer of help. Several calls came from doctor's wives who were no longer at the hospital. Ilse was frank with most of them, clearing the air, protecting her own reputation. She never did give the news people an interview. It was bad enough that their 'mess' was a public affair. Immediately after his 'resignation,' Robert was seen in public with Carrie. One person told Ilse they saw Robert with Carrie at a restaurant out toward

Roudensack. Another person said they saw the two coming out of Robert's lawyer's office together.

A week after his first visit to the house to collect some papers and get a long overdue lecture from Ilse, Robert arrived at the house, still walking right in like he was in charge.

Robert went to the family room and sat casually in one of the brown leather club chairs, swinging his leg over an arm, totally at ease. Ilse sat on the sofa. He didn't spend any time chitchatting. He got right to the point.

"This is kind of 'shitty,' he said, "but I have seen the lawyer and filed for a divorce."

What was 'shitty' Ilse thought, was that he didn't do it almost three years before! It was about time! She was ready for the fight. Ilse told him that she had retained a lawyer, a very good one.

Ilse was curious if Robert had given any thought to Ilse's future or was he only concerned about his own. She asked, "Where will I go? What will I do?"

Robert got a smirk on his face and then laughed his sick laugh when he replied, "You can always go back to Janesville!"

He couldn't or wouldn't let go of his original 'clever' plan that Ilse should have killed herself. The cemetery in Janesville is where Ilse's grandparents and father were buried and there are plots there for the rest of the family. *His sick sense of humor and his disregard for Ilse's life kept surfacing. It was sobering and sad that after all she had endured at his hands, he still wished she were dead.*

He didn't say much more except to point out that he had worked hard and made most of the money. Ilse told him that she would like him to call before he came over again. She didn't want him wandering in and out whenever he felt like it, checking the kitchen pantry on his way through looking for a snack. She would deal with him through her lawyer.

Before he left he said, "Oh, just one more thing. Could I have the key to the beach condo? I want to go down."

"Sure" Ilse said, "as long as you go alone. I don't want Carrie sleeping in my bed. She already did that here."

That made him angry enough to leave and he didn't go to the beach to regroup. At least she didn't know if he did.

Time passed, now with regular trips to see Mr. Donald. Ilse told him Robert would have to pay for the divorce. Her attorney told her that the way he read Robert, he had to be in control and he would balk at that.

"We'll get the money to cover it," he said. "We just won't earmark it that way."

All the work Ilse's brothers had done was put into play. Quite often, at the lawyer's office, Ilse would end up in tears. Robert's lawyer was full of ridiculous demands, which were countered by Mr. Donald. The appraisers had to come to the house to look at all the furniture, artwork, and tools. Ilse pointed out that Robert had taken a lot of tools and now had the John Deere riding lawn mower from the garage.

The lawyers met with their clients at a joint meeting with a young clerk. Both had determined the assets. The four went through the security check and were seated in a room, on opposite tables, with the 'judge' in the middle, a very young woman with the power to determine Ilse's monthly income and support until the divorce was final.

The paperwork came out. Right away Ilse saw that there was a lot missing on Robert's disclosure sheet. After they got started, Ilse pointed out there was a Toyota truck that Robert didn't mention under vehicles.

"Oh, I forgot that," he said.

When Ilse started to name all sorts of stocks that he hadn't disclosed, Mr. Donald nudged Ilse to keep still. He was determined that Robert would give up more if he weren't challenged. Robert acted surprised that Ilse knew about the stocks. She had been keeping track of every piece of paper work in the last several years, and he was surprised she was aware of his 'new' portfolio.

He directed his excuse at the young woman in charge because she acted as if she thought Ilse was picking on Robert, that she was trying to get more than her appropriate share.

"Those are things that recently came from my parents," he said. Ilse then backed off to let Mr. Donald do his job. She just wanted Robert to know she wasn't stupid about what he had been doing. His parents had not given them money throughout the marriage except the $2000 for a down payment on their first house.

They had given HIM the lifetime gift one week after he moved out of the house. *He had orchestrated the move to coincide with the time the lifetime gift was given so that Ilse could not claim*

336

any of that money. It was fine for him to claim a share of what her parents had given her all those years, Ilse thought. At least Ilse hadn't told Mr. Geiger, Robert's lawyer, that she knew about the lifetime gift or the truck when he conned her into telling many other things she knew.

In addition to the meetings with the lawyer, Ilse was still going weekly to the mental hospital where Dr. Morrison had her office. There were still times when she found talking about the marriage quite difficult, but now she was talking about the divorce preparations, and trying to think what she would do as a single, divorced woman.

29
Goodbye Letters

Robert's birthday was coming up and Ilse decided that she would give him one last gift. She found a frame with space for a variety of photos and decided that he would like to have some photos of him with his children and some pictures of his first grandson. He didn't have any except what he had taken from his office. When she thought of family pictures he had at his *office, Ilse wondered what he had done with the paintings that were hanging on his office walls. They were her best watercolors.*

She spent hours looking for pictures and found some of Robert with each child and nice snapshots of both Molly and Will, as young adults. *With thought, Ilse decided to call Robert and wish him a happy birthday and ask him to meet her so she could give him the pictures.* When she called, no one answered and Ilse assumed he was out with Carrie celebrating with a birthday dinner. She left a message asking him to call her in the morning.

After she left the message, she decided she would write a letter for him, a goodbye letter. It seemed appropriate after all the years they had spent together. Ilse worked on her letter into the wee hours of the morning, crying as she wrote it. It had to be letter perfect so he wouldn't have reason to criticize her or again call her stupid. She decided she would take it along and have Dr. Morrison read it, correct any spelling or punctuation errors, and approve it.

Robert returned the call the next morning. They had gone out for a wonderful birthday dinner. Ilse told him she was headed down to see Dr. Morrison, but she had something she wanted to give him for his birthday. She'd like to meet him near where he lived at a roadside café on her way back from her appointment. He said that was great, he'd look forward to meeting her.

Ilse told Dr. Morrison that she was meeting Robert to give him a gift, the photo collection that she had framed and wrapped in birthday paper for him.

Then she told Dr. Morrison about the letter and asked if she would mind reading it and telling her what she thought. Dr. Morrison started to read, stopped and said, "It's quite long Ilse."

"Yes," Ilse said, "I lived with Robert for a long time. It is personal but you already know everything there is to know about me."

Dr. Morrison began reading the letter again:

April 21st

Dear Robert,

    I'm thinking of you on this special day and I'm hoping that with your birthday will come new life. And of course, I hope you will celebrate with a lobster dinner and chocolate cake with that fluffy white frosting that you love so much! Nothing I ever gave you would be finer than the gift of Molly and Will, a "forever" gift that I freely gave to the man I once knew. It was a gift from the heart and soul that I hope you will forever cherish. You can be certain that every April 21st I'll be thinking of you. Now it seems you want to cast aside all friendships and memories of your past life. However, I hope my best gift to you will remind you of times that were filled with hopes, dreams, joy, and sincere love. With a grateful heart, I accepted your gift, which no one can take away. Thank you for giving me two wonderful, perfect children and for sharing a part of your life with me.

    I can't understand your bitterness toward me. I have a feeling that you'll cast aside this letter, as I have been cast aside. Please read it because I want to remind you how much I cared. This is hard for me, but it is my way of ending a part of my life so there can be a new beginning for me and for you.

    The dream to grow old and recall precious memories with you and our children is gone. For thirty good years, I was truly happy. For those years, I am grateful and I thank you. Your dreams and ambitions were also mine because I was a part of you. Fulfilled, I welcomed each day. Then something happened for which I am not grateful. The dreams disappeared and I knew the future I looked forward to was gone. Someone else would "cash in" on all my dreams and abscond with the love and comfort I deserved. Naturally, I am angry and you would be too if it happened to you.

When I tried to explain the pain from the depression that wouldn't go away, you said you were glad I hurt so I would know how you've often felt. Well, now I understand and my soul shares the agony you sometimes live with. You have never, however, had to suffer that pain <u>alone</u>—all alone with no one to hold you and comfort you. Whenever you were feeling depressed, you had someone to comfort you, someone to support you, someone putting their arms around you, hugging you, someone you could make love to—all the things that made your depression tolerable. You've never had to feel totally alone and unloved. Perhaps you can look at my pain in a new way if you realize how lonely I have been and perhaps will always be. My friends have been wonderful, but there can never be a replacement for the warmth and affection from the person you love. Knowing that you had transferred your affections to Carrie and she was giving you what I was not allowed to, made my pain even deeper. To be blamed and degraded as well as rejected was more than I could bear. Try to understand that the wound is so deep the scars may never heal.

For almost three years, I grieved for you as though you died. The Robert I knew is gone. The Robert I knew and loved wouldn't do or say the things this Robert has said and done. The Robert

I knew and loved had high standards and ethics, which he passed on by example to his family and others. And the Robert I knew valued his family. He would not condone the behavior and lies that the new Robert finds acceptable.

I see glimmers of the old Robert lurking. I hope and pray he reappears so he can regain his self-respect. I cry for what is lost - for you, for Molly and Will, our families, for me. Your family had the highest respect for you and took pride in your accomplishments. I hope your self-respect will return for Molly, Will and your grandchildren, and that they will learn from the tragedy they have witnessed.

Please care enough to read this and hear me. I could not have been more caring or faithful than I was to you. And my promise of "until death us do part" was real. I reluctantly have to face the death of a dear lover and friend. I grieve because I feel so deeply and still care for you. This does not have to be an ugly ending if we can treat each other with the consideration and respect we both deserve.

I wish you God's speed, love, and happiness. Thank you for the wonderful years. It's time to close the book and begin another, but I'll always remember the 'first volume.'

Much love to the "old Robert"—the Robert I knew and will love forever.

Ilse

Dr. Morrison read the letter carefully, while Ilse toyed with the engagement ring she had taken off. She was running it up and down a ridge on the side of Dr. Morrison's desk. The doctor wasn't making corrections and when she finished reading she simply said, "That's a very nice letter, Ilse."

"Do you think it is okay to give it to Robert?" Ilse asked.

"Absolutely!" Dr. Morrison said.

Before the session was over, the phone rang on her desk, but she didn't stop to answer it. She never took calls interrupting a session.

Ilse felt good about her letter. Writing it had helped to unburden her.

Ilse was almost at the parking lot when she heard Dr. Morrison's voice.

"Come back!" she called.

Ilse was confused. She had never called her back. I'll bet that Dr. Morrison was rethinking something about the letter.

Instead, Dr. Morrison said that the unanswered phone call was Robert. He knew Ilse was there for an appointment and he wanted Dr. Morrison to return his call. He needed to talk with her. She said she needed to have Ilse's permission to call him.

Ilse said that it was fine and started to turn back to her car.

"No! No! I want you to stay and listen to my end of the conversation." Robert picked up the phone immediately when she dialed.

Ilse couldn't hear what he was saying, but she heard Dr. Morrison calmly say,

"No. No. It's not like that. No, it isn't anything like that. Robert, I'm sure. No. She's okay."

About half way through hearing her end of the conversation Ilse, still standing beside the desk, began to cry.

She knew exactly what he was saying. He was worried that she was going to try to kill him when she met him. That is how he interpreted Ilse's comment that she had something for him.

She would never hurt anyone. Why would he think this? Because that is what Robert thinks he deserves, Ilse thought.

Dr. Morrison confirmed what he was worried about. After Ilse calmed down, she sent her on her way saying, "If it is going to upset you to see him, you don't need to go."

"I'm going," Ilse said. "I'm going to give him the last birthday gift I will ever give him and the letter I've written."

When she met Robert, he had a stupid look on his face and he said, "That wasn't so far out. People do that sort of thing."

She told him, "The idea was for me to kill myself, remember, not to kill anyone else. You know me. You know I would never hurt anyone."

They went into the café and sat down. There weren't many people there. He went to the counter and bought Ilse a diet coke. She didn't feel like eating anything. Ilse gave him the birthday gift first and he unwrapped it; he didn't speak, but seemed to like it.

Then she gave him her letter. He started to put it in the inside pocket of his sport coat.

Ilse said, "Please read it. I really want you to read it."

"Trust me. I'll read it."

She doubted he ever did, as she knew she would never trust him again.

Ilse and Robert talked civilly for a while. They discussed Will's graduation from medical school in one month. Ilse had insisted that he call the grown children and tell them he was filing for divorce. He said he recently told his parents. Ilse wasn't going to tell her mother yet. She would tell her when the divorce was final she decided. He had been to see Molly and Ed and the new grandson. Robert was busy trying to get another job. He seemed quite pleased with himself, quite happy. He was confident that with his experience he would land another excellent position.

Everything seemed to happen at once. Only a few days after the birthday get-together, a letter arrived at the house from Robert's parents:

April 20

Dear Ilse,

We just received a letter from Rob saying you had separated which greatly distresses us. How could that ever happen? It seems to us you were perfect together. I just can't believe it. How can we express our feelings? It doesn't seem possible. Surely, there is some way you can work it out, as you are both very intelligent people. Rob said you were hospitalized twice and still continue to struggle every day.

He told us about how remarkable Will is doing and continually receiving high grades and honors and that we should be very proud of him. He also said Molly had moved into a new house and that she's working in the neonatal intensive care unit at the University Hospital. She's a great girl and we enjoyed her so much when she was here.

I think you should make every effort to get back together again. You are so perfect together. "Forget and forgive" is the only advice I can give. Rob said he is going to call us soon and we are anxious to hear from him. He's a wonderful man and we love him, no matter what.

Love, Mother & Dad

Robert didn't tell his parents the whole truth. He told them about the separation after they'd been separated for two years. He made a point of telling them she had been hospitalized. He told them only what he wanted them to hear. Ilse decided she wouldn't respond to the letter.... until a second letter came. It was addressed to both of them. Robert must have written to them.

May 1st

Dear Ilse and Rob,

I've been waiting to answer your letter until your dad received a shot in his spinal cord region. He's been having severe pain in his hip when he walks. Dr. Devon suggested he have a special medicine that has been developed lately and has helped lots of people. To have a shot in the spinal region scares me but every one we have talked to about it thinks it's getting to be a common procedure. However, they are just ordinary people here and I'm afraid they don't know anything about it. I think you should ask some of the doctors there at your hospital what kind of success they have. Anyway, he had it today. He seems to be fine so far but not yet rid of the pain, although some better.

When writing this letter Granddad just opened Rob's letter we got today and the news has shocked us to pieces.

Ilse, I think you're in too many things and Rob is not getting the attention he needs. He's had quite a struggle in getting started as business manager of these two hospitals. He needs all your support. I thought your marriage was perfect. How could it go wrong?

(Failed to mail this letter. Thanks for the lovely Mother's Day letter).

(Then another note was added at the bottom in tiny print):

Couldn't you and Rob come to see us by plane soon so we can talk this over? I believe you are making a serious mistake this late in your lives with two children and a grandchild.

Dad

After all this, he's not telling his parents the truth and I'm not going to be the fall guy anymore! I'm writing them back and telling the truth. He has lied and lied to me, but he is not going to put the blame for this on me. Furthermore, he didn't tell them that he lost his job. His parents think it is all MY fault. Enough, already!

Ilse wrote to them:

May 18th

Dear Folks,

It is hard for me to write this letter to you. I do not want to transfer any of my pain to you, but if I am totally honest with you, I know you will be hurt and will find it difficult to understand what could create such devastation. I don't think I will ever totally understand what has happened, but I know I have to accept my loss and go on with my life as best I can. I know I did my best.

Perhaps this letter should have been written long ago, but I didn't write in deference to Robert. I felt it was Robert's place to tell you in his own way and in his own time--you are his parents. However, for more than thirty years you have been my parents too, my family and my friends. For this reason, because I care deeply for all my family, I have not wanted to see you hurt and disappointed as I have been. As I have discovered, there is more pain when we are deceived and not treated with the honesty that is deserved.

From your letter to me, I can tell that Robert told you very little. Sometimes people hide the truth by what they don't say. Maybe he won't even tell you now, but HE filed for divorce citing "irreconcilable differences.' He filed for the divorce this past February after leaving me more than two years ago. A year before that I knew he no longer cared for me and that he was involved with a woman who worked for him. He told me he never loved me and by the things he said about Carrie, I knew his affection had been given to her along with admiration and expensive gifts. I was devastated and had difficulty coming to terms with what I didn't want to believe.

As you said, "How could this happen?" My world was shattered as the thirty years of a good marriage had been cast aside for a woman almost twenty years younger than I am. The things I cared the most about were gone. I think you know that I loved Robert dearly and will always love the Robert I was married to in the beginning. He was kind to me. He gave me wonderful children that have grown into the finest adults. We struggled together and worked toward common goals for Robert's career and for a happy, loving family with high morals and ethics—with trust built on honesty, faithfulness, and integrity. We "had it all" and I felt we had accomplished many goals with our team effort.

Then the unbelievable happened and I doubt that I will ever understand the power that a woman can have over a man. Nor can I understand how a woman can destroy a happy home to satisfy her own whims and advance her career. But it happened, and as difficult as it is, we have to face reality. To deal with his own guilt, Robert denies any wrongdoing on his part. He mercilessly blames everyone else, especially me. It seems Robert wants to forget everything and everybody from his past and the easiest way to do that is reject everyone. That's why he rarely contacts you. That is why I have rarely heard from him in the past two years.

My depression and hospitalization was very real and the pain has been unbearable. To be rejected by the person I cared for and loved so dearly did make me deeply depressed. He told everyone I was suicidal. I was not. I do struggle everyday, but I have always known I have Molly, Will, and Kyle to live for. It is somewhat easier now that Robert has filed for divorce. For almost three years, I did not know what his intentions were and at first, I was hopeful that we could be a family again. The fact that I have let go and forgiven means I can wish Robert happiness. I will be okay. I have no choice as nothing I can do or say will change things.

Although Robert denied his affair with Carrie, I knew from the beginning. In a town like this, there are many rumors, especially when it involves someone as prestigious as Robert. Early on there were many rumors and much speculation. Whenever I confronted Robert he would say, "You're crazy, Ilse. Believe that if you have to, but it's not true." Robert's Hospital Board members confronted him with the issue and he denied it to them too. I could have accepted it easier if Robert had been honest with me. I'm sure I would have been depressed but probably not to the extent that I was. To live with cruelty and criticism and lies was very destructive for me. I think the board would have accepted his indiscretions with perhaps just a slap on the hand had he been truthful with them.

On Feb. 9th, Wills birthday, the chairman of the board called Robert in. He resigned immediately (they had the resignation letter prepared for him) after they presented him with a private investigator's report exposing his affair with Carrie. They were very kind to him in the papers. I was told about his 'resignation' by friends and by the 5 o'clock and 10 o'clock news reports. Robert showed up here a few days later to tell me he was filing for divorce. He now lives with Carrie and she still has her job, until she finishes a project. He had promoted her up to Senior V.P.

He has not been able to find a job yet. Hopefully he will soon. This has been such a scandal that it may be a stumbling block for a while, but he should be all right. He gave up a great deal for a woman—his family, his job, and his fine reputation. I'm sorry for you, for his children, for myself, for disappointing friends and I'm truly sorry for Robert.

This has become long and I'm very weary and sorry the ending couldn't be different. I want you to know I always supported Robert and I will continue to–but it has to be with truth and total honesty. I feel I did you a disservice to not tell you sooner.

Although Robert left me alone, I hope you will still consider me a part of your family and your friend. I hope you will keep in touch and let me know how you are. You have always been kind to me and I want to return that kindness to you. I worry about Molly and Will. This has been very difficult for them. They love their father and always will. And I know you'll always love your son. We don't need to approve of what people do to love them.

My love to you,
Ilse

There was at least one more letter Ilse needed to write to clear the air. She needed to write to Robert's sister and brother-in-law. She had always liked Amy and George. George was the one person who helped the most when Molly was married. *They deserved to know what had happened.* Ilse wrote a letter to them a few days after writing to Amy's parents:

May 20th

Dear Amy and George,

You've been on my mind for ever so long. However, in deference to Robert, I did not try to contact you and also I was insecure enough to be afraid of being rejected by you as well as by Robert. Until recently, I was still intimidated by Robert and his wishes and I was still trying to believe him, although I knew the truth in my heart all along. What happened is real and I have to face that reality and go on with my life. I haven't been "crazy" but very disturbed and very depressed over a situation I could not change and found unbelievable. I couldn't believe that such a good person, with such high ideals and moral standards for himself and his family and others would compromise it all for a woman. He's given up a lot—the things I thought were most important to him—his family and a prestigious position that he has worked for. Until his affair with Carrie was revealed, he kept telling me, "You're crazy, but it's not true." I had very little contact with him. I last talked with him the day you called here looking for him. Perhaps you got hold of him and can better understand what has happened. I'm wondering if I'll ever understand, but I know I have to accept what has happened. I'm sad about the effect on Molly and Will and for you and for your parents, for his friends and business associates, for myself—but I'm especially sad for Robert.

Quite a long time ago, I read a book that gave me some insight. You might want to read it: "Sudden Endings: Wife Rejection in Happy Marriages" by Madeline Bennett. When I read it,

I was going to recommend it to you in the hopes that you, too, may understand a little better what has happened.

Until recently, Robert had told your parents nothing. Maybe your mom will share his letter with you. From a letter from your mom a few weeks ago, I surmised that Robert told them very little and again I felt the blame lands on me. I can no longer tolerate the lies and deceit—often by what is not said. It is a cruel way to ease one's conscience as I truly think it is more destructive than the truth. I know your parents thought I was upset with them when I rarely wrote. I've hated living a lie and I think I did your parents a disservice by not being up-front with them. I finally wrote to the folks a few days ago. I hope that my letter won't upset them too much but I can no longer live the lie. I will continue to care about them even though Robert said they are no longer my concern and I should forget about them. They have been my family and my parents for over thirty years—and you have also. I cannot just cast everyone aside and do not intend to, but I understand that I may be rejected in the process. The two of you have always been high on my 'favorite people' list and I hope that we can still be friends. I am interested in what you're doing and what my nieces and nephews and all the children are doing. I will always wish you all the best. You are special to me and I will always remember, with fondness, our good times together. I have no regrets except the last few years. I was happy and I think Robert was. I enjoyed our team effort with our family life and his career. I was proud of Robert and his accomplishments. I'm happy I had Robert's fine children—we will never take them from each other. I loved Robert unconditionally and I will always love the Robert I was married to. The realization that he is a different person continues to make me sad. I'm saddened by my tremendous loss and the loss of the future I so looked forward to. It was a dream that has vanished for me and I feel lonely and alone. However, I'm grateful for wonderful friends that have supported me and literally kept me going when my depression sunk to all-time lows. My faith has been tested but it has made me stronger. I'm at a point now where I know I'll be okay.

For Robert's birthday, I put together some framed pictures for him of Kyle—he's a cute little 'devil.' I also wrote him a letter trying to express my feelings and I think it helped me 'let go.' Writing to the folks was also a catharses and I know writing this letter will also help. The healing process has been very slow and elusive for me, as I've held on to the dream too long. Until Robert filed for divorce, I just wasn't ready. I actually feel better now that I know what his intentions are and there will be some finality.

Ilse filled in her letter with chit chat about what they were doing, what Molly and Will were doing and then continued:

Over Memorial day weekend, I'm going to Molly and Ed's to take care of Kyle while they go to Florida. The day after I get back I'm leaving early for California to see my mom and I plan to tell her, as I've hidden it from her all this time and every Sunday she asks how Robert is, tell him 'hi,' etc. I had hoped to spare her but my brothers are afraid she'll find out inadvertently. James sent me an airline ticket so I can go. Tracy's son is getting married so I'll be able to go to the wedding. That should be fun. By the way, my brothers call Robert's Carrie 'chickie.' They help me see the humor in it all—and the more accepting I am of the situation- the more I can see the lighter side too.

The upkeep of the house and yard is keeping me busy. I have been trying to keep everything nice, as it will make a difference if I have to sell the house. I've been volunteering at the 'Girl's Club' in town the past several years. I think it's mutually rewarding. I also have been working with a Vietnamese family for about a year and a half. I just signed up to work on a Habitat for Humanity project sponsored by my church. I still volunteer for the hospital auxiliary. It keeps me busy and productive. My "Holiday Harvest" and "Spring Blossoming" craft shows have been big successes. I have about forty crafters and I make the downstairs of the house into an irresistible boutique. Many of my friends help. I take only the finest quality work, which gives the show a good reputation. I'm now getting crafters selected for my November show.

What else is new? I'm not sure. I do a lot of quilting. I've made Molly and Will each four quilts and two for myself and of course a few baby quilts for Kyle. I'm now able to concentrate much better so I'm beginning to read a lot again. Have you read The Firm *and* The Pelican Brief*—both by John Grisham? Those are the most recent fun books I've read: I'm always trying to read 'self help' books as I try to get my life back on track.*

I've rambled on long enough—please know I think of you often—hoping you're happy and I send my love to you and your extended family. Please help Mother Kelly to understand. I

*feel sorry for her and I know she is concerned
about Robert. Please try to help her realize that I
would have never left Robert because I loved him
dearly, but I could not alter the course of our lives.
Be sure she understands that I will be there for
her if she ever needs me.*

Love ,
Ilse

A few days after Ilse sent her letter off to
Amy and George, one came from Amy:

May 25th

Dear Ilse,
*George and I were so happy to receive your
letter. It sounds as if you are well on your way to
recovery. You deserve a good life and we know
you will find it again. Thanks for sending the
newspaper articles. All of our knowledge about
what has happened mostly has come from you.
Robert has said very little although he told us that
he had quit his job and was looking for a new one.
He also said that he had written the folks about
the divorce, but did not tell them about his job.
They did not call me after they received his letter,
but the last time I called them, Mother expressed
concern and surprise about the divorce and
wanted to know if I knew. I think they are very
sad about it, but they're okay. I didn't feel it was
my place to fill them in on any details except to say
that this was something Robert wanted—not you.
I'm glad that you wrote to them.*
*We would love to have you visit us and of
course, you will always be welcome in our home.
Please, please always feel welcome. As far as we*

are concerned, you will always be a member of our family.

The rest of the letter was family news, which always interested Ilse. Then Amy signed off saying:
Take care of yourself and let us hear from you. We would love to see you soon.

Love,
Amy and George

Writing letters to Robert, his parents and sister had been difficult, but it was all part of 'closure' that was necessary to move forward...just like 'disclosure' was necessary in preparing for the divorce. It was all painful but also unburdening. Ilse still had to go to California and tell her mother which she thought would be the most difficult of all. She knew her mother would be disappointed in her. One brother was divorced, and when it happened, it broke her mother's heart. With that divorce, a young daughter was involved. Ilse's children were grown and it would be somewhat easier for them. She would tell her mother, and if she didn't understand, it would have to be okay. There was no turning back, no reconciliation. Furthermore, Ilse was now anxious to finish the 'mess' and get on with whatever life she could carve for herself.

At the San Jose airport, Ilse rented a car. She had depended on her brothers quite enough to take care of her. She would have to become more and more independent. Although she had been on her own several years, she knew all the decisions would soon be totally hers.

Getting to the lovely retirement home was not a problem during the daytime. In the distance, Ilse could see the ocean and beaches she had visited as a child. Her mother was waiting in her apartment, still the same with family photos everywhere. *Ilse thought, Oh! She looks so peaceful and comfortable, it is a shame to tell her this disturbing news.* Anxious to get the bad stuff out and over with, Ilse began to blurt out her story, like a child making excuses to a parent over their unacceptable behavior.

Mother said very little as Ilse cried. She didn't reprimand Ilse, but clearly thought being hospitalized was not necessary.

"Couldn't you be strong enough to fight back? Why did you succumb to psychiatric care and hospitalization?" Ilse tried to explain that she had no choice. Robert forced the hospitalization. Psychiatric visits were another issue. Ilse thought she could benefit from that. The divorce did not seem to be an issue with Mother. It seemed she never had liked or really trusted Robert, but she never said anything negative to Ilse about him all those years of their marriage. *She was a smart woman not to impose her opinions and cause friction in the marriage.* Her problem with it all was that Ilse hadn't been 'strong.' *In the end, Ilse knew it was her innate strength that pulled her through, probably a strength inherited from her parents and their training.* There were a few money questions. *Ilse thought she would have enough to be okay, and if she didn't she would get a job. She had confidence in Mr. Donald, her lawyer.*

After the initial 'confession' to her mother, Ilse felt better. A weight was lifted and with her twin brothers she could 'unload' some more baggage and laugh about things they had done. They also laughed about 'Chickie' and what she was in for now that the "spooking around" was over. *It wouldn't be nearly as much fun and exciting for them since their secret affair was no longer a secret. It would be almost fun to see how their relationship turned out, since it was woven with so many lies to other people. It probably always would be.*

30
A Divorce? "No Big Deal?"

There were continual arguments about
money, through the lawyers. Robert put a price
on the beach house and the lot on the lake in
North Carolina. Ilse made a trip to see the lot
and meet with the realtor that sold the lot to
them before the lake existed. When they bought
it, it was speculative. They had visited the area
with their long time friends, Tom and Pam, and
both couples had purchased a lot, thinking they
would someday sit in their rocking chairs on
their decks overlooking the lake.

Throughout the years, as the developers
went broke several times, Robert would harass
Ilse about what a horrible investment it was. He
said he never should have let her talk him into it.
Tom and Pam still had their lot. Robert wanted
to buy two less expensive lots not on the lake, but
Ilse insisted that a lot on the lake (that wasn't yet
there) was the better investment. She said a
"lake lot or nothing." She won out and the lake
lot was purchased. Since then, the lake had
'come in', having been filled up from springs.
When Ilse visited the property after a stay at the
beach, the realtor who had sold it to them years
before remembered Robert well, and told Ilse

361

that it was worth more than the price that Robert had put on it. She could sell it for a profit, or just maybe, she would want to move there some day. In the end, Robert was agreeable and Ilse paid him half of the amount Robert thought it should be valued at. Since they owned the beach house with Steve and Liz, Ilse's brother, he put it on Ilse's side of the ledger. It was fine with Ilse that he didn't want any business connections with her family. She could keep the house in town, but would have to pay Robert half of the appraised value. That sounded okay but in the end Ilse lost a lot of money since the housing market dipped significantly.

Both lawyers wanted to avoid the expense of going to court. Although Robert had flippantly told Ilse, "You can have it all!" he tried to weasel out every dime he could. It was good for Ilse that her brothers had so much financial information to pass on. Robert tried to use Ilse's 'mental illness' and hospitalization against her, but it really worked against him. Ilse had her head together when it came to the finances. Robert had taken three years of her life to beat and degrade her. *She wasn't going to let him destroy her financially. She had worked as hard for the family income as he had.* The legal visits were not without heartache, however. Often she would find herself crying, but seldom shaking. The process seemed lengthy and drawn out.

When Will switched to pre-med in undergraduate school, Ilse was happy but she told him, "Just don't get a 'God' complex! I hope that being a doctor won't make you feel like you're better than everyone else." When she told her son that, she was thinking of the superior attitude the Kelly family had because Robert's father was a physician.

When Robert and Ilse were married her twin brothers, James and Jacob had stayed at the Kellys'. After they returned to California, they sent thank-you notes addressed to Mr. & Mrs. Kelly instead of Dr. & Mrs. Kelly. Ilse was pleased that they had the good manners to write a note at age nineteen, but the Kelly's emphasis was on the error. "How dare they not be addressed with the proper title?" Robert made a big deal of it. *Ilse thought they were the ones being rude with their high opinion of themselves. James and Jacob, raised in a modest family, were the ones with 'class' because they wrote notes with sincerity.*

One major issue and *concern for Ilse was the upcoming medical school commencement ceremonies for Will. Ilse was concerned that Robert would bring Carrie.*

Dr. Morrison said she didn't think Robert would bring her along and then as an afterthought said, "If he brings her, it shows that neither one of them has a conscience."

Ilse didn't want to go in to the city alone, but Will kept saying he didn't want her to bring any of her friends. Many had offered to go with Ilse. Ilse thought that Will was embarrassed by what his father had done and knew that everyone in town finally knew the truth. Jacob and Tracy said they would come from California. When Ilse told Will they were coming, he couldn't say no.

Granny Mueller had purchased gold cuff links for him, with the caduceus, the symbol for the medical profession. There had not been a medical doctor in Ilse's family until now. Will's MD degree made the entire family very proud.

The day before going in to the city for the ceremony, Jacob and Tracy went to Ilse's closet to help her decide what to wear, wanting her to look her best and feel confident. She told them of her concern that Carrie might be there, and they reassured her it would be fine...they were her bodyguards.

There was a special awards ceremony in the morning, before the afternoon matriculation ceremony. Will said maybe Ilse would like to go to that and Ilse asked if he was getting an award. It was a possibility, he said. He wasn't sure. Ilse sat next to Will. His beautiful new fiancée sat on the other side. Jacob sat next to Ilse, armed with his camera, and Tracy sat next to him.

Before the ceremony began, Robert came in with Carrie. *Dr. Morrison said that if he brought Carrie, it showed that neither had a conscience. Well, that answered that.* They sat in the far back of the room. Robert was a proud father but could not enjoy being right there to shake his son's hand as he received award after award. The last award was the most coveted award, given by a combination vote of faculty and students, "The Best Doctor" award. *Ilse thought Will had received many already and was thrilled, but surprised when they called Will's name again.* Jacob went crazy with his camera. *Is it possible to burst with pride?* On the way back to his seat, Will made eye contact with Ilse, with a half smile on his face, and then that shrug of his shoulder. *He would be the best doctor ever and remain humble too. Ilse was sure of it!*

After the graduation ceremony Ilse went right out to be the first to congratulate her son, along with Jacob and his camera, Tracy, and Will's fiancée, Jennifer. Already Robert and Carrie were there. Everyone was anxious to hug Will and get pictures so they threaded their way though the crowd. Jacob and Tracy had forewarned Ilse that they would be friendly and civil to Robert and Ilse would too for Will's sake. Ilse introduced her brother to Carrie and the extent of Robert's greeting was, "Hello, how are you?"

"Great," Ilse said, and she was. Robert and Carrie rushed off.

As they went down the escalator Tracy said, "Don't look at them. I'll tell you what they're doing. Carrie is trying to take hold of his arm. He's shoving it aside."

Will wanted to introduce his mother to some of the doctors and *Ilse felt good that he was proud of her. He always knew how to make her feel better.*

Carrie kept working to finish a project. Her office was at a building site where Ilse was going for a Grand Opening for pediatrics. Ilse waited for her friends in the lobby. They had tables set up for nametags and Ilse sat on a bench nearby. As she looked up, the elevator doors opened and out stepped Carrie, this time fully clothed, carrying her briefcase. She jumped slightly when she saw Ilse sitting there. *Ilse wasn't going to let her get by.* Loud enough so that the ladies who were signing people in for the reception could all hear Ilse said, "Well 'hi' Carrie! How are you?"

"Fine," she said, quietly trying to draw attention away from an embarrassing situation.

Ilse still wasn't about to let her off the hook. "And how's my husband?" Ilse asked.

Clearly shaken she answered, "Fine."

Just one more dig and then I'll let her go, Ilse thought. "Tell him I said hello and give him my regards. Tell him he knows what they are!"

"I will," she said.

Ilse's friends came in right after Carrie went out the door. They said they just saw Carrie and she was in tears. *Maybe she had a conscience after all or maybe she was feeling sorry for herself. She had it coming, Ilse thought, and more.*

In Nebraska Ilse visited Robert's parents to see how they were doing. In just the few months since Grandmother had written Ilse the letter, Robert's mother was confused and hardly knew her. *Ilse thought perhaps it was the divorce that made her deteriorate so quickly.* Dr. Kelly asked Ilse why she and Will had helped get Robert fired by joining in the private investigation.

When Ilse questioned him he said, "You know how you got involved with the group that got Robert fired." Ilse had tears in her eyes when she realized that not only had Robert told them she was 'mentally ill' and suicidal, he had also linked Ilse and Will to the loss of his job, telling his parents that she had participated in the plot against him. *Will it ever end? Ilse thought.*

Why does he have to continue to blame it all on me? Ilse left Robert's parents her phone number if they ever needed her help. It was a sad last meeting, but she knew she wouldn't see them anymore. Sending a card now and then, so they knew she thought about them, would be the extent of her contact with them.

Robert came over to the house one day to pick up a few things. Ilse told him she wanted his wedding ring returned to her and the nugget ring she had given to him after their 'marriage encounter' weekend. He had been wearing the wedding ring until he lost his job. Ilse knew he wore it to throw people off, to make them think he was still married to Ilse. She had continued to wear her rings, feeling naked when she took them off.

Robert said he'd give her his rings if she gave him her diamond. Ilse said, "No, I accepted them and wore them in good faith. You didn't." Then she told him she wanted him to return the last expensive watch she'd given him and the beautiful little carriage clock he had taken from his desk top. He said "no" to that too. When Ilse mentioned it to Mr. Donald, he said he'd write Robert a letter and ask for the rings for her. He said Robert would be more likely to comply if he asked him to gift the watch to his son, Will, and the carriage clock to his daughter, Molly. He agreed, but didn't comply. It became part of the divorce agreement. The rings were a matter of principle for Ilse and she was getting stubborn about it all.

The last visit with Mr. Donald was one of the hardest. He stood up and handed a little box to Ilse.

"The rings," he said. Ilse opened the box and was in tears when she saw that Robert had wrapped each ring in toilet paper. She had seen him do that before with something for Joe Hawk and they both thought it was funny. This time it wasn't. It was a message that didn't go unnoticed by Ilse or Mr. Donald. *He was still trying to hurt her and it worked.*

Ilse left the meeting with Mr. Donald and went directly to the jewelers. She gave him the rings and said, "I want you to melt these down into one great big COLD heart."

He said he'd never done that before, but he'd try. When Ilse picked the heart up, she gave him her diamond wedding bands and asked if he could make them into earring jackets. The jeweler thought that was a great idea, and began to promote both ideas for other women.

At the same time, Ilse's diamond mysteriously disappeared. It was during the time she was preparing for the 'Holiday Harvest' and she frantically looked everywhere for the ring. Everywhere. Others suggested that Robert had come to the house and taken it while she was sleeping. With the security system, she didn't think that could happen, but with everything else he had done, who knew?

He had to be prodded to give the Patek Philippe watch to Will. Carrie, with all her money bought him another one. Will really didn't want it, but Ilse insisted it was part of the agreement. Robert wrote a letter to Molly saying that he would bring her the carriage clock. He didn't want to send it. He never gave it to her. *Maybe they realized that it was something that Carrie couldn't so readily replace.*

Ilse told Molly she should ask for it, but she wouldn't. Neither Will nor Molly wanted to ruffle their father's feathers. He never fulfilled his part of the divorce agreement in every detail. *He was still going to do what suited him.*

When the stocks and money were transferred, the lawyer brought in some financial managers that handled all the paper work. Ilse had a meltdown when the final papers were completed and executed. The secretary came in and asked Ilse if she was okay, and *she was, just terribly, terribly sad. It was so final, so cold.* Her college roommate went with her to witness signing the final papers. *Ilse wondered if Robert ever realized who the witness was or if he even looked at the signature, finally totally rid of her.*

31
Finally...the Divorce ...1994

It was over. Ilse had been fired, just like he fired his employees. He could fire them and never talk with them again. It was as if they never existed. Now he had fired Ilse and probably would never talk to her again.

Ilse kept going to see Dr. Morrison almost once a week. It helped her to process feelings that no one except the doctor understood. There would still be hurdles to get over. Once the divorce was final, it was easier because Ilse could begin to plan a future. She could go where she wanted, do what she wanted, whenever she wanted. There was a new-found freedom. In some ways it was frightening, but if she could regain her self-confidence, she knew she would enjoy the independence. <u>She had been controlled for years.</u> She would have to be strong and positive to face the future alone. Dr. Morrison was encouraging.

Feeling better than she had in a long time, after the divorce was final Ilse was concerned that her depression would keep coming back. She told Dr. Morrison of her fears, saying that so many times over the past four years she had thought she was better and then she fell again into that dark hole of depression. Dr. Morrison told Ilse that she thought she would ALWAYS be fine. The marriage was the most important thing in her life and the loss of that dream was critical to her. She didn't think there would be anything else that would trigger a depression again. Ilse felt better with that professional opinion.

The day that Robert came over to the house after he lost his job, he was flippant when he told her, "You shouldn't have put all your eggs in one basket!" *What did he expect? They were all put in his basket and anything short of that would have been unthinkable to her.* He never would have allowed her to be unfaithful. *There were no regrets about doing what she thought was right as a wife.*

Ilse found a story. It reminds her of the struggle she faced with depression over that four-year period. It is called "The Frog Story." In the story, there are two frogs. Ilse is one of them.

The Frog Story

A group of frogs was traveling through the woods and two of them fell into a deep pit. All the other frogs gathered around the pit. When they saw how deep the pit was, they told the unfortunate frogs they would never get out.

The two frogs ignored the comments and tried to jump up out of the pit. The other frogs kept telling them to stop, that they were as good as dead. Finally, one of the frogs took heed to what the other frogs were saying and simply gave up. He fell down and died.

372

The other frog continued to jump as hard as he could. Once again, the crowd of frogs yelled at him to stop the pain and suffering and just die. He jumped even harder and finally made it out.

When he got out, the other frogs asked him, "Why did you continue jumping? Didn't you hear us?" The frog explained to them that he was deaf. He thought they were encouraging him the entire time.

The story teaches two lessons:

1) There is power of life and death in the tongue. An encouraging word to someone who is down can lift them up and help them make it through the day.

2) A destructive word to someone who is down can be what it takes to kill them.

Be careful of what you say. Speak life to those who cross your path.

The power of words...it is sometimes hard to understand that an encouraging word can go such a long way. Anyone can speak words that tend to rob another of the spirit to continue in difficult times.

Special is the individual who will take the time to encourage another.

Jumping out of that pit was the hardest thing Ilse ever had to do, but she kept jumping even when Robert was trying to rob her of her spirit. She had been fired from Robert's 'staff' but she was strong, resilient, and finally free. She would make a good life for herself and maybe help others by what she learned by being in the bottom of that pit and her struggle to become Ilse, the real Ilse, the survivor.

Epilogue - Moving Forward

There is a beautiful sunset almost every evening over the North Carolina lake where Ilse built her home. As Ilse sits on her back deck watching the setting sun she knows she will wake every day to a life filled with peace, laughter and love. However, this is definitely not the sunset of her life. There is a lifetime of experiences ahead of her: new friends and new business ventures. She is too young to 'retire' and will find constructive, productive outlets for all the energy that is still waiting to be unleashed.

Ilse did not keep a journal or precise calendar during the four year period she has written about. However, what happened is very clear in her mind although the time-line may not always be accurate. The letters were copied from the drafts she wrote, and letters she received which were saved in her divorce file...she's not sure why she kept them...perhaps to help her tell her story.

It has been fifty years since Ilse and Robert graduated from high school together, before their romance began. Both appeared last summer at their class reunion where a booklet was distributed with a 'blurb' from each classmate. One of Robert's comments was, "wonderful second marriage." He married Carrie, not long after the divorce, and chose one of Ilse's favorite spots, back in Clarkston, for the ceremony.

The reunion was awkward for not only Robert, Carrie, and Ilse, but for classmates as well, many of them mentioned in Ilse's story. Robert acted like he didn't even know Ilse, let alone sleep with her for twenty-eight years. Ilse approached them in an effort to be cordial, but there was little to say. There were comments afterwards like, "Did you see the size of Carrie's ring?" "Robert talked about how successful he was, how great Carrie is, and how much money they both made." Is that why they came to the reunion? Ilse wondered. To let everyone know that they were happy and financially successful? To show that they didn't do anything wrong? It was phony, Ilse thought...still about appearances, success and money. Several people commented that Carrie was much younger. They also commented, and Ilse noticed too, that Robert's eye and corner of his mouth were twitching, a dead give-away that he was nervous.

Robert and Carrie appeared happy and both had successful careers. Robert was able to rebuild his career, to again reach the pinnacle in his field of expertise. A few years ago, he retired. At his retirement dinner (Ilse heard from her adult children), he was touted as one of the best hospital administrators in the country. Ilse was always proud of him and happy for his success and would never deny the fact that he was an excellent hospital executive. His friend, Joe Hawk, was at his retirement dinner to give one of the speeches. His children and grandchildren were also there to honor him. They have a limited relationship with him, but there has been an effort from both sides to re-establish a bond. Robert is their father. He gave them life. That is reason enough to love him.

Joe Hawk remains a close friend to Robert. His ex-wife, Marilyn, now lives at the beach, so Ilse and Marilyn see each other often.

The reunion was only the second time Ilse had any contact with Robert since the divorce almost fifteen years before. The first time was when Will and Jennifer were married and he said, predictably, "Hello. How are you?" Ilse's standard answer is, "Great!"

Ilse has gone on to have a wonderful life, totally independent, enjoying every day, especially a freedom that she never realized was missing all those years. What she went through made her stronger with a new appreciation for her family and friends. It also gave her an additional awareness, and consequently more compassion, for others who fight depression. Her friendly approach to people continues to attract new and interesting friends.

For ten years after the divorce, Ilse actively sold fine fashion jewelry for a company introduced to her on a trip to Austria. Representing the company helped her get her confidence back. She worked her way up the ladder and often spoke at the conventions. She won trips to California, Florida, Nassau, Hawaii, London, Spain, and a Caribbean cruise. She was able to come out of her 'shell,' enjoying her success in the jewelry business.

Ilse is a "free spirit" as she travels the world, goes to the beach condo with Steve and Liz, or other friends, and enjoys her wonderful neighbors as they share the beautiful sunsets over the lake. She is in close contact with her supportive brothers and their wives, (Steve, the twins, Jacob and James, and the oldest brother,

Walter, who finally expresses his affection in appropriate ways). Although Ilse sees Tom and Pam once or twice a year, and still vacations with them sometimes, they sold their lake lot to purchase property closer to their family.

Meg is still a "best friend," always supportive and fun! They have traveled a long road together and it reflects a special bond, which dates back to the eighth grade when Ilse's family moved to Sidney. Ilse couldn't ask for a more supportive or compassionate friend. Meg is still pretty, young at heart, and a remarkable lady.

Ilse still sees Melanie, her friend from New Hampshire when the children were young. Not much has changed with their relationship. They still do crafts and laugh a lot but now they share their grandchildren's escapades.

The three "sisters' are often together at the beach, at Ilse's lake home, or at their homes in Clarkston. They're peppy, fun and looking for adventures, and they are still married to their wonderful husbands.

Jackie is now divorced which, like Ilse's divorce, was a shock. She has a story of her own. Mr. Donald, Ilse's lawyer, helped two of her friends with their divorces. He's the best.

Ilse still feels she hadn't needed to be hospitalized, but knows that Dr. Morrison's counseling helped her get through a difficult time. Ilse has the utmost appreciation and respect for her. She was able to soon get off all medication and since then, she hasn't needed further psychiatric help and has never regressed. There is no longer anything to be depressed about.

Alexis...such a dear, smart, beautiful, loving lady died a year ago. Ilse continued to keep in touch with her, misses her, and is forever grateful that she encouraged her and was her special friend, helping with her "private investigation." Ilse never knew if Alexis ever told her husband about their adventure.

Marie and Ilse see each other a few times a year and still go to Telluride. She is retired now and enjoys living in the sunny south.

Sadly, Sasha had to be put to sleep shortly after the divorce. She is not replaceable. She was a wonderful source of comfort as she truly sensed Ilse's sorrow.

The Lexus is still running with almost 300,000 miles to attest to Ilse's travels hither and yon. Now she calls the car "old gray" since it is twenty years old, but Ilse is anything but old. Almost five years after Robert and Carrie began their secret affair, Ilse began the best years of her life. She wouldn't, however, trade the two precious children and their growing-up years. They are a lasting blessing that came from the marriage, a forever gift from Robert and her precious gift to him.

Will lives in the north and Molly lives in the south, with happy, well-adjusted families of their own. Will and Jennifer have two children, a boy and a girl. Molly and Ed have three children, a boy and two girls. They are the finest son, daughter and five grandchildren anyone could wish for. Both are successful, contributing adults and happy with their careers and beautiful families. They visit Ilse's home on the lake and the beach condo, and Ilse travels to be with them often.

The independence and freedom Ilse feels is appreciated more because of the ordeal she survived. Her innate strength and the support of her family and good friends are gifts she is thankful for. She views every day as special with a reverence for life. Ilse is healthy, energetic, and now, ever so happy. Life is good. Perhaps if she hadn't experienced those depressing years, she wouldn't appreciate all she has. She HAS IT ALL! It's not about money. It's about freedom and the quality of life she lives. She looks at what she has, not what she had.

Ilse's wish is that her story will help other women (and men) recognize a pattern of emotional abuse early, and not tolerate or accept what is always wrong. No one EVER deserves to be treated badly.

Yes, Ilse did all right in the end. She endured, she healed, she conquered, and finally she stopped caring. However, one morning she woke up and thought, 'that louse should have gone to jail. If I knew then what I know now, he'd be doing time.' Her new sense of power made her smile.

Made in the USA
Charleston, SC
14 April 2015